Bob & Kathy Sundin
11163 Netherland Dr.
Boise, Idaho 83709

PEOPLE PROBLEMS

The Executive
Answer Book

PEOPLE PROBLEMS

The Executive Answer Book

JOHN B. MINER

Research Professor of Management
Georgia State University

RANDOM HOUSE BUSINESS DIVISION
NEW YORK

First Edition
987654321
Copyright © 1985 by John B. Miner

All rights reserved under International and Pan-American Copyright
Conventions. No part of this book may be reproduced in any form or
by any means, electronic or mechanical, including photocopying,
without permission in writing from the publisher. All inquiries
should be addressed to Random House, Inc., 201 East 50th Street,
New York, N.Y. 10022. Published in the United States by Random
House, Inc., and simultaneously in Canada by Random House of
Canada Limited, Toronto.

Library of Congress Cataloging-in-Publication Data

Miner, John B.
  People problems.

  Includes index.
  1. Employee counseling. 2. Communication in
management. 3. Personnel management. I. Title.
HF5549.5.C8M56 1985   658.3'85   85-8374
ISBN 0–394–55002–1

Manufactured in United States of America

Contents

About This Book

Our basic aim is to help managers meet one of the greatest challenges of managing: dealing with subordinates whose performance is unsatisfactory. This is not a theoretical book about *management* but a practical book about *managing*—intended for managers and aspiring managers who really want to assume the managerial role and not just the title,

Of course, there is more to managing than dealing with ineffective subordinates. But in most books about managing, this aspect is often ignored or treated superficially. We believe there is a distinct need for a reference book that answers a manager's questions about why some subordinates perform poorly—and discusses what can be done about it. Few would disagree that making the most of an organization's human resources is an essential function of managing.

The book is organized so that the reader can systematically identify every possible source of an employee's poor performance. Significantly, this includes the possibility that the cause of subordinate ineffectiveness may lie with the manager. One of the book's major goals is to guide the reader to improved managerial performance through an understanding of how certain managerial approaches can lead to unsatisfactory work by subordinates.

This book had its origins in a management development program presented to a group of research and development managers some years ago. Since then, the program has been further developed and repeated many times. Follow-up studies show that the program has achieved its goal of creating better managers: most of the participants have an outstanding record of success. We believe that the material used in the program—and in this book—can be an equally potent self-development tool.

*   *   *

All of the material in this book is based on thorough research by myself and others in the field—as well as on my own hands-on experience in dealing with the problems of unsatisfactory employee performance. Throughout this effort, I have had indispensable help from my wife, Barbara Miner. I am also deeply indebted to Peter Reid for his extensive editorial assistance and to Patricia Haskell and Alison Husting at Random House for their continuing faith in my efforts.

JOHN B. MINER

1

Managing as Dealing with People

Managing is often defined as the process or art of getting work done through others. Although this definition stresses supervising and the human resources of the organization at the expense of decision-making and financial or material resources, it does focus on an important aspect of managerial work. Managers spend a very high proportion of their time dealing with people—not only with their subordinates, but with their superiors, their peers, and a wide range of people outside the organization.

What Does a Manager Do?

For many years, managing has commonly been viewed in terms of such component functions as planning, organizing, staffing, directing, controlling, coordinating, communicating, decision-making, representing, investigating, motivating, and perhaps other activities. This is the management process approach. Most research has supported this approach: many of these functions have been shown to require sizable segments of time in a wide variety of managerial jobs.

The most important functions appear to be planning, organizing, directing, coordinating, and controlling. To a somewhat lesser degree, staffing and representing also are depicted as important aspects of the managerial job. The common denominator is that all of these functions may involve dealing with people to some extent, and such functions as directing, staffing, and representing relate almost exclusively to people.

However, this management process approach has come under considerable criticism in the past few years, notably from Professor Henry Mintzberg at McGill University. Mintzberg prefers to look at managerial work in terms of the various roles that managers play, and he presents some data and several persuasive arguments in favor of his approach. He casts the manager at various times as:

Figurehead

Leader

Liaison

Monitor

Disseminator

Spokesperson

Entrepreneur

Disturbance handler

Resource allocator

Negotiator

In my view, this approach does not preclude the management process approach; it is simply a different way of cutting the pie, although a very interesting and provocative one to be sure. Most importantly, this approach does not invalidate the strong emphasis on dealing with people that prevails in the process approach to the manager's job. Mintzberg explicitly describes the first three roles as basically interpersonal in nature. His descriptions clearly indicate that the other roles all include dealing with people as a sizable component and that some, like negotiator, are almost entirely of this nature.

No matter how one approaches the subject, then, dealing with people emerges as an important aspect of managerial work (although managing certainly has other important aspects as well). This means that a manager must understand people and the multiple forces that make them act and perform as they do.

One way of doing this is to concentrate on the problem of ineffective or poor performance. In one sense, dealing with ineffective performance provides a framework on which to hang the diverse factors that determine human behavior and job performance. But even more important, it represents a major problem that all managers face. There is nothing more demanding and time-consuming than attempting to deal with a subordinate whose performance is unsatisfactory in some respect. This is the very essence of the challenge of managing, and at the higher levels it can mean the difference between organizational survival and extinction. As Marvin Bower, former managing director of the international management consulting firm of McKinsey & Company, points out in discussing the will to manage, " . . . the primary deterrent . . . is the natural reluctance of most managers to discipline their subordinates or to injure their feelings." Thus, Bower presents a strong argument for the necessity of *dealing* with poor performance, rather than sweeping it under the rug.

Dealing with Unacceptable Performance

One assumption is basic to all that follows: to accomplish its goal, corrective action must be based on a thorough understanding of the factors causing the difficulty. The manager must become in one sense a diagnostician, devoting time and effort to finding out what has produced the poor performance. Only then will the manager be able to prescribe an appropriate solution and take the appropriate action.

In a way, the managerial job requires skills similar to those of an experienced automobile mechanic. Faced with a car that does not run satisfactorily, the competent mechanic asks questions of the driver, observes the condition of the engine, and makes various changes while noting their effects on operating efficiency. Only then does some kind of corrective action make sense. A good mechanic does not begin by replacing the carburetor, although this approach may occasionally prove successful. It may also prove highly profitable, at least for a brief period of time. But we would never consider a person who employs it a good mechanic.

The point can be made even more aptly with the practice of medicine. Again, diagnosis typically precedes treatment. Long gone are the days of such practices as bloodletting as an almost invariable treatment, applied without any attempt to determine what was producing the disorder. Medical practice has developed to the point where a more sophisiticated approach is possible, and the human lifespan has consequently been extended by many years. The field of management has begun to enter a similar stage. Just as biological research provided the knowledge necessary for advances in medical practice, social science research can provide means for improving managerial practice. We have reached the point where "managerial bloodletting" is no longer an acceptable approach. We have the knowledge and tools to extend the "occupational lifespan." The knowledge may be still somewhat rudimentary and the tools may sometimes be lacking in precision, but they are good enough to be of real help in supervising subordinates. They enable the manager to use a diagnostic approach and apply "cures" that have some relationship to known causes.

Although it is by no means the only aspect of the managerial job, handling ineffective performance is a major responsibility of management. Managers are people who have been assigned more work than they can do alone. They must therefore induce others to assist them if they are to be successful. To the extent that these others fail to perform effectively, managers themselves fall short of complete success. In practice this means that failing employees create a very special problem and consequently place unique demands on their superiors' time. Employees who do their job well do not make major demands on supervisors—they are capable of working for long periods on their own. Ineffective employees, on the other hand, usually require frequent attention, and their manager must often devote many hours to their difficulties. In the long run, having the skill to deal with poor performance should make a manager's job much easier and more satisfying.

Performance Failure in a Competitive Economic System

What is meant by poor or ineffective performance? The problem is a complex one, but understanding it is crucial. Individual performance is characteristically judged in terms of its contribution to the goals of the organization. These goals tend to be intimately associated with the values of the members—with what the members believe the goals should be. Although in any organization there are likely to be diverse opinions on goals, some degree of consensus usually prevails. In business, the organizational goal is generally considered to be continuing maximization of net profits within the limits set by the ethical and legal standards of society. Many contend that this should not be the objective of business enterprise, and they have proposed alternative or supplementary goals. But the vast majority of business managers still focus strongly on the ultimate criterion of profitability. And society as a whole, to the extent that it supports capitalism in any form, automatically commits itself to this position. By embracing capitalism we bind ourselves to the view that each individual business *should* compete for profits. It follows that the performances of individual members of a business organization must be evaluated in terms of contribution to the firm's profitability.

Other types of organizations will, of course, have completely different objectives, and performance within them will be judged on some other basis. Furthermore, any individual employee may also be a member of some other organization with objectives differing from, or even completely at variance with, those of the business. Nevertheless, within the firm itself the behavior of individual employees must be evaluated in relation to company goals. The same behavior may, of course, be evaluated in an entirely different way by some other group, such as a union to which the employee belongs. Some union members *may*, because of their commitment to their union, behave in a way that makes their employer call them ineffective.

When we speak of ineffective performance, however, more is implied than merely a relationship to profits. The use of the qualifier ineffective indicates some feeling that a person's behavior is unsatisfactory and has fallen below some standard. Since the standard that constitutes the dividing line between effective and ineffective performance is not always clearly defined, it is impossible to provide a perfectly precise definition of ineffectiveness. As a working guide, let us say that an employee has failed whose performance is *considered* unsatisfactory either by superiors or in terms of organizational standards. Although this definition lacks theoretical sophistication, it does have considerable practical value.

Performance Criteria and Standards

In the context of a management-by-objectives (MBO) system, performance criteria and standards may be determined to a considerable degree by the individual employee. However, as Professors Stephen Carroll of the University of Maryland and Henry Tosi of the University of Florida have shown, the extent of such employee participation has little relevance for MBO outcomes. More commonly, the standards for employee performance are established by an employee's line superiors and by certain groups within the organization that have been assigned this function. These groups characteristically include units with titles such as personnel, budget, methods and standards, industrial engineering, quality control, and so forth. The standards may be rigidly established numerical cut-off points or they may be highly subjective standards existing only in the minds of individuals and subject to frequent variation. Although objectively and subjectively established standards may not be equally desirable from the viewpoint of their contribution to organizational goals, they do have the same consequences for supervisor and subordinate. Once a manager defines a person as ineffective in some respect, both individuals have a problem that needs solving.

Of course, the manager or the organization might sometimes establish inappropriate standards that are clearly inconsistent with company goals. It is, in fact, possible that inappropriate standards might completely explain the ineffectiveness—that an individual might be ineffective by definition only. Even in such cases, however, there is still a problem to be solved. The employee has been defined as ineffective, and some action must be taken. The matter cannot be ignored because the standards were loosely and subjectively defined or because they were too high.

Standards are not characteristically established for an overall entity called "performance." Usually performance is broken into a variety of aspects, and standards of ineffectiveness are developed for each. A person may be said to be producing an unsatisfactory quantity of work, to be absent too often, or to be ineffective in some other respect. Companies have developed a great variety of criteria by which to evaluate people. In many firms, the same factor is used under different names. There are, however, four aspects of performance that appear frequently. These four appear to cover most major criteria that are used to evaluate work-related behavior and that can be logically derived from the goals of the business organization. There are, of course, many aspects of human beings and their behavior which are evaluated by other people but which have nothing to do with organizational goals and profitability. These are not included in the four categories. Also, it is clear that subdivisions can, and on occasion should, be made within each category.

Quality is an obvious first. Work is usually evaluated in terms of accuracy—that is, the number of errors made. However, in certain kinds of jobs, quality cannot be evaluated numerically, and other criteria must be used.

Quantity of output has achieved similar acceptance as a major dimension of employee performance. Employees are usually considered ineffective if they fail to complete a satisfactory amount of work within a designated time span.

A third dimension is closely related to the first two, but is widely used as an independent criterion. This is *time spent on the job.* It includes absenteeism, lateness, lost time, premature separation (before hiring and training costs are recovered), disabling accidents, and so forth. The employee who spends insufficient time on job performance is generally judged ineffective on that basis alone. Clearly, if employees are not present and working, they cannot produce an adequate quantity of work; or if they attempt to do so within an insufficient time span (perhaps they have missed three out of the five working days in the week), the quality of their work will inevitably suffer. Employees who spend so little time on the job that they cannot do their work satisfactorily should be considered ineffective, irrespective of the cause. An employee who has a serious illness and cannot work for a long period of time is an unsatisfactory employee insofar as contributing to company goals is concerned, even though by almost any other criterion that person would receive sympathy rather than disapproval.

The final aspect of performance is more complex than the preceding three. It concerns the degree of *cooperation* with others in attaining organizational goals. In a sense, this aspect contains two related dimensions. It means in part the impact of the individual on the performance of co-workers. The employee who in some manner reduces the quantity or quality of work done by other members of the group, or who reduces the time they spend at work, may be considered ineffective according to this criterion. This aspect of performance also includes the direct impact of the individual on the attainment of organizational goals. Some examples are employees who steal from the company, who incur court judgments against the company for damages, who frequently break equipment and waste materials, or who perhaps even engage in sabotage. All have a direct negative impact on profits.

This fourth dimension is, of course, particularly relevant in evaluating managers, since the managerial job requires taking action to influence the performance of others and making decisions that have a direct bearing on profits. If a manager's actions have a consistently detrimental effect on the work performance of subordinates, then he or she is likely to be labeled ineffective. Similarly, the manager who makes decisions that frequently prove to be costly blunders, or who seriously threatens the survival of the organization in some way, may well receive the same designation.

The Four Dimensions of Employee Performance

Quality of work

Quantity of work

Time spent on the job

Cooperation in attaining organization goals

It is now possible to answer the question of what is meant by ineffective performance. Ineffective performance is the failure to achieve minimal standards on those dimensions of performance that are relevant to organizational objectives. The standards may have been established by line superiors, by appropriate organizational groups, and perhaps by the individual employee at an earlier time. A person may fail in one of the four dimensions or in all of them; for the purpose of defining ineffectiveness, it matters little. Nevertheless, in terms of the problem confronting the responsible manager, the number of ways in which a subordinate fails is an important consideration. An employee who does high-quality work, never misses a day, and has a positive impact on others, but is excessively slow, represents a very different type of problem from the employee who is below standard in all four areas. Yet both are ineffective.

Dealing with Unacceptable Performance as a Control Function

In terms of the process approach to managerial work, dealing with subordinates whose performance is below standard primarily represents a control activity, although at times the directing function may be involved as well. Actually, the control concept provides a very helpful way of looking at performance failure.

Control is typically viewed as involving at least three component activites. These are:

- Establishing the standard
- Measuring the deviation
- Setting up a feedback process or some similar procedure to correct the deviation

This is much like management by exception, which focuses on the extreme cases that are most likely to affect results. One difference is that with performance failure, only negative deviations are given attention, whereas the exception principle in its entirety calls for dealing with positive deviations as well—usually by encouraging or rewarding them. Other than this, management by exception, the control function, and dealing with poor performance are essentially the same. In fact, correcting ineffective performance is often referred to as performance control.

Such performance control does require the three basic control activities, just as do production control, quality control, inventory control, cost control, and the like. However, there is an added ingredient that may not be needed in many other types of control processes. This is the diagnostic phase mentioned earlier. After the fact of a negative deviation from standard has been established, it must be determined what factors operated to produce the deviation. Only with this information can the manager introduce an appropriate feed-back process to correct the deviation.

To deal effectively with a subordinate's failure, the manager should first think of possible causes based on what is known about the subordinate. From this process will emerge a list of factors that appear to be contributing to the problem. Then the manager can select the corrective approaches that are most likely to strike at the causes identified.

Many good managers are able to exercise performance control and correct negative deviations almost intuitively. From long experience, they know what works with certain kinds of individuals in particular situations. But many other managers never achieve this level of intuitive effectiveness—and even if they do, developing such a skill by trial and error and observation is a lengthy process. For these reasons, it makes sense to spell out those thought processes which in many good managers are essentially intuitive—and to describe in detail all the causal factors that must be considered and the corrective actions that may be applied. In this way, a manager can develop skills in performance control quite rapidly. Later, the somewhat laborious problem-solving process involved can be replaced with the quicker intuitive approach as learning is consolidated. It is similar to learning to drive. First, each action is thought out in great detail, but before long everything happens automatically with no need to give conscious attention to the process.

Of course, handling problems of ineffective performance is not the only way in which managers and organizations deal with employee performance. Managers do try to stimulate *everyone* to perform at a maximal level, rather than merely focus on the poor performer. They do try to get employees who are already satisfactory to do better. And organizations use a variety of techniques such as training, pay incentives, safety programs, and the like to stimulate maximal performance or to prevent ineffective performance from ever occurring. Still, performance control remains *one* important function of all managers. Furthermore, learning about it has a side benefit: a manager may gain insight into his or her own potential sources of managerial ineffectiveness.

Screening as a Solution

At this point you may have certain questions and reservations as to the real need for dealing with performance failure along the lines we have been considering. Why is it necessary for a manager to analyze each instance of performance failure to determine the causes? Why, in fact, do managers have to face the problem of ineffective performance at all? Is it not possible during the hiring process to screen out all those who would subsequently fail? And cannot all candidates for promotion be similarly screened, so that any who would be ineffective in the higher-level position can be eliminated from further consideration? In short, cannot selection procedures lift the burden of dealing with ineffective performance from the backs of managers?

Unfortunately, we do not yet have techniques that are capable of screening out all potentially ineffective performers from a company's work force. Screening can and does significantly reduce the amount of poor performance. For instance, Professor Edwin Ghiselli, who was at the University of California at Berkeley for many years before his death, has clearly demonstrated the value of psychological tests in screening. Without such techniques, the number of problem cases confronting any manager would be much greater. And in all probability, more extensive and effective use of the techniques currently available could even further reduce the amount of performance failure. Yet in a practical sense, there are limits to what can be accomplished. Certainly screening and selection (the terms refer to opposite sides of the hiring process) face some obstacles which to date have proved insurmountable.

A major difficulty is that the available measuring devices are far from perfect. They do not always reveal a characteristic when it is present or the exact extent to which it is present. This is true in varying degrees of all the selection techniques currently in use: interviews, application blanks, psychological tests, reference checks, credit company investigations, physical examinations. All of these, whether they attempt to obtain a sample of typical behavior, a sample of physical functioning, or information on previous behavior, are subject to some error. People do not always reveal all they might during interviews, for example, and even some physical measures are sometimes unreliable. In spite of many advances, we still need further research in psychological and biological measurement and prediction.

Further, even when good selection techniques are available, they are not always used with maximum effectiveness. Perhaps they never can be. There is always an element of human error, always the possibility that the person applying the screening procedure will overlook something or make a mistake. When, for instance, psychological tests administered as part of an applicant testing battery are rescored later at a more leisurely pace, errors often show up. Most are of little practical significance—one or two points one way or the other. Occasionally, however, a sizable disparity is found. For example, a whole column of the answer sheet may have been skipped or counted twice. The same kinds of difficulties are found with other techniques: interviewers frequently forget important information; physicians fail to note important clues to diagnosis; X-ray pictures require considerable skill to interpret, and a tired nurse or medical technician can easily overlook a crucial sign.

In addition, cost considerations tend to limit the use of some available selection techniques. For example, relatively effective tests for epilepsy and other brain disorders have been discovered and could be included in the normal pre-employment physical examination. But the equipment is very costly, the time required considerable, and the incidence of these disorders within the labor force rather low. It is not economical to screen candidates for employment on this basis. Accordingly, such cases as do occur often go undetected. The same is true of psychological tests. A good selection battery for a given job is developed only after an extensive process involving comparison of test scores with various indexes of performance effectiveness. This is worthwhile only if the company hires sizable numbers of people in the position or positions for which the test battery was developed. Since most companies have many positions for which new employees are needed only occasionally, large numbers of people are hired across many jobs without the extensive screening that could be used if cost were not a factor.

Other Screening Problems

The failure of screening to totally solve the problem of employee ineffectiveness cannot, however, be entirely blamed on difficulties with the selection instruments themselves. There are also such factors as ambiguous definitions of performance and unstable standards. For example, two supervisors may utilize distinctly different criteria in evaluating the performance of subordinates. That makes it possible for two employees whose job behavior is practically identical to be evaluated quite differently. One may be considered ineffective, the other not. No amount of research on selection techniques alone can yield a way of correctly predicting how the performances of these employees will be evaluated.

Either we must develop some approach that will allow for differences in methods of judging performance, or objective and precise performance criteria must be consistently applied.

This problem is further compounded by the fact that the same employee may work under a succession of supervisors, all utilizing somewhat different performance criteria. Where objective measures of performance have been developed, usually by an organizational group such as industrial engineers or personnel research, these variations in evaluations are minimized. But there are many jobs, especially at the management level, where subjective judgments by a superior are all that are available. The usefulness of screening procedures is clearly dependent on the degree of precision and consistency attained in performance evaluation. We cannot achieve high levels of success in screening out ineffective performers when there is no certainty about what will constitute true failure at a given time.

Change is, of course, not restricted to standards. Any shift in the work environment, the composition of the work group, the individual employee, or the job requirements may invalidate predictions and thus result in less than perfect screening. Emotional and physical problems may develop in a person who was healthy when hired. Interests and motivation may change. Or the job itself may have to be adapted to a changing technology. So far, initial screening procedures that will predict and adjust for such changes have not been forthcoming.

There are also times when potentially ineffective performers are hired even though the selection process has clearly identified their problems. This often happens when the labor market is extremely tight. If shortages in an occupation are so acute that enough qualified people cannot be found, a firm may have to accept applicants for whom the probability of failure is known to be high. A few such people may prove to be better than expected. Others will perform in a satisfactory manner for a brief period of time. It is better to have someone doing something than to let a position go unfilled because no qualified applicants can be found. Also, a number of firms have hired socially disadvantaged people with a high failure risk in order to meet governmental pressures or to be socially responsible.

Since someone may fail in one aspect of the work while at the same time performing successfully in other areas, a company may hire someone despite known weaknesses. On occasion, it is expedient to accept deficiencies in order to gain the advantages of certain strengths. This is often true in the case of a staff specialist or a policymaker. The company will then usually make every effort to minimize the consequences of the individual's weaknesses. This does not relieve the person's superior of the need for dealing with the problem of failure, however. It only restricts the manager's freedom of action in dealing with the problem, since hiring occurred with a proviso that the person would be retained and in a job that makes maximum use of his or her talents.

In short, while screening can reduce the need to deal with unsatisfactory performance, it cannot relieve the manager entirely of responsibilities in this area. In this respect, as in many others, managerial work emerges as largely unprogrammed and full of uncertainties. It is just such uncertainties—and the need to cope with problems as they arise—that make managing so challenging, and for many so personally satisfying.

Firing as a Solution

Another approach, which eliminates the need for understanding and dealing with the ineffective performer, is to simply fire the employee. If all poor performers were fired as soon as their failings surfaced, there would be no need to determine the causes of the difficulty. This is an appealing answer and under certain circumstances an entirely appropriate one. Where there has been an opportunity to employ it, managers have frequently done so. Historically, firing has been the preferred solution in most instances of performance failure.

At present, however, the climate of public opinion and the external governmental controls under which organizations operate make retirement and disciplinary action for dishonest or antisocial behavior the only bases for forcibly terminating an employee that one can be sure will not meet resistance. True, layoffs are also generally accepted by the public, as a matter of economic necessity. Layoffs and retirements, however, usually have little impact on the proportion of the work force that is ineffective, and disciplinary firing is actually applied in a very small number of cases. Layoffs are generally carried out according to seniority rather than on a merit basis, so those with poor performance records are no more likely to go than anyone else. Retirements, if they are based on strict adherence to a predetermined retirement age, do not take differences in effectiveness into account. An exception is disability retirement, which, of course, is performance-related.

Why is it that firing for poor performance has become so difficult? As was mentioned, the pressure of public opinion is a major factor. More and more, management's right to "terminate at will" is being questioned. With increased realization that the individual may not be entirely responsible for failure, and that increased effort alone may not always solve the problem, there has come a feeling that dismissal may often be unfair. This view has without question helped to produce many of the limitations on a manager's freedom to fire.

Drawbacks of Dismissal

One factor restricting dismissal for ineffective performance is the necessity of paying for work not performed. Companies contribute to state unemployment compensation funds in accordance with experience rating procedures that in most cases result in larger payments by firms with a greater number of ex-employees filing claims. In addition, many companies have agreements, either formal or informal, requiring severance payments to any employee who is terminated after a minimum period of service. This means that firing creates costs, which may not be great but must be considered when dismissal is contemplated.

Other costs can result as well. If it is ruled that the firing represents an unfair labor practice—for example, that dismissal resulted from union activity—the company may have to reinstate the employee with back pay. Even if the company wins such a case, either before the National Labor Relations Board or in the courts, the process is likely to be time-consuming and expensive. The same considerations apply to cases where there might be discrimination on the basis of race, color, religion, national origin, sex, age, or handicap. Furthermore, any discharge may result in a grievance being filed by the union and perhaps arbitration. Or a strike may be precipitated. This is particularly likely when a no-strike clause has not been written into the labor contract. But even with such a clause, a wildcat strike or a slowdown is possible. With any of these eventualities, the costs to the company, either directly or in terms of lost production, may be sizable, and the original decision by management may have to be reversed—which means the employee may not stay fired.

Even if there is no intervention by a union, those who worked with the fired employee may feel that the dismissal was inequitable and react accordingly. The group may set out to get even with the company by making things difficult for their supervisor. This threat probably has been somewhat exaggerated by management, but it still represents a distinct possibility and therefore deters many managers who might otherwise resort to dismissal. This expectation of employee reprisal is similar to the expectation of consumer reprisal. People's sense of injustice may be so intense that they try to persuade others not to buy the company's products or apply for work there. Thus, both the product market and the available labor market can be reduced.

Other Factors Restricting Dismissal

There are other, less elusive factors. Training a new employee is always a costly process. When an employee is fired, the company not only loses any further return on its investment in that employee, but it usually must pay for training a replacement. For this reason, it is inefficient to dismiss anyone whose skills might be used and who might perform effectively somewhere in the organization. Transfer, if feasible, may make for a considerable saving. Therefore, most companies no longer permit the immediate superior to make termination decisions on a unilateral basis. Because of rising replacement costs resulting from the extensive training that a rapidly changing technology requires, and because the employee might be used elsewhere in the organization, firing has implications extending well beyond the immediate group. Furthermore, conditions in the labor force and within the company may make it difficult to find a suitable replacement. The individual manager may not be aware of these conditions—so termination has tended to become an organizational rather than a purely personal decision. The result is that fewer employees are being fired.

Finally, certain pressures within organizations tend to weigh against dismissal as a solution to ineffectiveness problems. Many firms have an unwritten policy that anyone who has been employed for a considerable length of time, perhaps ten years or so, should not be fired. Of course, an employee who has been unsatisfactory from the beginning should have been released long before, and therefore the company has itself to blame for the current problem. According to this argument, if the ineffectiveness is of comparatively recent origin, the employee should be retained out of appreciation for contributions in the past—for having given so many years to the company.

Firing on the management level has additional limitations. Management groups often feel that no one member should be responsible for the firing of another. It is always possible that political (and personal) rather than performance considerations will be given undue weight. Managers are, of course, forced out, but frequently only after much soul-searching. Managers recognize that firing someone in their group can mean negative social consequences or even near-ostracism. Loyalty to the managerial group is very important in any company, and discharging a fellow member, especially a popular one, may bring down heavy sanctions on the heads of those responsible.

These pressures are not, however, always purely external—they derive from inner values and beliefs that are widely held. It is not easy to fire a person, and the experience of guilt can be very unpleasant. It may well be that this guilt is the strongest deterrent of all.

Pressures such as these, some of them highly rational and pragmatic, others more personal and emotional, do operate to limit firings. In many instances, these pressures can have a positive effect because the manager will then try to deal with ineffective performance and figure out a solution. If, however, the manager cannot find a sensible, visible solution, not firing the employee creates a problem. The manager must continue to get the work done under the handicap of an ineffective subordinate. The employee is locked into a situation of continuing failure. It would seem that firing, and a new start, would be better for all concerned. A good manager will know when this point has been reached and will have the fortitude to act, even if it is unpleasant to do so and some resistance is anticipated.

But keep in mind that an ineffective employee should be fired only after a conscientious effort to deal with the problem internally and to determine the consequences of various courses of action. The causes of failure should be established and the feasibility of taking various corrective steps explored. If the chances of restoring effective performance look bleak and the consequences of firing are not too disproportionately negative, then the decision to terminate should be made.

Key Factors in Performance Failure

Work performance is a complex product, derived from the interaction of many factors inside the individual and in the surrounding environment. Performance control involves the identification of these factors or causes. What are the strategic factors that have combined to make an individual perform below existing standards? This is the diagnostic question on which all corrective action is predicated. In the following chapters, we will provide a framework for answering this question. We will describe aspects of the individual and the environment that may prove strategic and the various ways in which these aspects may operate to produce failure. We will also indicate when these factors can be altered and to what extent—and suggest ways of accomplishing this to bring about a satisfactory level of performance.

Performance control requires a manager to pose a series of questions. Is it possible that this . . . or this . . . or this aspect of the individual or situation may be causing failure? Such questions should then be checked against what you know about the individual's character and work. Some factors will be rejected as untenable; it is unlikely that the failure has been caused in this way. Other factors seem to fit the data and provide clues to what has gone wrong. These emerge as the key factors contributing to ineffective performance.

The number of possible strategic factors is large— so large, in fact, that a manager may have difficulty remembering all the questions that should be asked. It is possible, however, to categorize the various potential key factors under a limited number of headings and thus make the analytic process less cumbersome. The chapter titles in this book represent just such an approach: all possible strategic factors that have been identified to date fall into one of nine areas.

Although extended explanation at this point is unnecessary, a brief summary of the components of this analytic framework will show what we mean by a key factor. The first four categories refer to aspects of the individual. One, there may be some intellectual deficiency relative to job requirements: the person may be lacking in knowledge, intelligence, or mental ability. Two, there may be some emotional problem, perhaps a psychological disorder or illness affecting performance, or perhaps simply an incompatibility between job demands and characteristic ways of expressing feelings. Three, there may be a conflict involving motivations: strong motivations may be blocked at work, or they may be satisfied through activities that do not support effective performance. Four, there may be a physical disorder, deficiency, or characteristic that is detrimental to performance or perhaps incapacitating.

The next four categories refer to the various groups of which the individual is a member. Five, the family or some similar intimate group may precipitate problems that interfere with job performance. Six, the same may be true of the work group, which includes the immediate supervisor as one of its members. Seven, the cause of the difficulty may lie with the company, which, of course, performs a variety of acts and establishes a variety of conditions with a direct impact on individual employees. Eight, performance failure may result when some characteristic of the individual or the job does not fulfill, or is not in harmony with, the demands of society as a whole. These societal demands may be in the form of cultural values or formal laws.

The ninth category is one which might be called situational. It takes into account those nonhuman aspects of the environment—such as the work itself—which may be strategic to performance failure. This category also includes the actions of various groups that may influence the person's behavior even though the person may not be a member of those groups.

There is nothing sacred about this set of factors. It is simply one that has served well in dealing with failing employees and that has the advantage of being comprehensive enough to cover almost all that a manager needs to consider. Individual managers may prefer to develop their own lists of key factors. A similar approach has been taken by Professor Eli Ginzberg of Columbia University, and various consultants and writers also have offered their own alternatives.

Learning About Oneself as Manager

For both the prospective manager and to some degree the current manager who desires to improve and develop, the study of ineffective performance is a two-edged sword. First, would-be managers are cast in the managerial role—faced with the need to cope effectively with problems of subordinate performance failure. Through study, a person can gain some sense of how it feels to actively accept the requirements of a managerial position. Some prospective managers may view this challenge apprehensively or uncertainly, while others may find it provides considerable satisfaction and a sense of increased personal esteem. Either way, learning to deal with ineffective performance does permit you to learn about yourself as manager, by playing the role in your mind. Ultimately you should be able to decide whether you would be miscast in this role. One caution, however: unfamiliar roles often cause considerable discomfort at first. Later they may grow on us and gradually become a source of major satisfactions. This can be the case with managing. It takes time to learn.

For both prospective and current managers, there is a second benefit of learning to deal with ineffective employee performance; this is the other edge of the sword. It equips you to handle failures not only in others, but in yourself as well. Perhaps this is the most important part. Once you have developed a skill in performance control, you can apply it just as well to your own performance problems as to the problems of subordinates. These may be problems currently recognized by those who are already managing, or they may be future problems anticipated by those who expect to manage.

By turning the analytic, diagnostic process inward, you can identify key factors in your own performance problems and then take an active role in correcting them. Perhaps this is the ultimate challenge of managing—to actively control your own behavior so as to play the managerial role well and gain major satisfactions from it.

2

Dealing with Problems of Intelligence and Job Knowledge

Intelligence, mental ability, knowledge, aptitude, talent, literacy, I.Q. mental deficiency, learning ability, reasoning—these are all factors that involve the ability to think, to know, and to solve problems. How do these factors influence job performance—and more particularly, how can they contribute to unsatisfactory performance? Before trying to answer these questions, let us take a look at the nature of intelligence and mental ability.

What Is Intelligence?

Intelligence means the degree to which someone is ready to learn new things rapidly and reason correctly, often as a function of having already developed a relevant base of knowledge. Put somewhat differently, it is the developed capacity to grasp, relate, and use concepts. Thus, mental ability is largely a function of existing knowledge—at least, in so far as existing knowledge can be used to acquire and develop further information. Someone who knows almost nothing about thermodynamics will obviously be less able to deal intelligently with new materials in that field than someone who is expert.

There appear to be three major factors that influence a person's intelligence—native potential, motivation to learn, and environmental stimulus potential.

Native potential refers to a characteristic of brain structure or chemistry that serves to facilitate and limit the development of what is actually manifested as intelligence. Thus native potential is not synonymous with intelligence; it is a *possibility* for learning only. Differences in native potential appear to be already established at birth through heredity. But these differences are not likely to coincide with those found later in actual, manifest intelligence. Native potential does seem to influence the ease with which mental ability may be attained and appears to set a top limit on the possibilities for development. But whether or not development actually occurs depends on the other two factors: motivation and environment. No intelligence test can measure native potential. In fact, we have no way of measuring it at all.

Why, then, do we believe that native potential exists as a factor in intelligence? The evidence comes from two sources. It is known that injury to the brain may substantially reduce mental ability. This does not always happen, and the exact nature of the loss seems to depend on a variety of factors not yet fully understood. Nevertheless, injury to the brain can affect intelligence, and injuries to other parts of the body characteristically do not. It seems likely, therefore, that something about the brain influences intelligence level.

In addition, some people are born with a very limited capacity for learning. No matter how strong the wish and how great the opportunity, they are able to learn and retain only a minimal amount. Many must be maintained in institutions for the mentally deficient. This would indicate that there are differences in mental ability existing from birth which are comparable to differences in physique and physical capacities.

What about the role of motivation in intellectual development? The evidence for that is equally conclusive. People who are actively interested in learning and developing, who want to accumulate new knowledge, will in fact develop their native potential more fully, other things being equal, than those without such interests. This is particularly true in childhood. Children who are strongly competitive, who are sufficiently independent to initiate many activities on their own, who are motivated to achieve, and who persist in the face of failure are likely to increase sharply in I.Q. When children tend to lean frequently on others for help and take little interest in accomplishing things on their own, the development of intelligence is correspondingly curtailed. The belief that motivation plays a key role in intellectual development is strongly supported by a sizable body of research emphasizing the importance of striving and being motivated during the learning process.

There is also strong evidence on the third factor: environmental stimulus potential. The richer the environment, and thus the greater the opportunity for learning, the more likely people are to develop their native potential. Certainly, if the environment is intellectually barren, it makes little difference that native potential is high and motivation to learn strong. Learning will be curtailed and intelligence will suffer.

Children in England who had been brought up on canalboats were tested and the intelligence of those at different age levels compared. Until about the age of six, these children scored nearly as well as those living elsewhere. But the older children, who attended school only

5 percent of the time normal for English children, were markedly deficient relative to others of a similar age. Whereas most children have a constant exposure to new material as a result of their schooling and thus continue to develop their intelligence, the canalboat children had practically exhausted the potential for learning in their environment by the age of six. A similar drop in rates of learning has been found among children living in isolated mountainous areas in the southeastern United States.

The best available evidence suggests, then, that for optimal development of intelligence, a person must have a sizable native potential, must have strong motivation for learning that goes back to childhood, and must have been exposed during this same period to a rich learning environment. To the extent that any of these is lacking, intelligence will suffer and the speed of new learning will be reduced. Mental ability is definitely not a direct and unchanging product of hereditary conditions existing at birth.

Mental Abilities—Which Are Important to Job Performance?

As a result of differences in interests and motivation, as well as differences in opportunities for learning, most people develop abilities in certain areas and fail to develop them, or develop them to a lesser extent, in others. For example, a child whose father takes apart the family car and then puts it back together again nearly every weekend is likely to develop similar interests. Under these circumstances, one would expect a greater development of mechanical ability than in a child of equal native potential who spent most of his or her free time reading.

In a similar manner, many other abilities develop. Intelligence is the total complex of these special abilities as they exist in the individual. Any broad area in which people can become interested and learn can be the springboard for developing a special ability. In actual fact, however, four areas appear to be particularly significant in job performance. In order of their apparent importance for the prediction of job proficiency, they are:

- *Verbal ability:* a knowledge of words and their use.
- *Numerical ability:* skill in manipulating numbers.
- *Mechanical ability:* a capacity for dealing with mechanical objects and a knowledge of the principles that govern their operation.
- *Spatial ability:* skill in visualizing and relating objects in accordance with their shapes and positions.

Of course, tests of many other mental abilities have been developed, and many of these have been helpful in understanding some specific types of work performance. In addition, a great variety of tests measure some limited aspect within each of the four broad areas mentioned. For the manager, however, these four general abilities are the most important to understand.

Most people are somewhat more competent in certain areas than in others, and sometimes one or two abilities are *considerably* superior. But it is more typical for all of a person's abilities to be at approximately the same level. If one ability is well below average, the others are likely to be similarly depressed. This finding is not too surprising in view of the way intelligence develops. Although a person may be more interested in one area than in another, the real and important motivational differences are between people who are generally competitive, active, and curious and those who are not. Similarly, environments are characteristically rich or poor in the opportunities they provide for development in all areas. American elementary schools almost invariably offer the child a chance to develop verbal, numerical, mechanical, and spatial abilities nearly simultaneously, although the first two usually receive the greatest emphasis. These similarities between the levels of motivation to learn and environmental stimulus potential in all of the various ability areas apparently account for the substantial relationship among abilities that is found in most people.

Our discussion of how various abilities constitute intelligence raises a question about intelligence tests. There are several well-known tests usually considered to be measures of general intelligence or I.Q.: the Stanford-Binet, the various Wechsler scales, the Concept Mastery Test, and so on. But how can any test measure the general characteristic of intelligence if it is a complex of special abilities?

These so-called I.Q. tests do not really provide information on a single competence. They are, in fact, conglomerates that tap a variety of abilities and combine the results into a total score. Yet one ability invariably predominates: verbal. General intelligence tests are primarily measures of verbal ability, although several other abilities are almost always included.

There is good reason for this emphasis on verbal ability, since it appears to be the most important aspect of intelligence as recognized in our society. Verbal ability occupies a position that is in many ways unique. Words and verbal structures are our primary means of communication. In a society that is advancing rapidly as new ideas and technologies develop, the transmission of knowledge takes on tremendous importance. A society in which communication was severely restricted would progress slowly, if at all. Each individual would have to start over again, without benefit of the experience of other people who had been engaged in similar efforts.

In our society, then, information is transmitted largely through the written and spoken word. Teaching is primarily a verbal process. So is thinking: because we communicate primarily with words, we tend to think with them also. This situation need not exist in all societies; other abilities may assume this superordinate position and presumably have, on occasion, throughout history. But in highly industrialized countries such as the United States, the predominance of the verbal would seem to be a necessity. It is only appropriate that the major measures of mental ability should reflect this cultural emphasis.

The Importance of Job Knowledge

In addition to the four kinds of abilities we have already discussed, there are also more limited spheres of intellectual competence that tend to be specific to particular jobs or job families. These represent the intellectual skills and knowledge required to perform certain kinds of work. Much of this knowledge has become generally associated with a given occupation. One needs knowledge of accounting in order to perform accounting functions, knowledge of engineering in order to perform as an engineer, and knowledge of typing, shorthand, filing, and now often computer applications in order to be a satisfactory secretary.

But there is also job knowledge that relates to a specific company and the environment in which it operates. It can be important to know company policies, be informed about sources of services in a given area, know the local labor market, understand the biases and preferences of certain other people within the company, be perceptive about such matters as organizational climate or culture, and know customers. These things are not taught in school, but they are intellectual in nature and they do matter.

Much the same type of knowledge comes from what may be called cultural learning. A study for The Conference Board conducted by Alan Janger and Ruth Schaeffer indicates that the major problems causing poor performance among the culturally disadvantaged are lack of basic education or skills training, inability to manage one's personal affairs, poor knowledge of the general and specific requirements of the work situation, inability to defer satisfactions, suppressed hostility toward whites on the part of minority group members, and low motivation. Many of these problems are intellectual in nature, and a substantial number are related to deficient job knowledge in the broad sense, caused by a lack of cultural learning.

Job knowledge, defined to include knowledge of the organization's culture and of the factors influencing a company's operations, is perhaps the most underrated aspect of managerial work. It is vital to know the nature of the industry, the company's competitive situation, and the characteristics of the people with whom one must work. But these matters are too specific to be included in a general education, so they often have not received the attention they deserve.

Defects of Judgment or Memory

Before turning to the relationship between intelligence and performance, we should mention one additional aspect of intellectual functioning. Some people have considerable difficulty remembering things and using good judgment or common sense. Such people may, nevertheless, score relatively well on tests of mental abilities. Yet anyone who talks to them over an extended time is left with an indelible impression that there is something wrong with their intellectual functioning. They may fabricate stories to cover gaps in memory, or they may complain about their inability to remember things. They may come to almost nonsensical decisions regarding appropriate courses of action in certain areas, while still being able to make rational choices in other areas. They sometimes stop rather suddenly in the middle of a sentence as if they had forgotten entirely what they were talking about.

Such people are likely to be suffering from some physical or emotional disorder that has affected the intellectual sphere. We have already referred to brain injuries and disorders. Conditions of this kind can bring about defects in memory and judgment of the type just mentioned. Similarly, people with emotional disorders tend to eliminate from their consciousness anything that is excessively disturbing, thereby producing what appears as a gap in memory. And strong emotions may influence the processes of intelligence, resulting in decisions that seem totally devoid of common sense and rationality. In these instances, intellectual competence is reduced, but only because of factors known to be of physical or emotional origin. Brain disorder and emotional illness will be discussed at greater length in succeeding chapters.

Matching Verbal Ability Requirements to the Job

The generalization that verbal ability is the most important aspect of intelligence in our society certainly holds true for ineffective job performance. Every job has a minimum verbal level required for satisfactory performance. A person who falls below the level will probably fail in that type of work. Yet that person might easily qualify for another, less intellectually demanding occupation. Of course, many employees *exceed* the minimal verbal level of an occupation.

For practical purposes, the hierarchy of occupations may be broken into four groups according to how much verbal ability is required for effective performance. At the top are occupations such as accountant, industrial chemist, civil engineer, bank executive, lawyer, office manager, personnel manager, sales manager, treasurer, purchasing agent, and many others of a professional or managerial nature. These positions are held by about 12 percent of the labor force. It is extremely improbable that work at this level can be performed by a person whose verbal ability does not place him or her in the upper half of the working population. The specific lower boundary in terms of verbal ability will vary with the particular occupation and with the type of standards established in a given company. With one group of over forty successful officers of large corporations whom I tested, none had a verbal ability that fell below the top 25 percent. Presumably, some people of lower verbal ability are promoted into such top executive positions but cannot maintain an effective level of performance in competition with their more talented peers. As part of the same study, a number of distinguished professors in major colleges and universities were also tested. All were well into the upper 20 percent of the population in verbal ability.

The second level of occupations contains primarily skilled workers and lower-level supervisors: carpenters, clerk-typists, maintenance supervisors, service station managers, plumbers, sales representatives, timekeepers, credit investigators, surveyors, automobile mechanics, and so forth. This group includes about 32 percent of the labor force. Anyone falling in the lower 25 percent on verbal ability is very likely to fail at these jobs. Of course, because of standards established by specific employers, many of these jobs will require intelligence considerably above this level.

The third group is semiskilled and includes some 38 percent of the working population. Typical jobs are boilermaker, bulldozer operator, knitting machine operator, receptionist, truck driver, drill press operator, salesclerk, watchman, shipping clerk, and mechanic's helper. Anyone above the lowest 10 percent of the labor force in verbal ability should be capable of performing effectively in these jobs insofar as verbal intelligence is concerned. Below that 10 percent level, the failure rate can be expected to rise rapidly.

The fourth and lowest group includes 18 percent of the labor force. The work is all unskilled: construction laborer, elevator operator, loader, janitor, longshoreman, butcher's helper, packer, dishwasher, mason's helper, bootblack, and so on. Since the intellectual demands are minimal, these jobs can be filled by almost anyone. Most unskilled jobs do not require a high level of literacy; some require none at all. The only group that might be excluded from these jobs would be the roughly 2 percent of the population generally classified as mentally deficient. Even some people at this very low level can hold unskilled jobs; many more are institutionalized and thus are not even potentially a part of the labor force.

The Role of Special Abilities: Numerical, Mechanical, Spatial, and Verbal

Once minimum verbal demands are met for a certain job, other factors become important in influencing the level of performance. Some are intellectual; some are emotional, motivational, or physical. Here we will deal with the intellectual sphere and leave the other areas for later chapters.

The intellectual factors other than verbal ability which are important to performance tend to vary with different occupations and jobs. Numerical ability, for instance, must be at a relatively high level in occupations such as accountant, office manager, production manager, pharmacist, treasurer, and comptroller. Mechanical ability is required among airline pilots, contractors, electricians, mechanics, and certain types of engineers. Spatial ability is crucial for architects, artists, civil engineers, and surveyors. Verbal ability not only generally determines occupational level, but is also a special ability of great importance in occupations such as college professor, industrial relations specialist, lawyer, corporate officer, and writer.

A lack of any one of these special abilities may well prove to be a factor in performance failure. Thus, a manager seeking to determine what has caused ineffective performance must know something about the abilities required for various jobs in the unit. The examples noted in the preceding paragraph were drawn primarily from higher-level occupations. What about other kinds of work?

To some extent, an intimate knowledge of job duties will provide a picture of the necessary abilities. Especially when starting to direct a new activity, a manager will find that perusing job descriptions and specifications can be very helpful, even when they do not actually state intelligence requirements. In addition, the United States Employment and Training Administration has accumulated a great deal of information about the ability requirements for various occupations through its extensive use of the General Aptitude Test Battery.

Identifying Intellectual Factors in Poor Performance

Identifying intellectual factors that are strategic in ineffective performance is not always easy. When such factors are suspected, the ideal procedure is to compare the individual's test scores with those of people performing similar work. Does this employee score relatively low on a measure of general intelligence or verbal ability? Or low on tests of special abilities known to be important in performance? How about achievement tests tapping the specific job knowledge required? Does the employee fail to measure up to others on tests of memory functioning or judgment?

Unfortunately, it's not always possible to make this kind of comparison based on the specific factors thought to be strategic. Observation of work behavior and discussions with the employee may be the only sources of information available. Or psychological testing may be appropriate only for checking one hypothesis, such as the possibility of insufficient verbal ability, while the testing of other hypotheses may be limited to whatever can be learned from conversations and observation of behavior. Fortunately, studies conducted by myself and by others concerning the accuracy of intelligence estimates made during employment interviews do indicate that in the hands of experienced managers, such nontest approaches can be quite valid.

The usual signs of intellectual difficulty on the employee's part are an excessive number of mistakes and slowness in learning. People lacking the required mental ability characteristically take an unusual amount of time to learn new tasks. This slowness in learning the unfamiliar may stand in marked contrast to a considerable competence in dealing with material to which the employee has had long exposure.

In early stages of a new job, the diagnostic task is made more complex by the problem of determining whether trouble is due to lack of ability or insufficient job knowledge. If normal training has been completed yet learning is inadequate, the answer is probably a deficiency in intelligence. However, if training has been short-circuited but there is evidence of previous intellectual accomplishment such as a college degree or a military commission, job knowledge is probably deficient.

The manager's diagnosis problems are compounded by the fact that slow learning of job duties and "silly" mistakes are not the only manifestations of intellectual difficulties. Employees may attempt to avoid tasks they don't understand or that they know they cannot handle intellectually. As a result, they may appear to be "goofing off" or insubordinate rather than lacking in mental ability or knowledge. In such instances, the manager should try forcing compliance and observing the results, to determine what would happen if avoidance were not possible.

In other cases, people may appear insubordinate because they lack the mental ability to grasp company rules and regulations rapidly. Workers, for instance, may consistently disobey safety regulations simply because they do not understand them. Often, in such situations, the manager involved cannot believe that "anyone could be so stupid." The assumption is that the problem is basically of an emotional or motivational nature—that the worker is a troublemaker. Therefore, the manager fails to ask direct questions that would reveal the extent of actual knowledge.

There are other ways in which intellectual deficiency relative to job demands may manifest itself. Faced with a situation that makes them feel constantly inadequate, people who lack the needed verbal ability, special ability, or job knowledge may become emotionally upset. It is not a pleasant experience to be continually expected to perform tasks that are beyond one's intellectual capacity. Eventually the feeling of being in over one's head is likely to take its toll. Severe emotional disorders do, on occasion, result from such situations. More frequently, the emotional reaction is transitory. The person is touchy, gets mad with little provocation, or often feels anxious and upset. In any case, the underlying intellectual factor can be masked by the emotional problems, which, although they may also be contributing, are not the most important determinants of the failure.

Dealing with Overplacement

The intellectual factors that can influence performance have been discussed separately because there is no universal solution to difficulties arising out of intellectual causes. What will work with one kind of problem will not necessarily work with another.

If necessary verbal ability is lacking, demotion appears to be the best answer. Studies conducted by British psychologist Philip Vernon established that performance in a new job was best predicted from a knowledge of the person's effectiveness in very similar positions. But where such comparisons could not be made—as when similar prior experience was lacking—a measure of general intelligence or verbal ability was the most valuable indicator. Furthermore, if a person failed in a job, a transfer to some other type of work at the same level frequently proved unsatisfactory. The individual was very likely to fail again even when interest in the new position had been expressed. Demotion, on the other hand, characteristically produced both effective performance and, in the long run, a happier individual.

For the manager, it is not easy to shift a person to a lower position and either reduce the salary level or place a lower limit on future salary increases. In fact, demotion is probably the most difficult personnel action that a manager can take. Firing can be easier, since the individual is quickly gone and any guilt and remorse that the manager may experience are more easily forgotten. In the case of demotion, the employee is constantly present to serve as a reminder of the unpleasantness involved.

For this reason, many firms rarely demote an employee, even when the individual involved would prefer such action to remaining in the present position or being dismissed. In one case, when a company psychologist recommended a sharp reduction in grade to overcome the difficulties associated with an employee's overplacement, those responsible for the decision could not bring themselves to carry out the demotion. This was in spite of the fact that the man wanted to be demoted and would have been much happier if the action had been taken all at once. It took two years of gradual demotions and continued ineffectiveness before the man was finally placed in a job at a low enough level to permit him to contribute effectively. Such instances are not uncommon. Perhaps demotion is more easily accomplished if the manager realizes that there is no other practical way of salvaging the employee as an effective performer—as is usually true when there has been overplacement in terms of verbal ability.

The Use of Transfer and Training

When an employee clearly is on the right job level but is still failing, the various special abilities become important. If there is a deficiency in this respect, the employee might be transferred to another position, one at approximately the same level but more consistent with his or her particular constellation of abilities. This should be done with knowledge, not on a random basis. It should be clear that the employee is failing in the present position because of inadequate spatial, mechanical, or numerical ability, or lack of the extra verbal ability needed for the particular job. It should also be clear that the employee possesses specific abilities that will contribute to success in a new position on the same level.

These recommendations are based on the assumption that mental abilities in adults are essentially static and that therefore the job must be adjusted to the individual rather than the individual to the job. However, this is only partially true. The very sizable body of research in this area has been reviewed by Professor Joseph Matarazzo of the University of Oregon Medical School, and the following discussion is based on his conclusions. Intelligence level does change. If abilities go unused for long periods of time and there is no opportunity for practicing what has been learned, some decline may occur. Even verbal ability, which under normal circumstances receives constant use and practice, may diminish slightly if there is considerable isolation. However, other research indicates that verbal ability normally tends to rise slowly throughout the adult years in a sizable segment of the population.

But these are all gradual changes. Is it possible in a relatively short time to raise people's abilities so that they can perform effectively in a job for which they previously lacked the necessary intelligence? Or are there instances in which intelligence level has decreased markedly over a period of a few months? Allowing for the measurement errors inherent in testing instruments and the conditions under which they must be administered, sizable short-term decreases probably occur only when there has been some damage to the brain. Increases, on the other hand, do apparently take place in certain individuals who receive concentrated training. The optimum conditions seem to be a very low initial level of ability and a situation where the deficiency is caused by limited opportunity rather than insufficient native potential.

Thus, intensive training *can* raise people with mental deficiencies to at least a satisfactory level. In actuality, however, such increases in ability appear to be very rare. Among working adults, opportunities and motivation for extensive, concentrated new learning are at a minimum. If people are holding jobs, they cannot devote the same amount of time and effort to learning as they did in earlier years as students.

The implication is that companies probably can bring about changes in the mental abilities of employees if they are willing to assume sizable costs for lost work time and training. Under normal circumstances, however, demoting or transferring people and replacing them with qualified workers is more likely to produce an effective performance level while keeping costs to a fraction of what they would be with a special training program. This is only true, of course, when replacements with appropriate abilities are available. In other instances, such as when a company is operating in an underdeveloped country and must rely on the local populace for manpower, an investment in extensive educational programs designed to raise intelligence levels may be the only possible solution. Also, as Professor Peter Doeinger of Harvard University reports, certain companies are getting involved in remedial education programs for the culturally disadvantaged.

Usually, companies must furnish any training that is unique to the particular firm or industry, largely because society is generally unwilling to do so. In times of occupational shortages, a firm may have to move into more general occupational and professional training also, in order to compete for personnel. Certainly where performance failure is attributable to a lack of specific knowledge, the appropriate solution is some type of training or education. Whether this will be provided within the company, outside the company at company expense, or entirely through outside resources depends on many factors—the availability of training, the length of training, employee interests, and so on. When the employee has no desire to increase his or her knowledge of a job, or when training is not feasible because of insufficient facilities or excessive duration, the answer may be transfer rather than training.

In summary, performance is most likely to be improved by demotion when there is a lack of verbal ability, by transfer at the same level when job-related special abilities are insufficient, and by training when inadequate job knowledge is the cause of performance failure. However, when deficiencies in memory or judgment are caused by brain disorder or psychological problems, the intellectual problems can be handled only by taking some action to deal with the underlying physical or emotional factors.

3

Dealing with Emotional Problems

In this chapter we will discuss emotional problems as they affect job performance, while the next chapter will cover motivational problems. Many people lump all these problems together under the label of personality—they speak of personality traits without differentiating between those of a primarily emotional nature, such as chronic pessimism, anger, and nervousness, and those that are basically motivational, such as the desire for power, the need to conform, and dedication to work. The reason for making the distinction here and treating emotions separately from motivation is purely practical. To use a single concept, personality, would mask differences that are important in taking the correct managerial action to improve performance.

Since we are interested specifically in those emotions which may cause ineffective performance, we must emphasize the less pleasant ones—anxiety and fear, shame and guilt, grief and depression. We will also touch on anger, hatred, jealousy, and extreme excitement. The more positive emotions—such as love, happiness, and joy—will get only fleeting reference. Much of the discussion will be devoted to emotional illness, because it is often this problem that has the greatest influence on job performance.

The Manager and Emotional Disorder

Some readers may be concerned about the propriety of discussing topics generally considered to be the exclusive province of clinical psychologists and psychiatrists. You may feel that the diagnosis and treatment of emotional disorders should be specifically reserved to the professionally qualified and that not even limited information should be given to those without specific training in the area. In other words, "a little knowledge is a dangerous thing."

This is a valid position if you are talking about the detailed diagnosis and treatment of severe emotional disorders. These tasks should be reserved to those with professional training. It is also true that some people with a limited knowledge of abnormal psychology have said and done things that have negatively affected the emotional adjustment of others. But a manager needs *some* knowledge in this area to perform effectively. And by judiciously applying such knowledge, a manager can benefit individual employees as well as the company. In the discussion here, every effort will be made to provide guidelines that minimize the possibility of inappropriate application.

The point simply is that the manager is on the firing line and in a position to see emotional problems as they evolve. Clinical psychologists and psychiatrists become involved only when someone takes action to get them involved. Managers are in a key position to do this, but they have to know what emotional illness looks like and what its symptoms are. Also, when an emotional disorder interferes with work performance, managers need to know that this is the true nature of the problem, and what can be done about it.

Finally, managers themselves are not immune to emotional problems, and because of the nature of their work any emotional illness is likely to affect their performance. Managers need to know about emotions and emotional disorders in oder to cope with potential problems of their own. (A valuable discussion of the role of anxiety in a manager's life and work, and the methods of dealing with it, is contained in Alan Schoonmaker's *Anxiety and the Executive.*) Thus, for job effectiveness, both in handling subordinates and in handling oneself, managers should be able to know an emotional illness when they see one.

What Is Emotional Disorder?

It is important to distinguish between the term *emotional disorder* and the more widely used *mental disorder.* In a general sense, the two terms refer to the same thing. Mental disorder, however, has a somewhat broader connotation. It includes intellectual deficiencies and disorders involving specific brain damage as well as conditions directly attributable to emotional problems. Since it is only the latter that concern us here, the more specific term *emotional disorder* is appropriate.

The borderline between emotional health and illness is difficult to establish. Basically, emotional disorder is defined in terms of symptoms, but the relationship is not a simple one. Certain types of emotional responses, behaviors, ideas, perceptions, motives, and physical conditions are considered signs of illness. But what these symptoms are can vary from society to society, and even among groups within a single society. Cultural relativism is involved. An example is a man who was discharged from the military service as insane, because he had delusions and hallucinations, but who was able to become a successful minister shortly after returning to his hometown. He retained that position and was treated as an honored member of his community even though for some time he continued to exhibit the same symptoms that had brought about his discharge. In fact, it was largely because of these "symptoms" that he was selected for his job by the congregation; they were viewed as reflecting the minister's close ties with God.

Clearly, there is no single, all-inclusive definition of emotional illness based on the classification of symptoms alone, even though many such definitions have been proposed. Almost invariably these definitions emphasize one group of symptoms at the expense of others. Consistency and severity of manifestation must also be taken into account, and perhaps other factors would be included in an ideal definition as well. Certainly, symptoms which are not persistently evident cannot be considered indicative of a true disorder; neither can those which have little impact on the individual's pattern of life. Anyone can occasionally manifest what appears to be emotional illness. Many people generally considered stable are not entirely free of symptoms, and some suffer from a rather large number. The presence of symptoms alone is not sufficient to warrant a diagnosis of emotional illness.

If we observe people who are considered emotionally disturbed, however, one factor appears to be consistently present. There is a lack of flexibility, a rigidity, that makes it impossible for such people to adapt to the demands of the world around them. The individual not only possesses certain symptoms, but the symptoms appear to take over and exercise almost absolute control. They disrupt the ongoing process of life and impose new patterns, irrespective of what might otherwise be the person's wishes. These new patterns are compulsively inflexible; they do not change with changes in the existing, real world.

This disruption of the ongoing processes of existence may occur in one or more areas—work, love and family life, social relationships generally, recreation and enjoyment of leisure, responses to legal controls. Although from a managerial viewpoint, disruption in work is the most significant, symptoms frequently spread from one area of life to another, so that events in a nonwork area may subsequently affect job performance.

People whose symptoms do not disrupt the ongoing process of life in this way are not usually considered emotionally ill. They may retain sufficient flexibility to continue their normal life patterns with minimal change and to adapt to varying circumstances as they occur. Although such people may not be diagnosed as emotionally disturbed, they may gain very little happiness from life. Similarly, people may possess symptoms which are so attuned to the demands of their exisiting situation that no disruption occurs. The minister described earlier presumably maintained what was considered an adequate adjustment because his symptoms fitted the expectations of his parishioners. Unfortunately, such people generally lack the flexibility necessary to adapt to changing circumstances. Should their worlds change, their symptoms will almost certainly make it impossible to adjust to the new circumstances, in the same way that the minister was unable to adjust to military demands.

Neurosis and Psychosis

The most important distinction within the emotional disorders, from a managerial viewpoint, is between psychosis and neurosis. The two affect performance differently and they offer somewhat different probabilities of recovery. In one sense this is a matter of severity. In psychosis, the person is so bound up in emotions and the process of defending against them that responsiveness to the demands of the outside world becomes minimal or is totally lost. Emotion is experienced with overpowering intensity, and equally drastic defensive processes are mobilized. Distorted ideas or perceptions are always present, and there is usually strong commitment to them. Interpretations that are inconsistent with reality are not regarded by the psychotic person simply as possibilities. They are beliefs, held with absolute conviction—even though there has been no attempt to check on their validity. These distorted thoughts and perceptions may sometimes manifest themselves in very bizarre behavior and speech.

It is this loss of contact with external reality which distinguishes psychosis from neurosis. In neurosis, a term that we will use to cover all remaining emotional disorders, this break with reality does not occur; individuals do not lose themselves entirely to intense emotion and the process of defense. Instead, they adopt methods for warding off emotion that are generally consistent with the demands of social convention and the need for survival. This conception of the factors distinguishing psychosis and neurosis receives support from a study conducted by Professor Silvan S. Tomkins (now at the University of Pennsylvania) and myself of the personality characteristics of over 400 patients under treatment for psychosis and over 200 under treatment for neurosis. Two features appeared with unusual frequency in all the various types of psychotic groups studied, but rarely in any of the neurotic groups: a marked tendency to perceptual deviance and distortion, and an intense fear of bodily mutilation or disease.

Both neuroses and psychoses can be differentiated by the predominant emotion or emotions present. Intense anxiety or fear is probably most frequent.

Depression (often combined with guilt) is somewhat less common. Instances where anger or extreme excitement predominate are even less frequent, although they certainly do occur. In some cases there is a shift from one predominant emotion to another as the disorder progresses.

The Symptoms of Emotional Problems

What kinds of symptoms are likely to indicate emotional problems? The list that follows is based on a study of over seventy people suffering from many different kinds of disturbances. It does not include every possible manifestation of emotional illness, but it is sufficiently comprehensive to provide a working knowledge in the area. These symptoms may be classified as being primarily emotional, physical, behavioral, or cognitive.

The first type of symptom involves the persistent and intense experiencing of certain emotions—anxiety, fear, panic, depression, grief, guilt, shame, worry, anger, jealousy, belligerence. At such times, people may describe themselves as upset, nervous, tense, or irritable. They may have a feeling of "going all to pieces." They may experience an intense yearning for the presence of certain other people, such as a parent or spouse. Fears can be focused on almost any type of potential catastrophe—death, injury, illness, going crazy, losing control of one's bodily functions, and so on. The emotion may be precipitated by many different kinds of situations or by the thought of being in a particular situation. Typical examples: flying in an airplane, loud noises, darkness when alone, high places, being in the water, closed and stuffy rooms, school examinations, being criticized or reprimanded, crowded places, traveling in buses or trains, being ordered to do something.

Since such emotional experiences are extremely

unpleasant, we characteristically develop defenses that are successful to varying degrees in warding off these experiences. Such defenses act to insulate us from situations that might arouse intensely unpleasant emotions. A person's symptoms may reflect this attempt to avoid feelings, or they may involve a direct manifestation of emotion. Most frequently there is a combination of the two.

Physical symptoms that may arise from emotional problems include:

- Headaches, nausea, and vomiting, especially after meals
- Feelings of pervasive physical weakness, often combined with dizziness or fainting
- Constant fatigue, to the point where getting out of bed in the morning becomes extremely difficult
- Constipation and diarrhea, frequently alternating
- Inability to speak, or a speech defect such as stuttering
- Various skin rashes, especially on the face and hands
- Hand and body tremors, occasionally combined with more specific uncontrolled jerking movements involving muscles of the face or body
- Rapid breathing or difficulty in breathing, often with pounding of the heart
- Stomach pains or cramps, sometimes associated with ulcer formation
- Sudden loss of weight
- Aches and pains in various parts of the body, mainly the lower back and legs
- Frequent motion sickness
- Blurring and sometimes loss of vision
- Numbness of specific parts of the body

All these symptoms may, of course, have physical rather than emotional causes. In addition, a person may have quite bizarre beliefs and feelings concerning the body and physical functioning. Such symptoms are much more likely to be associated with a psychosis than a neurosis.

Another group of symptoms involves overt behavior. To the extent that dysfunctional behaviors have become inflexible, they may be considered possible signs of emotional illness. Examples are:

• Attempting suicide

• Excessive drinking

• Sleepwalking

• Excessive use of drugs

• Outbreaks of uncontrolled rage, perhaps involving homicidal attacks or the breaking of objects such as furniture

• Exposing the genitals in public

• Restlessness and agitation, such as constant pacing or movement of the arms

• Rape

• Banging the head against a wall

• Excessive accidental injuries

• Washing part or all of the body at regular and very frequent intervals

• Shrinking away from people

• Standing woodenly in one place or position

• Writing threatening letters to people in high places

• Sulking and brooding

• Peculiar and childish behavior such as writing on walls or smearing feces

• Compulsive theft

In addition, some behavioral symptoms involve an inability or refusal to do certain things, such as:

- Engage in social activities
- Bathe
- Leave home or a bed
- Go to sleep without long hours of wakefulness
- Eat or drink
- Engage in sexual activity
- Read or write
- Sit down in a chair
- Control bodily functions
- Dress properly

On occasion, apathy, listlessness, and indifference may become so pronounced as to produce an almost total lack of responsiveness. The person appears completely preoccupied and withdrawn from the world or becomes comatose. Such extreme cases clearly indicate psychosis.

Finally, other behavioral symptoms involve speaking or communicating:

- Talking to oneself
- Crying and sobbing for no apparent reason
- Making frequent threats of suicide or homicide
- Inappropriate smiling and smirking, which sometimes develops into senseless laughter
- Excessively rapid speech that continues without interruption for long periods
- Wild and inappropriate yelling
- Incoherent muttering, occasionally combined with drooling
- Shouting or screaming during sleep

- Constant bemoaning of one's lot or protestation of guilt
- Continued and senseless lying, frequently with a view to self-aggrandizement
- Confused and incoherent speech, often involving references to religion, family members, or death

There may also be cognitive symptoms—that is, disturbed thoughts, perceptions, or beliefs—some of which were mentioned briefly in the preceding chapter. Either emotions distort intellectual processes so that intelligence is not fully utilized, or distorted thought processes serve to defend against the experiencing of disturbing emotion. Often there is a complete failure of intellectual functioning: inability to concentrate or pay attention; inability to think through problems to any solution; failure of memory either of recent events or of personally important events of the past; elimination from awareness of thoughts, wishes, and events that might produce unpleasant emotional experiences; inability to decide between alternative actions.

Or the symptoms may involve certain ideas or beliefs that lack foundation in fact. The degree of conviction may vary from a mere notion that such a thing might happen to absolute certainty that it has already occurred. Such ideas vary widely. Some examples are:

- Having a tight belt around one's chest
- Feeling something crawling over one's flesh
- Receiving a visitation from God
- Being constantly watched by other people
- Living in a strange and unreal world
- Having a venereal disease
- Being talked about and made fun of behind one's back
- Having no body

- Being already dead
- Having one's body gradually rot away
- Having some individual or group such as the FBI or "the Communists" try to bring about one's death
- Being taken advantage of and abused by others
- Having a devil inside which propels one's actions
- Being controlled by some mysterious external force
- Being totally invisible
- Having committed some terrible crime
- Being covered with an evil-smelling liquid
- Being an unrecognized genius
- Knowing that the continents are being gradually inundated by the oceans
- Being a famous person
- Being God

Such beliefs may be coupled with constant suspiciousness, confused thinking, the blaming of others for one's own shortcomings and failures, nightmares, or periods of delirium. There may also be distortions of perception, as, for instance, hearing voices shouting and cursing, seeing people or objects in the dark, being visited by a loved one who has died, or hearing someone try to seduce one into homosexual activities.

In all these instances, it is assumed that the perception or belief lacks foundation in fact. However, the manager who suspects that an employee has an emotional disorder would do well to check on the facts before jumping to conclusions. There was the case of a man from the hill country of the Hatfields and McCoys who was hospitalized because of his repeated contention that someone shot at him every time he used the toilet. Belated investigation revealed that the outhouse near his home had in fact been under fire for some time; there were numerous bullet holes.

Be warned that many emotional symptoms, even some of the most bizarre beliefs and behaviors, may not be manifested in the presence of superiors at work. Therefore, an emotional disturbance may go undetected for a long period of time as a cause of unsatisfactory work performance. I remember with some chagrin two occasions when I failed to note severe emotional symptoms in secretaries doing work for me. In both instances, the nature of the difficulties did not become apparent until the young women asked for help in obtaining treatment. Clearly, a person may be severely upset inside and yet give very little evidence of it. Eventually, however, the problems come out.

Experienced managers, especially those who have spent considerable time as first-level supervisors of large groups of subordinates, invariably report numerous instances when they have had to deal with symptoms of the kind we have described. The symptoms can become evident in a number of ways: during a discussion of lateness or absenteeism; when there's a severe failure in performance; as a dramatic psychotic outbreak that is evident to everyone; or during an exit interview at the time of a premature and unexpected separation.

How prevalent are symptoms of neurosis and psychosis? Answers vary depending on, among other things, the groups studied and the diagnostic methods used. Professors Bruce and Barbara Dohrenwend of Columbia University and the City University of New York, respectively, have reviewed the many studies involving this question. In urban areas of the United States, the average rate of emotional illness appears to be approximately 20 percent; in rural areas it is a few percentage points lower. Recent findings published in the *Archives of General Psychiatry* confirm the roughly 20 percent figure. There appears to have been little change over the years. Without question, the incidence of emotional illness in most work situations will run lower than in the population as a whole, simply because of pre-employment screening. Even so, we are dealing with a substantial number of people, especially when the supervised group contains large numbers of employees from the lower socioeconomic levels, where the incidence of emotional illness tends to be higher.

What Causes Emotional Problems?

What are the factors leading to emotional problems and breakdowns? What aspects of the individual and the environment coalesce to produce such severe and inflexible symptoms that the ongoing process of life is disrupted?

One factor is the number of situations which are seen as directly threatening or which stir up potentially disturbing thoughts, emotions, and impulses within the individual. Different people tend to be emotionally reactive to different kinds of situations. Just how these specific sensitivities are developed has not been definitely established, but that they exist is clear. The greater the number of such personally stressful situations, the more likely it is that a person will be exposed at some point to a potentially disturbing environment. The range of these specific sensitivities within an individual may be very limited, as is presumably the case in most people we would consider emotionally stable. But it may also be very large, to the point where anxiety is a constant presence in practically every environment.

A second factor is the frequency or duration of actual exposure to stressful situations—or the number of times a person feels that such exposure is imminent. Of course, if people can avoid upsetting situations without seriously disrupting the course of their lives, they may minimize the probability of emotional breakdown.

Or they may not have to expose themselves to their particular problem situations for long periods of time. For example, some people are excessively sensitive to hospitals with their aura of sickness, injury, and death. Consequently they may decide at an early age that a career in medicine is not for them. Or they may have been offered so many inducements to enter the business world that alternative courses, such as a career in medicine with its potential for triggering emotional disorder, may never have been considered seriously at all. In instances such as these, avoidance of hospitals could not be taken as indicative of emotional illness. However, a person who requires hospitalization for a physical illness and continually refuses treatment would not be considered satisfactorily adjusted. The same would be true if that person were to enter the hospital and subsequently develop emotional symptoms that interfered with the normal processes of treatment and cure.

Another factor is the intensity of the emotional experience aroused by the situation. If the intensity is low, then frequent exposure for long periods may not actually be debilitating. On the other hand, a single extremely intense emotional experience, such as the death of a loved one or some act of unaccustomed personal violence, may be sufficient to set off a lengthy period of illness. The intensity factor must, however, be evaluated together with the individual's capacity to withstand unpleasant emotion. Some people can handle considerable anxiety without resorting to defensive maneuvers or allowing the emotion to disrupt normal behavior. Others seem to be affected almost immediately and react in drastic ways to the slightest tinge of fear. What produces these differences we do not know.

Specific Emotions and Performance

From what we have said so far, it is clear that emotions and emotional disturbances may or may not affect job performance. The effects vary with the emotions aroused, their severity, the type of defenses employed, and the specific nature of the work situation. Without question, some people perform *more* effectively in certain jobs as a result of their emotional problems. They may, for instance, be driven to an intense concentration on work in an effort to ward off anxiety and guilt. Under many circumstances, however, anxiety, depression, anger, and other emotions cause performance failure. Similarly, the various techniques people adopt to defend against disturbing emotions frequently serve to decrease their effectiveness.

Research on anxiety reported by Professor Harold Basowitz of New York University and others has revealed a number of ways in which it may affect performance. Visual perception is likely to be disturbed, with a resulting increase in errors on tasks such as those performed in clerical occupations, inspection jobs, and the like. This reduced perceptual efficiency is also reflected in a general reduction of speed of performance. There is likely to be difficulty in learning new things. The anxious employee characteristically needs a much longer period of training when introduced to unfamiliar job duties, and even then learning may be incomplete. Skill is decreased in tasks requiring dexterity and muscular coordination. Intellectual processes are also affected: memory is poorer, and reasoning and problem-solving tend to suffer. Apparently the person experiencing severe anxiety finds it so difficult to concentrate on other matters that job demands are not fulfilled.

Depression and guilt have similar effects on performance. In addition, the depressed person tends to slow down markedly, with reduced quantity of work output. There may also be much self-deprecation and a pervasive, almost total loss of confidence. As a result, decisions may be inordinately delayed and the capacity for independent action without constant prodding may be minimal. Where guilt predominates, glaring errors may be made with a view to *provoking* criticism. People may actually bring punishment down on themselves in order to allay their emotion, although they are unlikely to be aware of what they are doing.

Anger may have a different impact on performance. For one thing, the direct and appropriate expression of anger is not common in people suffering from an emotional illness. When anger is found in emotional disorders, expression of it is often delayed to the point where it is very difficult to determine the original precipitating event. Or the anger is intertwined with anxiety and emerges as petulance, sulkiness, negativism, or a constant irritability and moodiness. If negativism predominates, the quality and quantity of work may be impaired because of what amounts to a refusal to do what management wants. Anger and resentment can, on occasion, have a direct disruptive effect on the quality and quantity of the person's work. More frequently, however, the result of chronic anger is a negative impact on the work of others. The individual appears to be a troublemaker, always stirring up fellow employees and interfering with their work. Such general antagonism may also manifest itself in breakage, theft, or other behavior that has a direct detrimental effect on profitability.

These findings do not mean that all emotions have a detrimental effect on performance. Studies reported by Christopher Poulton of Cambridge University in England make it clear that up to a point, emotions have an arousal effect that facilitates performance. At some level, however, the emotion becomes distracting and stressful, and adverse effects on performance emerge. Interestingly, routine, relatively automatic tasks that have been well learned can be performed effectively under much higher levels of stress than can highly skilled activities, such as managerial decision making.

Emotions and Performance at Different Job Levels

This susceptibility of managerial decisions to the effects of emotional stress is important. Certain kinds of managerial decision making can be severely hampered by emotional problems whose existence may not be apparent. It is always difficult to determine exactly what other people think of us. Managers with feelings of inadequacy may not know whether other people also see them in this way. Faced with this ambiguity on such an important issue, such managers tend to fill the gaps in their knowledge with assumptions that may be based on minimal information. Should they develop intense feelings of inferiority and guilt, their job makes it particularly easy to ward off these feelings by a process of selectively perceiving the world around themselves— by utilizing certain sources of information and not others. They may thus defend against their feelings of guilt by forming a conviction that they are really outstanding managers with tremendous capabilities.

Managers are in an ideal position to do this because they can base their ideas about themselves entirely on the statements of their subordinates. Employees are dependent on those above them for salary increases, promotions, even continued employment. As a result, comments by subordinates about their immediate superiors, insofar as they reach the superiors' ears, are likely to be uniformly favorable irrespective of actual performance. Accordingly, a manager can reject, as purely a matter of company politics or sour grapes, any less favorable comments made by other managers at an equal or higher level. On occasion the denial may be total—the manager may completely fail to hear criticism.

As a result of this process of selecting the evidence, managers replace feelings of guilt and inferiority by first a hypothesis, then a conviction of what may border on omniscience. They are sure they have a special skill, a superior business acumen. They become so certain of their marked superiority that they make less and less effort to base their business decisions on actual facts. Each decision becomes a testament to their personal and unique ability. They do not need to collect and evaluate information in order to arrive at a conclusion; they know. There can be little question that when the defensive process attains such proportions, actual job performance suffers drastically. If the manager is at a high level, the impact on company profits because of unwise decisions may be considerable, as Professors Manfred Kets deVries and Danny Miller of McGill University have shown.

Two sources of emotional stress in managerial work have been investigated quite extensively and have been shown to have marked negative effects. Both seem to cause increased feelings of tension, anxiety, and anger. The first source of stress has been studied by Professor John Rizzo of Western Michigan University, among others. It occurs when managers either are totally unsure of what they are supposed to do, or are getting two or more conflicting versions of what they should do from sources that make a difference to them, such as two superiors. The second source of stress was given particular attention by Professor Stephen Sales of Carnegie-Mellon University before his death. He found that when managers are faced with obligations that require them to do more than they can in the time available, they do in fact produce more but at the expense of increased error rates and more physical and emotional stress.

The Impact of Emotional Illness at Lower Levels: This evidence suggests that symptoms of emotional illness are particularly likely to interfere with work when the employee is in a higher-level position. Jobs requiring only limited skill are much less vulnerable to emotional disruption. In one series of studies by Morris

Markowe among semiskilled production workers in a British factory, no relationship between psychiatric ratings of emotional health and job-performance ratings was found at all. Workers with a number of symptoms were no less effective than those who were symptom-free. On the other hand, studies of skilled workers and supervisors have consistently produced results of a very different kind. Indexes of emotional illness predominate among those who are unsuccessful.

My own follow-up study of men discharged from the army during World War II because of incapacitating emotional illness provides further evidence. Employment status approximately ten years after separation from military service was determined for a group of men who had been diagnosed as psychotic and for a group diagnosed as neurotic. Included in the study was a comparable group of men who had not experienced emotional disturbances while in service and who had been discharged during demobilization when the war ended. Among those who had formerly suffered from *psychoses* and who were employed at the time of the follow-up, the level of jobs held was comparable to that among the men who had not experienced an emotional breakdown. There was no evidence that occupational adjustment had suffered from a severe emotional disturbance initiated during military service. However, almost half of those who had been prematurely discharged for psychosis were not working at the time of follow-up. This percentage was almost seven times as large as that in the group demobilized at the end of the war. About a third of the unemployed were in mental hospitals; most of the remainder were still severely disturbed emotionally, even though not hospitalized. Characteristically, the latter had held a number of low-level jobs interspersed with long periods of unemployment. Apparently, either a psychosis subsides relatively rapidly, to the point where a person's career may be resumed, or it lingers and has an almost totally disruptive effect on occupational adjustment. Where symptoms remain of psychotic or near-psychotic proportions, performance is likely to be poor irrespective of job level.

Among those who had suffered from a *neurosis* at the time of discharge, the picture was quite different. Almost all the men were working ten years later. But they were much less likely to be in skilled and supervisory positions than were the men who had not been separated from the army for emotional disorder. Presumably, either the neurotic symptoms had remained long enough in a number of cases to interfere with performance in higher-level positions and thus make demotion necessary, or the symptoms had prevented these men from being selected for employment at higher levels in the first place. In any event, this evidence, combined with that noted previously, makes a convincing case for the theory that neurosis tends to have its greatest impact on work above the semiskilled level.

Apparently, as long as the job remains automatic and routine, workers can almost "do it in their sleep." Under such circumstances, emotional symptoms have little impact. When, however, concentration and attention are required, emotion does interfere and performance is disrupted. Since jobs above the semiskilled level cannot as a rule be performed automatically, emotions and emotional symptoms are more likely to have a detrimental impact on performance. The greater the amount of new learning, thought, and decision making required in a position, the more probable it is that ineffectiveness will be produced by intense emotional experience.

What Should a Manager Do?

Counseling by those without extensive psychological training can be accepted by employees and can contribute to improvement of ineffective performance, as Professor Ivar Berg of Vanderbilt University has demonstrated. On the other hand, a superior often cannot deal with the problem and should refer the individual to an appropriate source equipped to do so. In such cases, try to restrict any comments to matters closely related to the individual's job performance. The same holds true when an emotionally disturbed person returns to work after treatment. You can contribute most to restoring effectiveness by stressing the worker role and performance rather than the patient role and illness.

Obviously, most managers cannot treat emotional problems. They are neither qualified nor in an appropriate position to do so. They can, however, be a vital link between the subordinate and possible treatment sources. It is in this area that some of the greatest difficulties arise. There is an aura of shame and condemnation surrounding the idea of psychiatric treatment, to the point where many people often react negatively to any suggestion that they need help with an emotional problem. Efforts to get someone into treatment are most likely to succeed when the person is experiencing severe anxiety and unhappiness. People are also more receptive to the idea of treatment when they recognize the impending or actual breakdown and the existence of symptoms having emotional origins. Physical symptoms that derive from emotional factors are not likely to be included in this category. Where physical symptoms predominate, people will generally consider their problems to be medical rather than psychiatric and will strongly resist any advice to the contrary. Another factor in attitudes toward treatment is educational level. The higher this is, the more likely that emotionally disturbed people will respond favorably to a suggestion that they might benefit from professional help.

The Need for Caution: Because of the widespread resistance to any idea that problems may be of emotional origin and sufficiently severe to require treatment, it is advisable to be extremely careful in dealing with situations of this type. Efforts born out of the most humane motives can frequently backfire and drastically increase your difficulties. In general, it is probably best not to recommend treatment unless performance has suffered or unless the individual has introduced the subject of emotional problems. Should you announce such a diagnosis to a subordinate when the person's performance is satisfactory, you risk arousing considerable resentment not only in that individual but in the group as a whole should the subordinate share your diagnostic opinion with others. And the individual's condition may deteriorate as a result.

On the other hand, if work has been severely disrupted, managerial initiative of this kind is entirely appropriate—providing, of course, that there is some possibility of success. There is little to be gained by recommending treatment to an employee who will almost certainly reject such a suggestion and who is not sufficiently disturbed to *require* hospitalization. In such cases, where the probability of resistance is very high, some solution other than professional treatment must be formulated.

One further caution: Although many emotionally disturbed people try to keep their superiors from becoming aware of their problems, this is not always the case. Sometimes a subordinate will want to pour out his or her problems to anyone who will listen, or will specifically seek out a supervisor for this purpose. Under such circumstances, it is not easy to turn a cold shoulder. Yet the manager who can send such a person to a more appropriate listener may save much future trouble. The managerial job involves recognizing the need for help and making every effort to see that help is obtained. Should this role be extended, so that the manager-subordinate relationship resembles that between a doctor and a patient, the emotionally disturbed individual can well begin to make special demands on a boss that the latter may find hard to resist. Or in refusing to give such special considerations, the manager may provoke resentments that further aggravate an already difficult situation.

Becoming closely, and perhaps emotionally, involved in a subordinate's problems can have another unfortunate consequence. As the employee pours out problems, much may be revealed about marital difficulties, personal animosities, and so on that will subsequently be regretted. Guilt and shame may follow the discussion, and the subordinate may become so disturbed by the thought of what the superior now knows that all personal contact is avoided. At this point the manager has become a direct source of anxiety to the subordinate, and the work relationship is inevitably and unnecessarily impaired.

Recommended Action: The specific person in the organization to whom emotionally disturbed employees should be referred depends on the company and the nature of the work situation. It should be someone familiar with treatment resources in the community, such as a company psychologist or psychiatrist, a physician in the medical division, or someone in the personnel department. In recent years, a number of organizations have established employee assistance programs for this purpose. But in many instances, such intermediaries within the organization will not exist, and the manager will have to direct subordinates to someone outside the company. If a qualified professional specialist—that is, a clinical psychologist or psychiatrist—is not specified, the employee will probably turn to a clergyman or a physician without psychiatric training. Although such individuals may be able to help when the emotional disturbance is relatively mild, they cannot generally provide treatment for disorders of a more severe nature—the kind that are likely to be present when work performance is disrupted. If conditions reach psychotic proportions, some type of treatment within a mental hospital is usually required. In any event, whether the disorder is a psychosis or a neurosis, the individual should ultimately be seen by a professionally qualified person. Otherwise, it is very unlikely that effective performance will be restored on anything approaching a permanent basis.

For humanitarian reasons, managers may be tempted in cases of emotional illness to adjust their expectations and accept what they would otherwise consider unacceptable performance. In this connection, it is worthwhile to consider the conclusions reached by Professors James Belasco and Harrison Trice of Cornell University following a management development program that dealt extensively with performance failure and emotional problems. The participating managers developed:

1. Significantly greater knowledge about problem employees.

2. Attitudes that reflected less favorable evaluations of problem employees.

3. More favorable action programs, in that they were more likely to deal with problems effectively.

4. Increasing identification with management.

Thus, the managers learned more and developed a greater capacity to deal with the problems, while they became more "hard-nosed," more conscious of their managerial responsibilities, and more likely to do something about the situation. In general, the more managers learn about dealing with problem employees, the more they tend to act in ways aimed at solving the problem, even if this is not what the employee wants, and they are less tempted to be excessively humanitarian, which may only perpetuate the neurosis or psychosis by implicitly endorsing lower standards.

Actions within the Organization

Psychiatrists in the armed forces have found that a high percentage of those discharged for emotional illness readjust rather rapidly. A crucial factor in this high rate of cure seems to be that these individuals were forced out of the situation in which their disorders had become manifest and had to seek a new environment where they could continue their lives. They were aided in finding relatively stress-free situations by families, friends, employers, the Veterans Administration, other veterans' organizations, and educators, but very rarely by any kind of psychotherapy or psychiatric treatment.

Similar readjustments can be made within an organization if sources of stress can be identified and removed. Sometimes a job can be changed to eliminate the causes of anxiety. Sometimes the employee can be shifted to another type of work, another work situation, or another supervisor where the specific sensitivities will not be activated. Frequently, assigning more routine tasks that require less concentration and decision making will permit the employee to perform effectively despite the symptoms. For this approach to work, you must find a situation in which either stress will be minimized or symptoms will not interfere. At the same time, the employee should be induced to begin treatment if this is appropriate and feasible. Often, demotion to a less emotionally demanding position is required, although sometimes promotion to a job that carries more status and reduces shame and embarrassment can help. The course you take must be based on the nature of the symptoms, the type of emotion, and any specific sources of stress that may be present at work.

In many instances, of course, this kind of organizational action will be severely restricted by the options that are actually available. It may well be, especially where symptoms are of a severe nature, that after all possible means of retention have been explored, employment will have to be terminated, or at least a leave of absence arranged. Further investment in the employee may be unwarranted when the possibilities for future effective performance in an appropriate job are realistically remote.

Should a terminated employee subsequently appear to have recovered, there is always the possibility of rehiring. The experience of companies in hiring former psychiatric patients is mixed, as one might expect: some are cured, some are not, and some will readjust gradually as they move into the world of work. Studies conducted by Professor Donald Searls of Colorado State University and his colleagues provide some guidelines on the characteristics of former psychiatric patients who are likely to fail. They found that the most pronounced behaviors and characteristics for those who did not adjust were:

- Misses appointments for placement or counseling interviews
- Resists or refuses to accept job referrals
- Has incomplete or no vocational or technical training, and no education beyond high school
- Displays inappropriate behavior during placement or counseling interview
- Appears to have low physical vitality
- Has difficulty making himself or herself understood (poor communication of thought)
- Indicates preference for being a follower rather than a leader

These multiple signs of ineffective performance in coping with the employment process largely point to a lack of an active drive to work. Where these signs are not found, there is every reason to believe that former patients will be able to work effectively.

Alcoholism

Because of drinking on the job, hangovers, and anxiety, alcoholics often turn out insufficient work or work of poor quality. However, absenteeism is the major source of poor performance among alcoholics. Absenteeism rates two to three times those of other workers are typical. Alcoholics also tend to have high accident rates, especially involving off-the-job accidents, which result in considerable lost time.

When combined with the vitamin deficiency that almost invariably goes along with it (due either to an inadequate diet or a failure to eat at all during periods of intoxication), excessive drinking may result in incapacitating physical disorders. Permanent brain injury involving severe memory defects is frequent. For some individuals, alcoholism may well end in death.

How important is managerial action in this area? You can get some idea from figures I developed from data collected as part of an American Society for Personnel Administration–Bureau of National Affairs, Inc., survey of 100 companies. Among the following average estimates of the proportions of employees in various job categories with different types of emotional problems, alcoholism is in first place:

	Office Employees	Production Employees	Managers
Alcoholism	1.9%	3.2%	1.9%
Excessive marijuana use	.7	1.2	.1
Hard-drug addiction	.1	.4	.1
Emotional illness	1.4	1.4	1.3
Totals	4.1%	6.2%	3.4%

Probably the most difficult problem in managing alcoholism is identifying the problem. Employees typically cover up for their friends who have been drinking too heavily. Every effort is made to keep management from finding out about it; often even the immediate supervisor is involved in the conspiracy. Many alcoholics are good workers when sober. They are likely to be "nice guys" and a lot of fun. No one wants to expose them to the risk of being fired, and so nothing is done. They continue to work intermittently—and at times poorly—year after year, until the condition becomes totally incapacitating and continued employment is no longer possible.

A study by Professor Harrison Trice based on extensive questioning of approximately 200 members of Alcoholics Anonymous provides valuable information that can help in identifying alcoholism. Absences are likely to be frequent and the total amount of time lost considerable. Leaving work during the morning or not returning to work after lunch is particularly common. The absenteeism is generally explained by a variety of excuses, some of which are improbable and peculiar. Inconsistencies appear in these stories, and there is frequent mention of colds, flu, stomach upsets, and virus conditions. On the job, the red eyes and flushed face of a hangover are often in evidence. So too are hand tremors and the smell of either alcohol or breath cleansers. Work tends to be accomplished in spurts and slumps. There may be occasional temperamental outbursts and an unusual amount of suspiciousness. Also, problems outside work are likely to eventually reach management; financial difficulties involving loan companies, mortgages, and charge accounts; marital discord, sometimes with a request that paychecks be sent directly to the spouse; conflicts with neighbors or the police.

Dr. M. A. Block discusses a fivefold classification system for alcoholics that is particularly valuable because it relates the alcoholism to job performance. Alcoholics of the first type continually rely upon the effects of alcohol for relief of either physical or emotional pain. They display no loss of self-control and are in fact capable of abstaining, even though their drinking does have a disruptive impact on their family and work performance. Generally, the disorder does not become progressively worse.

In the second type of alcoholism, physical symptoms develop (gastritis, cirrhosis of the liver) as a result of excessive drinking. The major incentive for drinking is social, but the various physical effects can have a substantial impact on job performance. Yet, as with the first type, there is no loss of self-control, and few withdrawal symptoms are evident when drinking ceases.

By contrast, alcoholics of the third type exhibit a definite dependence on alcohol, accompanied by craving, loss of control, and withdrawal symptoms. Behavioral changes are clearly noticeable and job performance suffers severely. There is little capacity to abstain and a gradual deterioration occurs.

The fourth type is quite similar in some respects, but the loss of control is less pronounced and these alcoholics are unaware of their dependence on alcohol and inability to abstain. Many are regular wine drinkers— and because wine is widely used in their culture, they have no thought of not drinking regularly. Yet performance does suffer.

Finally, there are the periodic alcoholics who drink heavily for a short time and then cease either because they pass out or because they are forcibly stopped. Weekend alcoholics are in this category—they lose part or all of the workday on Friday and require Monday to recover. This category also includes individuals who disappear into an alcoholics' society such as a skid row for weeks or even months. In some cases, the drinking is restricted to nonwork periods and performance does not suffer; more frequently, there is an impact. Extended periods without heavy drinking do not make these employees any less alcoholic.

Dealing with Alcoholism: An employee who has been identified as alcoholic and who shows clear evidence of performance failure should be asked to discuss the problem. On the other hand, if performance is adequate, including the amount of absenteeism, there is little basis for managerial action. The employee is unlikely to accept advice to get treatment when there is no justification for such action in the work record itself. In fact, getting an alcoholic to agree that there is a problem that needs treatment is difficult even when there *is* a performance failure. If possible, the matter should be handled by someone in the company with medical or psychological training.

Frequently, the best course is to put the employee in touch with the local chapter of Alcoholics Anonymous. Many companies have AA members on the payroll who are contacted when an employee is known to have problems involving alcohol. The organization is generally willing to do anything that can possibly help in such cases, and the rate of cure is relatively high—higher, in fact, than that for psychotherapy with alcoholics.

If all efforts to get an alcoholic employee to obtain help fail and if poor performance continues, the next step should be a probationary period, with the understanding that failure to improve will mean dismissal. In some cases, an employee may contend that help has been obtained for the problem. A check should be made to ensure that treatment is in fact going on, because emotionally disturbed people are not always entirely truthful about such matters. If the difficulties continue during the probationary period, the employee should be fired. This is the most appropriate action from both a company and a therapeutic viewpoint, because the shock of "hitting bottom" may motivate the employee to seek treatment. Of course, many alcoholics are very skillful in extracting another chance by promising that they will never take another drink. But when these pleas are finally ignored, they will turn to alternative courses of action and may well seek help with a problem they now recognize as more than they can cope with alone. When they are fired, they should be told that they will be taken back when and if they can demonstrate that alcoholism is no longer likely to interfere with their performance. This is an important incentive to seek treatment in many cases, especially if the employee knows of people who have in fact been restored to employment by the company in this manner.

In managing alcoholism, it is important to differentiate between an occupational cure and a clinical cure. Alcoholism, and emotional disorders generally, can exist without having an impact on the job itself. Individuals may learn to control their drinking sufficiently so that absenteeism is minimal and other aspects of performance satisfactory, even though they do not totally overcome the disorder. They may continue to drink heavily off the job, especially on weekends. In such instances, it is easy to *assume* that performance is still inadequate without actually carrying out a reevaluation.

Increasingly, companies are establishing formal alcoholism control programs that typically operate along the lines suggested here. Managers are informed of company policies and procedures for referral, trained to spot work behavior that indicates alcoholism problems, instructed on using discipline to motivate employees to seek help, and advised to avoid discussing drinking with the employee except to indicate that the company handles problems in this area like any other health problem. The emphasis is on having the manager remain clearly focused on work performance.

The more successful programs appear to emphasize that drinking is a health problem, stress early identification through impaired performance, involve union participation, make consistent efforts to be sure that managers actually do act when performance declines, use absenteeism rates and other data to aid identification, and emphasize the effective use of discipline. Former Health, Education, and Welfare Secretary Wilbur Cohen reports recovery rates of from 65 to 85 percent for such programs, as compared to 30 percent for the general public.

Dealing with Drug Problems

Because drug problems are newer in this country, less is known about performance effects and means of control than in the case of alcoholism. Among companies that have information on the topic, the American Society for Personnel Administration–Bureau of National Affairs data indicate a sharply increasing frequency rate of drug use. However, most companies don't seem to know much about drug problems and take little action to deal with them. Relative to other emotional disorders, including alcoholism, these companies clearly feel little confidence in their capabilities for handling drug problems.

Marijuana typically impairs the work performance of chronic users much less than that of occasional users. In the latter group, major changes in intellectual functioning and muscular skills do occur. As the amount of marijuana increases, there is a shift from initial feelings of tranquility, apathy, and mild elation to distortions of perception, especially regarding time, and finally, with large amounts, to disorientation and hallucinations. Among regular users, identification is difficult because a type of adaptation effect appears. However, reports from countries with much longer experience—and, recently reports in this country as well—indicate that long-term use of marijuana tends to produce an overpowering lethargy, to the point where job performance is greatly impaired, if it is possible for the user to hold a job at all.

The amphetamines yield a symptom picture not unlike marijuana. In addition, amphetamines tend to produce an exaggeratedly positive self-appraisal and sense of personal competence, with the result that the individual takes much greater risks. There may be delusions of grandeur or persecution. Those who start using amphetamines on the job are likely to continue doing so in order to maintain this sense of competence.

In contrast to drugs such as marijuana and the amphetamines, opiates such as heroin tend to create a physical addiction similar to that of some alcoholics. Heroin provides the user with relief from frustration, panic, and hostility by creating a pervasive feeling of well-being. The impact on work and employment is likely to be massive. In a follow-up study of fifty-three addicts by L. B. Delfleur and colleagues, 43 percent were following permanent criminal careers selling drugs and stealing; another 34 percent were following sporadic criminal careers interspersed with short periods of legitimate employment, usually in low-level jobs; and an additional 6 percent were supported by their families. Thus, only 17 percent were able to maintain full-time employment. A number of these held relatively high-status positions where they not only earned enough to support their habit, but also had the freedom to adjust their work schedules to it.

Ideally, the handling of drug problems would be similar to that for alcoholism, with emphasis on the health aspects and impairment of job performance. Yet formalized company programs on drug use are less common than for alcoholism. Legal considerations add a major complication, because drug use can bring a felony conviction. Drug problems are much more likely to bring immediate termination than other types of emotional problems. Referrals to outside resources such as psychiatrists, psychologists, hospitals, and clinics are much less frequent; and so is inside counseling. Without question, many companies will have to develop more effective programs to deal with drug use and addiction, since there is little likelihood that the problem will just go away. In the meantime, managers should use the same guidelines as they would apply to alcoholics, to the extent that legal considerations and company policy permit.

4

Dealing with Motivational Problems

This chapter will be concerned with human interests, needs, wishes, impulses, drives, wants, intentions, motives, desires, and attitudes. Much of the research dealing with these topics has been devoted to work performance. As a result of this research, it is no longer necessary to use descriptive concepts such as laziness, lack of pep, inadequate competitive instincts, and so on. More meaningful approaches have been developed which give us greater understanding of the specific factors in individual motivation that can provide keys to ineffective performance.

Positive and Negative Emotions in Motivation

Human motivation is largely an emotional phenomenon—our behavior comes almost entirely from the interaction of positive and negative emotional states, both anticipated and experienced. When we act and talk as we do, it is in part to bring about events and conditions that will give us pleasant emotions. This might be an immediate condition—for example, when we say something we hope will bring praise from our listener. Or it might be tied to a future event—a young man or woman carrying out certain job activities in hopes of someday being appointed to a vice presidency.

But not all motivation is positive. We also act in response to anticipated negative emotion, trying to avoid behavior that we think will provoke anxiety or distress. When these unpleasant emotions are unavoidable, we will do everything we can to reduce their duration and intensity.

As with positive motivation, negative emotion can be either short-term or long-term. You may swerve your car when you see another one coming at you in the same lane—or you may refuse a promotion to manager out of fear that you might eventually be called upon to do something that would antagonize your subordinates and make you unpopular.

This attempt to avoid negative emotional states is similar to the defensive process used by people with emotional disorders. But symptoms of emotional disorder involve only specific kinds of behavior and threats of *extremely* unpleasant feelings—not just distress, but intense anxiety or deep sorrow. Most important, these symptoms are inflexible and overpowering. In extreme conditions, the symptomatic behavior takes place regardless of reality and no matter what other motives may have been activated. The inflexible, disruptive character of symptomatic motivation is what distinguishes it from other kinds of negative motivation. The person gives up everything that might otherwise be desired in order to satisfy the insatiable demands of the symptom.

Different motivations within us often conflict, of course. A variety of anticipated pleasures and distresses interact to produce our behavior. We have all experienced the conflict between long-term, delayed rewards and instant gratification—and our behavior is based on excluding one motivation to satisfy the other. For example, our immediate fear of a current situation may give way to the anticipation of some future happiness that we can attain only by facing the present problem. Or the pleasure from spending money on a luxury item may be given priority over the long-term rewards to be gained from investing the money.

Our Motivational Hierarchy

Each individual has a personal hierarchy of motives: relatively stable patterns of dominance which determine, at least in a general way, the type of motivation that is likely to win out. Emotional symptoms of the type discussed in Chapter 3 are, by their very nature, likely to have a high position in the hierarchy. Other motives, such as fear over the prospect of deviant behavior (conformity) and the anticipation of happiness upon achieving the symbols of success (ambition), may also predominate. In our discussions of the relationship between motivation and performance, we will primarily be concerned with the more dominant motives.

Research has not yet revealed how individual motivational hierarchies are developed. We do not know how to combine various bits of information about a person's previous experiences in order to predict which motives will predominate, just as we cannot predict who can withstand intense anxiety and who will succumb at the first twinge. But it is clear that these patterns, and the individual motives which make them up, are primarily learned rather than instinctive. They change from time to time, especially during the years of developing maturity, and there are sizable differences between people with similar heredity. Emotions must be attached to specific events, and expectancies must be built up. This is essentially a learning process.

It is also clear that human motivation does not fit any model for rationality. People often behave in ways that seem senseless and unnecessarily detrimental to their interests. Symptoms of an emotional nature are particularly likely to be irrational. In many areas of life, the prospects of immediate satisfaction often serve to overwhelm long-term goals. Much of the response to advertising, for instance, can be accounted for only in terms of emotional reactions of this type. Many people are attracted to advertising material dealing with complex technical subjects (such as chemical ingredients and mechanical processes) *after* they have already made the decision to buy the product. Apparently they need a logical explanation for their behavior and hope that the advertisements will provide it.

This caution on the potential irrationality of human motivation is particularly relevant when it is applied to our responses to monetary incentives. To support their theories, economists have developed the concept of the economic being—an individual completely informed, infinitely sensitive, entirely rational in his or her decisions. This person is assumed to consistently make choices that will maximize expected utility. With regard to performance management, this has often been taken to mean that subordinates will consistently make choices calculated to maximize monetary income and will be motivated in proportion to the expected financial reward. Although the concept of the economic being may often be adequate for predicting behavior, it is no more universally valid than the legal concept of a reasonable and prudent being. There is a wealth of evidence indicating that people will not always make decisions calculated to maximize their financial return. Many people who have reached the top salary bracket for their jobs and who have no hope of promotion continue to work just as hard as they did when merit increases were still possible. Others are apparently unwilling to exert themselves no matter how much money they are offered. Readers who are particularly interested in the position of financial motives in individual motivational hierarchies and in the evidence on pay/performance relationships should consult Edward Lawler's *Pay and Organization Development*.

Conscious and Unconscious Motives

While much human motivation deviates from rationality, motivation is also on occasion inaccessible to consciousness. We say and do many things from motives of which we are completely unaware. We often act almost automatically with no idea why. Sometimes we know that we ought not to engage in certain activities but nevertheless experience a compulsion to go ahead anyhow. After the fact, we may devote considerable time and effort to developing logical explanations for our behavior.

When it is impossible to become aware of the true motives behind our actions, it is safe to assume that the chain of events is somewhat as follows: Through our experiences during the maturing process, pleasant emotional reactions become attached to certain acts and events. Anticipations are created and a motive is formed. Many such motives may, however, subsequently prove to have negative implications. We learn that certain words and acts are socially taboo, that our motives are unacceptable to others. Giving them expression may result in considerable anxiety and embarrassment. The most common solution to this problem is to eliminate the original motive from consciousness so that the anxiety produced by thoughts or behavior associated with it need no longer be experienced.

Over time, this process results in the accumulation of many unconscious motives or impulses, which may break through the barriers we have erected against them and determine our behavior. Yet the motives underlying the behavior remain inaccessible to us. If it were otherwise, we might have to face things in ourselves that we would consider, at the very least, quite unpleasant. As it is, we are able in a sense to have our cake and eat it too. We gain the satisfaction of expressing certain impulses and wishes while at the same time minimizing, at least under optimal circumstances, the anxious feelings that have become associated with them.

As Sigmund Freud demonstrated many years ago, unconscious motives of this kind are often behind a great variety of errors such as making a slip of the tongue or pen, misreading something, failing to hear correctly, forgetting names and intentions, mislaying things, breaking objects "accidentally," and so forth. Such slips are most likely to emerge when we are tired or emotionally upset. Much ineffective job performance is caused in this way. It does little good in such cases to ask subordinates why they lost an important paper or broke an expensive machine or miscalculated a customer's bill. They will frequently offer a reason, usually one minimizing their own accountability, but it will rarely be the correct one. In actual fact, they do not know why; yet their own motives are clearly responsible.

Dominant unconscious motives can also exert considerable influence on the choice of an occupation. Many people choose work which will provide them with an outlet for their unconscious motives. Others take up activities which will help support a conviction that such motives do not exist. For instance, in one study conducted at Harvard University by Robert Harlow, personality tests were administered to a number of young men who devoted much time to weight lifting. The tests provided rather convincing evidence that for many, the weight training and resultant development of physique helped to ward off unconscious feelings of masculine inadequacy and inferiority. These men devoted considerable effort to establishing their maleness, yet they did not appear to be strongly attracted to women and tended to prefer male company. Unconsciously, at least, they believed other people must be very critical of them, and they considered themselves incapable of handling their problems without help from some external source. They needed strength and sought it in weight lifting.

Fear of Failure and Pleasure in Success

In a classic study by Professor Frederick Herzberg and colleagues, accountants and engineers employed by nine large concerns in the Pittsburgh area were asked to describe occasions when they had felt exceptionally good and exceptionally bad about their jobs. From an analysis of these stories it was possible to determine what factors most frequently contributed to their pleasure at work. Achievement—the successful completion of a job—was by far the most prevalent. Personal recognition or praise came next. The opportunity to do interesting, creative, challenging, or varied work was the third. Being permitted to exercise responsibility for one's own work or that of others was fourth, and promotion was fifth. Among these five sources of work satisfaction, three are clearly criteria of personal success on the job: achievement, recognition, and promotion. The opportunity to perform interesting rather than routine activities and to exercise responsibility or autonomy might also be considered a criterion of success, since higher-level positions usually are associated with these characteristics. Thus, the interviewees were clearly saying that attaining success in one form or another was their major source of pleasure in the work situation.

The primary sources of *dissatisfaction*, on the other hand, were not personal but external. They involved claims that the individual had been a victim of inadequate company organization and management, had suffered as a result of malevolent personnel policies, or had been exposed to incompetent supervision. Although the elimination of these external deficiencies might have reduced the employees' unhappiness, one cannot help wondering whether personal failures were not also involved. Could it be that many of these employees were describing occasions when they had come close to experiencing a sense of failure—and were able to avoid the resultant anxiety only by shifting the blame to another source? The study does not tell us this, but Professor Edwin Locke at the University of Maryland has marshaled data and argued persuasively to this effect. His results certainly support the view that failure is a major source of fear and distress in the world of work. Rarely does a person admit feeling bad because of his or her own incompetent job performance—this usually happens only when one is depressed and overcome with guilt. Much more frequently, at least part of the blame is placed on someone or something else.

Additional evidence for the dominance of pleasure in success and fear of failure as motivating forces in the business world comes from an unlikely source, a survey devised by Eugene Heaton, now a vice president at Opinion Research Corporation, and myself to determine what types of articles published in a company magazine were most widely read. The major finding of this study, carried out in the Atlantic Refining Company, was that articles dealing with the company's economic position, organization, products, equipment, methods, services, and advantages as a place of employment were much more widely read than those having little to do with the operation of the firm. A closer look at these company-oriented articles reveals an interesting fact. Some of these widely read items deal with personal success (list of promotions). Others describe the success of the company (an article about new products and the increase in sales they produced). Still other items refer to company programs and procedures designed to protect employees against the experience of personal failure (an item on the stability of the company retirement system and another listing service anniversaries for the numerous employees who had been with the company for many years). In contrast, readership was relatively low for articles unrelated to occupational or economic success and failure (a list of recipes, an article on stamp collecting, etc.). It appears that the motivating effects of success and failure are not restricted to engineers and accountants—they are spread throughout the organization. Ninety percent of Atlantic Refining Company employees, for instance, read about such things as promotions.

How Pleasure in Success Can Cause Unsatisfactory Performance: Ambition—the anticipation of a pleasurable emotional experience through attainment of success—is without question a major source of motivation at work. It usually contributes to effective work performance as long as events serve to reinforce the expectation of achievement—that is, when some degree of success is experienced.

However, when the individual's level of ability, or the nature of the job or the organization, or the actions of superiors serve to remove the possibility of experiencing success, ambition probably will not contribute to effective performance. In fact, when challenge is lacking or ambition frustrated in this way, anticipation of pleasure in success can only be a detriment and may contribute to failure. It may also lead the individual to seek employment elsewhere. An analysis of turnover figures in one company revealed that those hired with a graduate degree (master's or doctoral) rarely remained for more than a few years. They expected more than the situation provided, and went elsewhere to satisfy their ambitions.

Turnover is not the only way in which frustration of success may manifest itself. There are many alternative reactions, most of which contribute to ineffective performance in some way. Employees may stop trying to attain satisfaction of their desires on the job. They may stop exerting themselves almost entirely while assuming a "What's the use?" attitude. They may work slowly and disinterestedly, if at all. Work provides no "kick." Or, on the other hand, strong emotional reactions may be aroused. Employees may accuse others of blocking their development. They may condemn the company. Their work will suffer not so much from inadequate effort as from the disruptive emotions aroused by the blocking of a strong drive. Under these frustrating conditions, they may become real troublemakers and exert a strong negative influence on the performance of others.

Another type of response involves an important concept which we have not yet discussed. We have assumed that people enter employment expecting to attain happy feelings that they have associated with their particular concept of success. We have assumed further that they will try to gain this success through activities which contribute to effective performance. Unfortunately, this last assumption is unwarranted. Someone may enter a position having already developed techniques for achieving success that are sharply at variance with job requirements. Their behavior in pursuit of success and its associated pleasures may conflict directly with work demands or leave insufficient time for effective performance.

For example, employees may moonlight outside their regular job—which provides a real sense of accomplishment, but leaves them too tired or with insufficient time to perform adequately in their main job. Or they may devote their energies to attaining success through political activity within the company, spending so much time making friends and influencing people that the actual work suffers. They may bypass merit and promotional increases as a means of increasing their income and instead use company facilities or time on the job (perhaps even company cash reserves) to gain personal financial success through an outside business. Or they may attempt to satisfy their desires through fantasies and daydreams of success, to the point where their work is severely disrupted. In all these instances, there is no integration between the expected means of attaining success and actual job demands.

Lack of integration between behavior and job requirements may be a response to the frustration of more job-integrated attempts to attain success. Instead of quitting, losing interest, or reacting with intense emotion when efforts to achieve are persistently denied, an employee may seek other channels through which to attain goals and thus become increasingly ineffective as job behavior departs further and further from what is desired.

Employee Standards for Success: An additional complication is that people use their own standards to define personal success. *They* determine what level of accomplishment, what types of reward, will suffice. This is not to say that external standards have no influence. It may be generally understood in a company that a person on the way up *should* achieve a certain grade level by a specified age, or that a satisfactory performer in a given job *should* have attained a certain pay rate after being employed for a specific period of time. Standards of this kind are often internalized by individual employees and serve to influence their personal expectations. Nevertheless, people also take into account their own capacities as they see them. Many students are quite satisfied with a C average. Others will settle for nothing but an A. Satisfaction with pay rate is clearly conditioned by the specific individuals with whom employees compare themselves and by how they expect to stand relative to these individuals.

If employees define success in terms of very low standards, they will experience satisfaction at a low level and will have no incentive to improve. On the other hand, they may set such *high* standards for themselves that they will constantly fail to reach them, even though they perform at a satisfactory level by normal standards. Their continued personal "failures" and resulting disappointment may eventually frustrate them enough to produce strong emotional responses, loss of interest in work, or unintegrated behavior. At this point, performance actually will begin to fall off and may eventually become ineffective, even though the standards remain unaltered.

To summarize, here is what we know about the relationship between intense ambition and ineffective performance: *First,* employees may begin to perform ineffectively if their job-integrated strivings toward success are consistently frustrated. This is true whether personal standards of success are high or low. Excessively high standards are especially likely to ensure frustration and thus eventual failure.

Second, employees may perform ineffectively by employing techniques for achieving their concept of success that are not integrated with the requirements of the job. It does not matter whether their standards are high or low or whether they achieve success in their own terms; their performance will still be ineffective.

Third, employees may perform ineffectively according to external standards even though they use job-integrated means and actually do succeed by their own standards. If their standards are too low and their performance does not rise above them, the employees are considered ineffective by their superiors. A handicapped worker, for instance, might establish low personal standards and take pride in meeting them but might still fall well below acceptable managerial standards.

How Fear of Failure Can Cause Unsatisfactory Performance: To turn from positive motivation to negative motivation, fear of failure interacts with performance in somewhat the same way as pleasure in success does. Fear of failure frequently exists among very successful managers and executives, and can be a major factor contributing to their achievements. In attempting to avoid anxiety associated with what they consider failure, they may in fact achieve considerable success. For this to happen, a person must use job-integrated means for avoiding failure and must establish strict, although still entirely realistic, standards of failure. In school, such a person might feel distressed by receiving a grade of C. In the business world, the possibility that one among some twenty or thirty reports prepared during the year might bring a mild criticism from a boss would be quite upsetting. As might be expected, such people, although often extremely successful by any objective criterion, often do not experience much happiness. They gain little satisfaction from their work; it is sufficient that they have once again escaped the gaping jaws of calamity.

Ineffective performance can easily result if such individuals consistently produce work that is below their own strict standards. They are likely to experience intense anxiety or guilt, which in turn can disrupt performance. The actual level of the standards matters little in instances of this kind. Another possibility is that unsuccessful efforts to avoid failure may cause people to give up, decide to suffer the distress and unpleasantness of failure, and in the end find that things are not as bad as anticipated. Since failure does not have the strong emotional impact they expected, they lower their standards, perhaps dropping them entirely. This is not uncommon among the long-term employed. A type of relearning occurs, and failure is accepted as a fact of life.

Ineffective performance can also result when the means chosen to avoid failure are not integrated with job demands. As with ambition, unintegrated behavior may be brought to the job as an established pattern, or the pattern may be created on the job because integrated approaches are inadequate. The possible forms of such a pattern are myriad, including many symptoms of emotional illness. But one of the most common patterns of unintegrated behavior is avoidance of the work situation with its aura of criticism and punishment. People who adopt this pattern will be absent frequently and complain of numerous illnesses or other circumstances that make it seem inappropriate to hold them to adequate performance standards. Some people will invoke almost any kind of excuse in order to convince themselves and others that standards of work effectiveness are not really applicable to them. Thus, since they cannot be evaluated, they cannot fail. Frequently the blame will be shifted to some external event or person. "It's not my fault this thing didn't work out, he (or the company, or my wife, or the market) is to blame. . . ."

Among managers, there is another common source of ineffectiveness caused by lack of integration between job demands and the procedures used to avoid failure. Many sales managers devote their energies almost entirely to actual selling, even though this is supposed to be left to their salespersons. As a result, their managerial activities are seriously neglected. Although such behaviors can stem from several types of motivation, the managers are often seeking to avoid failure by doing everything themselves to make sure that things are done right. Unfortunately they overestimate their capacities and find out too late, if ever, that they cannot do the work of five or ten other people in addition to their own. This type of behavior is not unlike that of people who have developed failure-avoidance techniques which involve meticulous attention to detail and accuracy. Although such perfectionism may represent a thoroughly integrated approach in some jobs, there are other jobs where time consumed in constant rechecking makes it impossible to complete the work on schedule.

Finally, some employees do avoid the experience of failure through job-integrated behavior, but only because their personal standards for failure are very lenient. They won't appear very happy about their work, but neither will they appear particularly anxious. In fact, they may be rather difficult to deal with, since they will be convinced that their performance is adequate and may consider their boss's demands excessive.

Other Motives Affecting Performance

Although motives involving success and failure are most likely to be dominant on the job, many other types of motives may also contribute to ineffective performance. In fact, almost any motive that can be manifested at work may be strategic for failure, either because the means to its attainment are not integrated with job demands or because its satisfaction is blocked. Probably negative motives outnumber the positive. The variety of factors in the work situation that can provoke anxiety, guilt, shame, or some other distressing emotional state is almost infinite. When feelings of this kind are persistently activated, they will usually affect performance adversely unless some more dominant motive serves to counteract them.

Substantial evidence indicates that people who are distressed or dissatisfied because of work factors will frequently seek to avoid the source of their displeasure through absenteeism and job changes. Research findings indicate that fear of failure is not the only negative motive contributing to such behaviors. In fact, fear of failure is actually much *more* likely than other types of negative motivation to result in job-integrated behavior.

In addition to absenteeism and turnover, other unintegrated responses may appear when disturbing factors at work lead to dominant negative motives. Avoidance may occur within the work situation itself: absence from the work area, dispensary visits, refusal to perform certain job duties, and so on. All of these responses may, if carried to extremes, seriously affect the amount of work accomplished or its quality. Performance failure among salespersons is often caused by a distaste for interaction with other people. On the job, such salespersons tend to avoid social contacts whenever possible, and what conversation they do engage in is likely to be stilted and short-lived. Their shyness makes it impossible for them to get close to other people, and as a result their sales suffer. Similar types of avoidance can occur in nearly all jobs.

Positive Motives: Positive motives may have equally detrimental effects, and again the possible routes are numerous. In my experience there are, in addition to pleasure in success, four positive motives that are often strategic for performance failure when they become dominant. One of these is pleasure in dominating and controlling other people—what has been called a strong power motive. This motive often contributes to seeking a career in business management, particularly in line departments, and to successful performance in many such jobs. But a desire to dominate others can also lead to failure. The desire may be frustrated, even in line management. Union or subordinate reactions to managerial control can, on occasion, block the attainment of such control. People may just refuse to be dominated, or higher management may refuse to provide support. As Leonard Sayles has pointed out in *Managerial Behav-*

ior, managers in today's organizations seldom have the authority they think they need to get the job done.

Frustration is most likely, however, when the individual with a desire to dominate is in staff work or in a subordinate position without authority to direct others. The individual may then exhibit one of the usual reactions to frustration: emotional outbreaks, loss of interest in work, unintegrated behavior. The last often takes the form of persistent attempts to control the behavior of others in all kinds of situations. The other people become angry because they resent being pushed around, the person devotes excessive time to thinking up ways to gain obedience, and performance suffers all around. Often the attempts to control extend well beyond the workplace itself. Unlike motives involving success and failure, the desire to dominate others may not be satisfied on an integrated basis within the confines of a particular job. Many positions contain neither supervisory responsibilities nor an opportunity to exercise the power inherent in specialized knowledge. The only integrated approach possible in such situations may be for the person to put intensive efforts into qualifying for another position in which the type of desired satisfaction can be achieved.

A second positive motive that may cause job failure is the anticipation of pleasure at being made to feel accepted and liked by other people at work. The person wants above everything else to be popular. Where this desire is frustrated, due either to characteristics of the individual or to the actions of others, the usual reactions may occur. For some people, the whole work environment becomes a meaningless shell if they cannot obtain frequent indications of popularity. The strategies employed to secure these indications may vary tremendously. They may be entirely integrated: the person carries out certain job duties and in the process achieves a sense of acceptance. This need not be the case, however. Attempts to achieve a feeling of popularity by disruptive, attention-getting behavior are not uncommon. Anything that provokes attention from the group may contribute to a feeling of acceptance. In managerial work, an intense wish to be liked by others can result in abdication of responsibility and an inability to issue anything approaching an order to subordinates. Should the two motives conflict, the manager's desire for popularity with subordinates may predominate over any wish to fulfill the demands of the job.

A third key motive is social interaction sought for its own sake. A person may wish above almost anything else to be with others, to talk to them, and to participate in social activities, whether work-related or not. Preference may be primarily for the opposite sex, for the same sex, or for both; for small groups, for large groups, or for one other person. Activities directed to this goal may be thoroughly integrated with the job. The studies noted by Professor Henry Mintzberg indicate that the typical manager spends considerable time in meetings and other forms of social interaction. There are jobs, however, where employees cannot achieve satisfaction of social motives. For example, they may have to remain alone for long periods to carry out their job duties. Or they may be deprived of the specific kinds of relationships with people that are important to them.

Some people can suffer this kind of deprivation without undue negative results, presumably because other motives outweigh purely social ones. Others are completely unable to perform effectively. Unintegrated responses characteristically take the form of ignoring job demands in order to seek the interaction with other people that is desired. The techniques are many, and the experienced manager will be familiar with most of them. For example, a machine operator may spend considerable time wandering around the shop talking to people and neglecting the work that must be done. Or coffee breaks and lunch hours may be extended. Frustration of social motives is a common source of difficulty. Any supervisor of employees who must spend long periods of time without talking should be sensitive to the problem. Mere physical closeness to other people is usually not sufficient to satisfy this kind of motivation. If conversation is not possible, the presence of others may serve only as a source of frustration.

A fourth positive motive is the desire for assistance and attention from superiors—and it probably causes performance failure as frequently as any of the four. Managers may gain a feeling of happiness from being accepted by their superiors and enjoy the opportunity to get help with their problems. Such a desire can be fully integrated with job requirements, because in attempting to satisfy this motive a manager may become a hard and willing worker. This motive can lead to a smooth working relationship with superiors, with the manager perceiving their wishes almost before they are aware of them.

But sometimes things do not turn out that way. The superiors do not, or cannot, respond to such job-integrated efforts. Then managers with this motive become angry and upset, or lose momentum, or turn to unintegrated methods of getting what they want. These methods may take many forms. Often the managers resort to behavior that leads their boss to consider them "pests." They constantly demand assistance, instruction, praise, and attention. They disrupt their own work and that of their superiors. Once they get into the boss's office, it is almost impossible to get them out. Or they may deliberately get into difficulty in their work or with fellow employees so that supervisory attention is constantly required. They may become show-offs, at least when there is any possibility of gaining the attention of the boss.

This is not, of course, a problem unique to management. People at any level can develop a strong desire to lean on others whom they consider stronger and more powerful than themselves. And when such desires for assistance and attention exist, employees may try to satisfy them in ways which decrease the quantity and quality of their own work as well as that of others.

Many other types of motives may contribute to ineffective performance, such as an interest in solving new and stimulating problems, a wish to indulge in fantasies and daydreams, a need for constant changes of environment, a drive to incessant activity, a desire to take risks, or a preference for work requiring minimal physical activity. All these motives may be frustrated on the job for a variety of reasons and may, as a consequence, result in emotions and behavior that contribute to failure. All may be satisfied through either integrated or unintegrated behavior, although both possibilities may not exist within the same job.

Another Way of Looking at Motivation: Work Motivation

So far we have discussed specific motives and how they can affect job performance. But there is another useful way of looking at motivation on the job. That is the concept of *work motivation.* It involves focusing on the net effect of the various specific motives which may contribute to a person's work performance—or lower that performance. Such a concept makes it possible to bypass the specific motives involved and look at the end result only, in terms of the general level of motivation contributing to the effectiveness of performance. People are lacking in this work motivation when they have few, if any, positive dominant motives which they believe they can satisfy through work-integrated activity—and when, in addition, the anticipation of fear or some other unpleasant emotion does not lead them into integrated effort. They may also be considered unmotivated if their standards are so low that they can achieve their goal with little exertion. In such cases, the pleasure of success is achieved or distress avoided so easily that it hardly seems to require any motivation at all.

To complete this picture, there is also the person who not only seems totally uninterested in work, but behaves in ways that indicate an actual desire to fail. Such motives do exist, usually on an unconscious level. People who deliberately set out to fail on the job are likely to be considered irresponsible in our society, so they usually protect themselves from recognizing that they have such motives by keeping them out of consciousness. Nevertheless, schoolchildren often do unsatisfactory work in order to get even with their parents for real or imagined wrongs. And guilt-ridden people may deliberately make a mess of their lives in order to punish themselves, sometimes going so far as to confess to crimes they did not commit. In the business world, people can satisfy such motives by getting themselves fired or by being known as failures. Such people are generally grouped with others who are said to be lacking in work motivation, although they might more appropriately be described as taking pleasure in failure.

The term *work motivation* has also been employed somewhat more narrowly to summarize the effects of the particular motives that contribute to what might be called industriousness or perseverance. It is in this sense that the phrase is most widely used by social science researchers. When employed in this way, it does not cover all possible motives that may contribute to effective performance, but only a limited group of these motives closely related to putting energy into one's work.

This view of work motivation as the willingness and ability to devote energy to one's work was used by Mark Lifton and other researchers from Wayne State University in a study comparing line and staff managers. They found that work motivation was much more crucial to the performance of line managers; those who lacked such motivation had a very good chance of failing.

Among the staff managers, work motivation appeared to be less important to overall job performance than expertise, creative ideas, and the like.

Work Motivation—General and Specific: However work motivation is defined, it is usual to distinguish between general work motivation and work motivation as it applies to specific jobs. Thus the person who is failing because of low motivation in a specific job might or might not have low motivation if placed in some other type of work. But if the person has what is termed *general low work motivation,* then there is no other job in which that person's motivation would be higher. Whether this is the case can only be determined from the person's employment record. A number of almost identical failures in a variety of positions suggests that the motivational deficiency is general. However, this can never be proved conclusively; there *might* always be some job that would arouse interest. If, on the other hand, the person has had other types of jobs in which failure attributable to motivational causes did not occur, the motivational difficulty is probably specific. This distinction between the general and the specific has important implications for remedial action. Unfortunately, where the work history is sparse it is very difficult to make this distinction with any certainty.

Specific work motivation is often identified in terms of areas of interest rather than individual motives. Thus, among 464 managers studied in connection with a management appraisal program, strong specific motivation was found to be present in areas such as computation and working with figures, scientific matters, persuasion and selling, literature and reading, and supervising others. However, these managers did not show strong positive motivation toward outdoor and agricultural work, mechanical activities, and clerical tasks.

The same study attempted to determine the average levels of motivation in certain specific areas of managers of different types. In particular, managers responsible for research activities were contrasted with the heads of other kinds of major units. Most in this second group were line managers, but some headed large staff groups. As might be expected, the research managers were very much interested in scientific activities. They gave no evidence of particular motivation for selling and persuading and seemed to lack any desire to supervise others. The nonresearch managers, on the other hand, were strongly motivated to persuade and supervise others but did not have marked interests in the scientific area. This same study found that while supervisory and persuasive interests generally contributed to managerial success, strong positive motivation for scientific pursuits did not. As might be expected, therefore, the research managers were rated well below the other administrators on their management appraisals. Presumably, since they were more oriented toward scientific matters than managing, they employed unintegrated means in their efforts to gain success. They apparently sought recognition as scientists rather than as managers and thus emphasized one segment of the job to the exclusion of others.

This kind of correlation between performance effectiveness and the level of work motivation in special areas is more common in positions toward the top of the occupational ladder. Unskilled and semiskilled workers are less likely to fail in their jobs because they lack the appropriate interest patterns than are skilled, professional, and managerial workers. Probably one major difference between high- and low-level jobs lies in the importance of positive motivation generally. Fear of failure, quite irrespective of the specific kind of work involved, would seem to be somewhat more important as a motivating factor in lower-level jobs. At that level, not many people may have strong positive motives which they are able to satisfy through their jobs, but they may nevertheless perform adequately because the threat of failure is very real. They may see no prospect of getting into something more enjoyable, and they may be anxious to keep what they have rather than go without any work or move to something similar or worse, with less seniority. At higher levels, more individuals would be likely to decline in effectiveness once they found that their dominant motives were being frustrated in a given type of work. Their chances of shifting eventually to something more in line with their interests would be considerably better, so fear of failure would have much less motivational impact.

Dealing with Motivational Problems

When you believe that a motivational problem exists, your first step is to determine what motives are dominant. What does the person want? That is the crucial question, but simply asking it will be of limited value. Some strong motives are unconscious; others are unlikely to be disclosed to a superior. Careful observation of behavior can provide useful clues, however. So, too, can a competent professional psychological evaluation based on personality testing and depth interviewing. If these resources are available, a manager would be well advised to call on them, in the same way that intelligence test data would be used in explaining intellectual factors.

In dealing with motivational problems, your basic objective is to induce the ineffective worker to satisfy appropriate motives through job-integrated behavior while employing realistic standards of success and failure. Let us start with the satisfaction of motives.

One possibility is to rearrange the existing hierarchy of motivations so that motives suited to the specific job achieve a dominant position. To take a rather extreme but nevertheless instructive example, suppose that Tom Roy, a truck driver who works alone, is doing poorly in his job because he constantly stops to talk to people and therefore fails to meet delivery schedules. He is so drawn to others by the anticipation of pleasure in conversation that he fails to do his work. Suppose further that Tom's supervisor has succeeded in blocking this unintegrated behavior by assigning him to an after-midnight shift when there is no one around to talk to. This could produce a very bitter and resentful individual who constantly makes mistakes because he cannot keep his mind on his work.

Ideally, a person in this kind of job would drive from place to place with practically no social contacts, while actually deriving pleasure from the chance to be alone. But this solution would require that a completely different type of motivation replace the desire for social interaction in Tom's hierarchy of motives.

Obviously, this sort of change cannot generally be accomplished by an individual manager. Usually such a change could only be induced by a clinical psychologist or psychiatrist in successful long-term therapy. In fact, one goal of such treatment is to dislodge symptoms from their positions of dominance. And when a person is failing because of behavior associated with an emotional disorder, the appropriate solution is to provide treatment that will change the dominance relationships among motives. In most cases, however, the motives and behavior involved are not symptomatic of emotional illness, and such drastic personality changes are not appropriate.

Moreover, to provide this kind of treatment requires extensive training, some desire to change on the part of the subordinate, and a great deal of time. This makes it an impractical option for the business manager. When an unconscious motive—a wish to fail, for instance— ranks high in a person's hierarchy of motives, the chances of a manager bringing about any real motivational change are almost nil. Less-well-entrenched motives can shift position in an individual's hierarchy, however. It is not known exactly how this may be brought about, but certain kinds of management development efforts appear to produce this result—and at present such procedures offer the best hope of a solution to the problem of motivational change. They can be particularly effective when the training group consists entirely of people whose performance has suffered because of motivational factors and when the major goal of the training is to shift a limited number of motives, perhaps only one, to a dominant position.

Satisfying Existing Motives: An alternative approach involves providing on-the-job satisfaction of existing motives. If blocks and sources of frustration can be removed by changing working arrangments, then an individual might achieve satisfactory performance without undergoing a major personality reorganization. In essence, this means changing conditions to satisfy important motives rather than changing motives to match existing conditions. Of course, this solution is not possible where the factors restricting the satisfaction of motives are within the individual; for example, a person may be unable to achieve the success desired because of lack of intellectual competence. But often the blocks are external. They result from job requirements, supervisory actions, or organizational decisions that can potentially be changed.

If a person wants something very much, and if it can be provided on the job, there is a good chance that the person's performance will attain a satisfactory level. Suppose, for example, that Rachel T., a technician, desires above almost anything else to avoid criticism from her supervisor. But she finds that no matter how hard and carefully she works, criticism always follows—presumably because her boss assumes that the more people are pushed, the harder they will work.

Finally she gives up. She cannot achieve the freedom from criticism that she wants, and so her performance level declines. Removing or minimizing criticism under such circumstances can produce an amazing change.

Similar results can be attained by providing a sense of achievement for an ambitious individual whose progress has been blocked. But this cannot always be accomplished within the employee's present position. For example, consider employees who are failing because their lower-level jobs do not allow them to be as successful as they would like to be. They can perform effectively if they are given more demanding positions.

Our lonely truck driver provides another example. On his current job, he could hardly satisfy his desire for protracted conversation and still perform effectively. It would require a complete redesign of his job—perhaps more along the lines of a delivery salesperson's work— or a transfer to a new position to give him what he wants from his employment and at the same time obtain satisfactory performance. Similar changes may be required to satisfy dominant motives such as a need to avoid some anxiety-producing aspect of a job, a drive to dominate others, a wish for attention from those at higher levels, or a desire for group acceptance. But a careful judgment must be made as to whether the new job will in fact provide what was lacking in the old.

Dealing with Nonintegrated Activity: The job changes we have discussed so far are intended to help an employee satisfy dominant motives through job-integrated activity. What about the individual who is already achieving the emotional states desired, but through activity which is not integrated with job requirements—and which therefore results in performance failure? An example would be our truck driver, who obtained the social interaction he desired by stopping and talking with people, at the expense of job performance. Transfer may, of course, be the only solution when an integrated means of satisfying a dominant motive cannot be found within the present job. But there are also ways of substituting integrated for unintegrated approaches, of inducing a person to get what is wanted through more "desirable" methods. This does not require reorganizing the motivational hierarchy but only changing the means employed to satisfy existing motives.

Although such changes can be achieved, it is not easy. The first requirement is that the unintegrated techniques be blocked so they cannot satisfy an employee's desire. Take employees who are avoiding failure by refusing to compete—perhaps by avoiding work either through absenteeism or constant excuses. They must be convinced that they are really failing, that their behavior is not justified and does not, in fact, protect them from being considered ineffective. At the same time, they must be given a way to avoid failure through a more integrated approach, and must be persuaded to use it. They must learn that it is possible for them to meet the criteria of satisfactory performance on the job. The procedure, then, involves blocking one route for the attainment of what is desired and channeling behavior into an alternative route. If this can be done, the same motive which has previously contributed to failure may instead contribute to a satisfactory level of performance.

Accomplishing this change requires that the manager do three things: make the unintegrated activities fail to achieve their ends, ensure a greater degree of success for integrated efforts, and exercise great powers of persuasion. The subordinate must be convinced that when the unintegrated strategies have failed, it would be more beneficial to shift to an integrated approach than to some other, unintegrated approach.

To make this approach work, the manager must have good credibility with the subordinate involved. Unfortunately, a subordinate may question whether the manager is actually trying to help. Instead, the manager's actions may be viewed as manipulation designed primarily to help the organization. In that case, performance improvement won't seem that desirable to the subordinate, and the manager's persuasion is unlikely to succeed.

Motivational problems may also arise when an employee sets excessively low personal standards that permit failure to be avoided and/or success experienced while performance is still below established expectation levels. In recent years, we have learned much about the effects of setting explicit production goals. This research tells us that if unsatisfactory workers whose problems stem from their low standards can be induced to set or accept higher production goals, their performance will improve. Such goal setting may be on an individual basis or as part of a more comprehensive management-by-objectives program. The goals need not be set by the individual; satisfactory results can be achieved when they are set entirely by a superior, provided that the individual accepts them as attainable and legitimate.

What is required here is to move unsatisfactory employees away from their existing minimum standards to a commitment to some higher goal. Managers should emphasize not the negative consequences of failing to meet explicitly stated goals but the positive satisfactions associated with meeting them. This approach has the best chance of working with a person who experiences considerable pleasure in success, but who for some reason has been operating with very low standards.

So far we have covered many individual motives that may contribute to the level of specific work motivation in various areas of interest. But what about employees with general low work motivation? As noted earlier, these employees typically have a long string of failures preceding their present employment. In such cases, the chances of finding a solution are slight, and there is little that can be done other than separate them as soon as possible after their performance failure has been established. For subordinates who have no known motivation that might induce them to work productively, little can be gained by experimenting with a variety of possible solutions.

Do Threats and Discipline Work?

On the assumption that either economic incentive or fear of failure will always motivate an employee, some believe that ineffective performance can be handled by offering the opportunity to earn more money or by threatening severe punishment. It is true that these approaches have achieved some degree of success. But they have failed many times, too. Fear of the work situation, a desire to dominate, the wish to be popular, strong social needs, dependence on those at higher levels, and many other motives can be equally important to a person. Furthermore, the degree to which behavior is job-integrated and the level at which standards are set may serve to make financial incentives and the threat of failure relatively valueless. A more differentiated approach to diagnosis and correction is clearly required if a greater number of ineffective performers are to be restored to a satisfactory level.

It has become increasingly difficult to arouse a fear of failure and punishment, and thus to induce negative motivation and job-integrated avoidance efforts. In the past century, society has imposed many limitations on the negative sanctions available to management. With our higher standard of living, even those threats that can be employed have lost some of their emotional impact and motivational force. This does not mean that negative motivation is disappearing from the business scene, but only that it is less subject to control by individual managers. Unions and legal restrictions have increasingly deprived them of some of their more traditional techniques for getting the work out.

Yet after all these disclaimers, cautions, and qualifications it is apparent that threat and discipline can work, as Professor Gene Booker of Western Michigan University has demonstrated, and as many experienced managers have learned. The important questions are when and with whom does it work?

This approach appears most useful when employees have low standards of conduct or productivity and when fear of failure is at least reasonably dominant in their motivational hierarchy. It may also apply when motive satisfaction is being achieved in non-job-integrated activities, again when some meaningful level of fear of failure exists. It is important that these two conditions be present; when failure is attributable to intellectual or physical factors, punishment can actually do considerable harm.

The usual approach is for the manager to demand improved performance, coupled with a threat that negative sanctions will be applied if change does not occur. The alternative, and often the end result in any event, is formal disciplinary action carried out according to company policy or the union contract; the usual sequence is an official warning, suspension without pay, and ultimately discharge.

One area in which threat has been used with positive results is in controlling excessive absenteeism. Spot checks at home by visiting nurses or by management, coupled with discipline where appropriate, can help solve such problems, if motivation is the key factor. Some firms have introduced point systems with different types of absences resulting in different numbers of points being charged against the employee and with discharge the ultimate consequence if the point total goes too high. The drawback here is the lack of flexibility for dealing with various individuals.

Threats and discipline have already been discussed in the context of alcoholism and drug problems. They do not help much as a direct solution because the emotional disorders and their related motives are too dominant. However, threats and discipline can be used to motivate employees to seek assistance and treatment, which in turn may provide a solution.

In a study of over 100 discharged emotionally disturbed employees, Professors Harrison Trice and James Belasco of Cornell University found that 55 percent of the discharges were subsequently reversed by an arbitrator. Thus, employment was restored, but without treatment. The evidence indicated that this brush with the disciplinary process rarely had a positive effect. Many of the employees were fired again later or continued to be ineffective.

For discipline to be effective, it must be focused on very specific types of motivational problems and the manager must clearly indicate what types of behavior will serve to make further discipline unnecessary. In addition, the manager must convince his or her subordinate that threats will be carried out and that the discipline is not arbitrary, but a legitimate function of the managerial position. All this requires a certain coolness under emotional fire and a sense of assurance in dealing with such situations. Given this, managers can gain a good deal of satisfaction from carrying out a disciplinary action effectively, where it is clearly called for and appropriate to the needs of the employee and the organization. On the other hand, if a manager identifies too closely with the person who is to be threatened or disciplined, the situation can be a trying one.

5

Dealing with Physical Problems

Physical Illness and Job Performance

Most of us are familiar with symptoms of physical illness. From childhood on, we are taught to recognize and describe various signs that may provide a basis for medical diagnosis. So most managers are quite capable of identifying sickness in a subordinate—at least insofar as observation and listening to the person can provide clues. But this does not mean that the manager is qualified to make a specific diagnosis. About all that most managers can determine is that deficiencies in performance are attributable to sickness. After that, the problem is one for those with specialized medical knowledge. The manager's important role is to be a link between the subordinate and the physician. Although this role is much more easily fulfilled when the disorder is physical than when the symptoms are emotional, it may still present certain difficulties. Not all people will seek medical help when they feel ill or when they are injured—and many will even resist when someone attempts to persuade them to do so.

Although it is common for an employee to plead that seeking treatment indicates weakness, the basic problem in these cases is almost always fear. Some people feel that an illness does not really exist until it has been diagnosed; if they can somehow forget about it, it will go away. It is not surprising that managerial efforts to interfere with this denial process may sometimes meet with active resistance. Other people may be afraid to face the various things a physician might do to them: surgery, blood tests, shots, and the like. I remember one young man who shortly after induction into military service had his first exposure to the art of dentistry. Although scheduled for a second session, he never did attend. After forgetting several appointments and exhausting all other legal alternatives, he finally went AWOL rather than face the buzzing drill again.

In some respects, the impact of physical disorder on performance is self-evident: the major reason for failure is extended absence from the job. The number of times an employee is absent from work is not nearly so important as the total amount of time lost. It is true that frequent short-term absences are usually a greater supervisory headache, because the work needs to be covered on short notice and there is constant uncertainty as to whether the employee will be present on any given day. But the total amount of time away from work is the major determinant of lost productivity and of direct loss through payments for work not performed.

In dealing with someone whose performance is inadequate because of excessive absenteeism, it is important for the company to maintain contact during the time away from work. It is entirely appropriate to take steps to ensure that adequate medical care is being provided and that the company will be notified when the employee is physically able to return to work. True, the company has no right to compel a person to work, but it should be informed when the reason for absence has shifted from physical factors to motivational factors. Excessive absenteeism is an appropriate basis for establishing performance failure, and when it is caused by physical illness, the condition becomes a legitimate matter for company concern.

Employing a visiting nurse can reduce the time lost from work. Although this can be expensive, especially when employee homes are spread over a large area, the expense can be reduced by covering only people with records of excessive absence. In such cases, employee and union opposition is likely to be minimal, since the impact of the illness on performance is easily demonstrable. Resistance is most common when the employee has not been excessively absent and may interpret the nurse's visit as a totally unwarranted accusation.

If visiting nurses cannot be employed and the time lost is excessive, the manager should do everything possible to maintain contact. Telephone calls are apparently not sufficient; they have little effect on absenteeism rates. If possible, someone should actually see and talk with the employee. This should be handled tactfully, however. There is little to be gained by arriving at the door and virtually announcing that the purpose of the visit is to determine whether the employee is a malingerer. With tact, contact can be maintained, especially with those whose absenteeism constitutes a real problem, without employee reactions becoming strongly negative.

Absenteeism is not the only problem that can be caused by physical illness and injury—they can, of course, affect the quantity and quality of work directly if the individual continues on the job. A study conducted by Glynn Coates and co-workers at the University of Louisville dealt with this problem, concentrating in particular on the effects of feverish conditions and high temperatures. On the average, performance did suffer, and the higher the temperature the poorer the performance. Even more significant, however, was the finding that some people who have fevers become grossly ineffective, while others show no performance effect at all. Clearly one cannot assume that unsatisfactory performance always will result from colds and similar illnesses, but in some people it certainly will.

People who have many physical symptoms are also likely to have many emotional symptoms. One reason is the impact of physical illness on an individual's emotional life. Many people become anxious and afraid when they recognize physical symptoms in themselves. The emotional reaction may even grow into panic and become a symptom in its own right. Or the techniques that a person employs in an effort to ward off the anxiety may develop to the point where they constitute symptoms of emotional illness. Physical symptoms may also induce depression, although this is less common. In any event, these emotions and emotional symptoms may be as detrimental to performance as the physical symptoms themselves.

In fact, relatively minor physical changes, perhaps not even important enough to be called symptoms, can set off severe emotional breakdowns. Anything that might suggest the presence of a venereal disease can well initiate an intense emotional response. Similarly, an individual may interpret certain "signs" as indicating heart disease or cancer. I know of several people who restricted their work for years, some to the point of actually being considered ineffective, because they were convinced that they suffered from severe heart conditions. Yet when these people finally did seek medical help, no evidence of disease was found.

Physical Handicaps

With handicapped employees, physical factors can be particularly strategic if performance should fall below acceptable levels. Among those in the labor force are people with heart disease, amputations, crippling disabilities due to accidents or disease, deafness, blindness, arrested tuberculosis, and epilepsy. Certainly all people with these physical conditions do not become employed—a number are totally incapacitated. But many do seek work and, in spite of sizable obstacles, find positions. In general, handicapped workers tend to be concentrated disproportionately in lower-level positions. The physically normal person who becomes permanently disabled is very likely to return to the labor force in a job below that previously held. Thus, it is the first-line supervisor who usually must deal with problems of ineffectiveness caused by physical handicaps.

All available evidence indicates, however, that when a person is capable of steady work and is put in the right type of job, there is no particular reason to associate a handicap with ineffectiveness. Particularly useful studies in this area have been provided by Professor Roger Barker of the University of Kansas. Absenteeism among handicapped workers is actually lower than among physically normal workers. Accidents are not particularly frequent, although the total time lost when an accident does occur may be greater. Turnover is characteristically low. Quality and quantity of production are comparable to those of workers in general. A few studies have noted slightly poorer work records, but the differences are always small. Certainly there is no basis for assuming that a handicap means ineffective performance. In fact, there are many firms (in addition to those sheltered industries having rehabilitative as well as economic objectives) that make it a practice to employ physically disabled workers.

There are, of course, problems connected with specific disabilities. People with heart conditions may have somewhat higher rates of absenteeism and may have to avoid strenuous physical work. Amputees often become very proficient with artificial limbs, but certain tasks remain impossible. The deaf may learn lip-reading or use hearing aids, but performance of duties such as stenography is likely to be seriously impaired. Blindness is often incapacitating when it occurs in adulthood because of difficulty in adjusting to the disorder. When they are adequately trained, however, blind people can perform certain jobs very well. Arrested tuberculosis usually leaves the person with limited strength. As a result, frequent rest pauses may be necessary and absenteeism may be above average. Epilepsy, too, may cause a person to lose more days from work than normal.

When handicapped people do become ineffective for physical reasons, it is almost invariably because they have been placed in jobs where their handicaps make it impossible for them to perform adequately. The solution is to get them into more appropriate jobs as quickly as possible. This should be done with medical advice, because it often takes extensive knowledge of the condition to judge whether the person can do the work. In addition, the placement should ensure that handicapped employees will not be a hazard to themselves or others. Those who operate motor vehicles or potentially dangerous equipment must have the ability to protect themselves and others who work with them. Deaf workers cannot hear warnings; blind workers cannot see a potential source of danger; heart attacks and epileptic seizures may cause a person to lose control of his or her actions.

The ease with which handicapped people can be appropriately placed varies markedly with the nature of the particular disorder. A high proportion of jobs are inevitably closed to those who have lost the use of both legs and to the totally blind. On the other hand, blindness in one eye, loss of fingers, hearing difficulties short of deafness, and inability to use one foot are not nearly as restrictive. The majority of workers who have been hired with physical defects or who develop them later can achieve satisfactory performance levels without becoming a burden on anyone, if appropriate duties are assigned.

Undoubtedly, some companies will have to dismiss certain handicapped workers who would in other contexts be employable, because within that particular organization no suitable position is available. In such cases, most personnel departments will assist the person in obtaining approprate work elsewhere.

Another factor to consider in addressing the job problems of handicapped employees is that some employers are required by law to take affirmative action for people with handicaps. This is an obligation of all employers who do contractual work for the federal government, and of subcontractors to those employers. Affirmative action for handicapped people means making "reasonable accommodation" to their physical and mental limitations so that they can perform jobs for which they are otherwise qualified.

In a company with these obligations, all managers are expected to make special efforts in dealing with the problems of handicapped employees. These efforts could include:

Providing special equipment

Making changes in the physical layout of the job

Eliminating certain duties of the job

Modifying working hours

Providing special access to the job location

Managers should also be aware that the job problems of handicapped employees sometimes stem from lack of support and acceptance from co-workers. The manager's role here should be to prepare the new employee's co-workers, who may not be used to working with handicapped people. If the manager anticipates special problems, these should be explained so employees won't be taken by surprise. Tell employees how they can assist the new hire or help in the adjustment, and urge them to include the handicapped employee in coffee breaks and other social activities. Suggest to them that they avoid pity or condescension toward their new co-worker. Often initial problems stem from anxiety that the handicap provokes in co-workers; it makes them think that something similar could happen to them. This type of anxiety often disappears with time.

Organic Brain Disorders and Damage

So far in this chapter we have discussed employees who fail to perform effectively because of physical symptoms. Where there has been some damage to the brain, however, there may be no physical symptoms. Many of the symptoms associated with brain damage are similar to those of emotional disorder. Yet there are important differences in outcome. Emotional disorders can be cured, and in most cases the individual then is able to perform adequately in some type of work. The symptoms eventually disappear or become less constraining, although it may be many years before this happens. This kind of reversal of effects may also occur in some brain disorders. Many conditions are of an acute but temporary nature. The symptoms of alcohol intoxication and concussion, for instance, do not characteristically produce a prolonged lowering of performance. These acute brain disorders are not of much interest to us here for this very reason. Unless the condition is produced repeatedly, they are not causal factors in ineffective performance.

Some brain disorders, however, are permanent. Performance may be impaired and the difficulty may continue indefinitely. At present, little can be done medically to restore people with permanent structural brain damage to their previous levels of effectiveness. When the disorder is progressive, it may be possible to arrest its course, but that is the best that can be hoped for.

The sources of damage are many. Congenital or hereditary factors may result in defects that continue throughout life. So too may head injuries produced by falls, auto accidents, and the like. Diseases such as syphilis and encephalitis attack the brain. Various toxic drugs and poisons may be involved—alcohol, carbon monoxide, illuminating gas, lead, arsenic, mercury. The last three are particularly likely to be a source of brain damage in certain industries, because they have been widely used in paints and dyes. Permanent effects on the brain may also occur in conjuctions with heart attacks, epilepsy, diabetes, brain tumors, glandular disorders, and nutritional deficiencies.

In addition, certain changes associated with aging may cause progressive brain impairment in some people. Certainly not all people suffer this type of damage as they grow older. Nevertheless, it is by far the most frequent source of brain disorder. The process is characteristically gradual and frequently does not progress far enough to have any significance for management. On occasion, however, it may have considerable impact at a time when the person is at the peak of a career. The probability of this condition becoming strategic for failure increases steadily from the age of fifty on. If an employee over seventy becomes ineffective, the possibility of brain damage associated with old age should be one of the first hypotheses to consider. This does not mean that the hypothesis will be confirmed, however. Indeed, recent research indicates that aging in itself may not be responsible for deteriorating brain power in many older people.

The specific symptoms resulting from brain disorder are much the same irrespective of their source. The major differences are associated with the various stages of the disorder. When disease, aging, or progressive poisoning is involved, the symptoms usually develop in gradual progression unless there is medical intervention. When a head injury or some other injury occurring at a single time is responsible, the symptoms may be minimally incapacitating or they may be very severe, depending on the extent and type of damage.

In the early stages, it may be hard to tell from the symptoms that brain damage exists. There may be reduced speed and effectiveness of actions, especially when the person is dealing with unfamiliar situations; things may be done somewhat impulsively, without adequate planning; emotional states may change rapidly from irritability to depression to anxiety; neatness, honesty, and kindness may give way to more self-centered attitudes; at times the person may appear forgetful and rather vague about things that should be familiar. Unless one has known the individual well, these changes may not seem particularly significant. As the condition progresses, however, it becomes increasingly clear that something is wrong. Intellectual processes and memory may become obviously disturbed. Afflicted individuals may forget what they are doing or saying, where they are, or what has happened to them in the past. To hide these gaps they may make up stories and be convinced of their validity even when they are obviously ridiculous. On occasion they may repeat the same idea or phrase at frequent intervals. Judgment is at first merely poor, but later it can turn into complete confusion. The person may then appear restless, very talkative, and delirious. He or she may hear nonexistent voices or see fleeting images that have no correspondence to reality.

The problem of differentiating these symptoms from those of an emotional disorder is complicated by the fact that people suffering from brain damage may be emotionally upset over their deficiencies. Experiencing intellectual failure is an extremely powerful threat to emotional stability. The resulting anxiety, and efforts to deal with it, can cause a catastrophic reaction that develops into a full-scale emotional disorder of either neurotic or psychotic proportions.

A manager may sometimes wonder whether a present failure may be caused by changes that took place long before. For instance, a person may fail in a new, higher-level position after many years of effective performance. Could a head injury or the effects of some arrested disease be responsible? Where these are suspected, a search of the medical history can be fruitful. Although such searches rarely prove the case, they can provide strong presumptive evidence, especially if substantiated by psychological testing. Where the individual is failing and permanent brain damage is seriously suspected as the cause, demotion to a less demanding position can often be an adequate solution.

Physical Disorders of Emotional Origin

The close relationship between the experiencing of emotion and certain physiological changes has been recognized for many years. Among other things, there may be elevated blood pressure, dilated pupils and nostrils, and increased sweating. In addition, changes may occur in the glands, and various biochemical substances may be circulated in the blood. These physiological changes may contribute directly to the formation of symptoms if certain emotions are persistently aroused. More frequently, the process is indirect and involves efforts to avoid experiencing an unpleasant emotion.

One such mechanism operates like this: We noted previously that certain unacceptable motives break through to influence behavior in the form of slips of the tongue, "accidents," etc. These actions represent wishes that were once openly expressed but later became associated with anxiety. The person learned that to anticipate satisfaction in such activities was bad and would bring on disturbing feelings and events. Apparently, physical symptoms may also become a method of expressing these unconscious motives. Illness provides a perfect disguise and thus serves as an ideal means of warding off the anxiety that would result should a particular desire become conscious. It is entirely acceptable to have a symptom of physical illness, whereas it is not so acceptable to do certain things of a sexual or aggressive nature. And so the individual unconsciously attempts to cope with the threat of such desires by developing physical symptoms such as protracted vomiting or manifestations of heart disease. Under such circumstances, the symptoms are often totally effective in warding off the unacceptable motives and unaccompanied by anxiety, despite the presence of a severe physical disorder. The individual has no more idea why he or she is ill than what is behind a slip of the tongue. In some cases, however, the process is only partially successful, and the person experiences considerable emotional upset in addition to the physical symptom.

A second mechanism operates somewhat differently. The individual employs the disorder directly to avoid unpleasant emotions. Any illness that will serve to remove people from a disturbing situation, without forcing them to recognize their own inability to deal with the situation effectively, can serve this purpose. A sick headache may always develop whenever a young secretary has a date, and may make it impossible for her to come to work the next day, too. A faint feeling may overcome an account executive every time a presentation must be made to a client. In such cases, the symptom need not win out, of course. Some motive other than the avoidant one may assume a dominant position, and the person may continue on to face the situation with the added burden of the symptom. In severe neuroses, however, the symptoms do control behavior.

Sometimes this defensive process operates in a much more complex manner, as in the formation of a stomach ulcer. Because the earliest childhood experiences of being taken care of are associated with being fed, eating itself may provide a feeling of security or love and may act to ward off anxiety. This motivation operates frequently in overweight people. The ulcer sufferer, who may face frequent and potentially intense anxiety, does not avoid emotional upset by actually eating. But, whenever disturbing situations arise, there is a desire to be fed. This triggers the appropriate physiological mechanisms, including the secretion of acid into the stomach. The resulting acid concentration eventually erodes the stomach wall and contributes to the formation of an ulcer. Thus, a physical response adopted to avoid disturbing emotions has unfortunate side effects. Ulcers can in severe cases be fatal.

Almost any physical symptom can be evolved in one of these ways. Unfortunately, current knowledge of why people develop the specific symptoms they do is very incomplete. In some cases, hereditary factors seem to predispose the person to use certain parts of the body in forming disorders. In other cases, the symptom clearly is a learned product of life experiences. In any event, physical symptoms of emotional origin do appear to be based on specific physical sensitivities that vary from individual to individual.

Studies have established the role of emotional factors in many disorders, including epilepsy, diabetes, excessive fatigue, arthritis, constipation and diarrhea, backache, high blood pressure, hives and other skin diseases, disturbances of urinary function, impotence, asthma, hay fever, headaches, visual anomalies, and fainting. This is not to say that these conditions are always caused by emotional factors, or that physical causes may not interact with the emotional. Differentiating causes in any specific case is very difficult. Sometimes, for instance, a person will acquire a physically incapacitating condition, such as a sprain, as a result of nonemotional causes, only to have the disorder perpetuated indefinitely by emotional factors.

Managers should know that there are important distinctions between strictly physical symptoms and those which also have an emotional aspect. The treatments differ in nature and duration, and the prospects for ending the poor performance will differ, too. If an emotional factor is involved, the appropriate solution may require treatment of the underlying emotional causes.

It is unlikely that most managers can make the necessary diagnosis. When a physical symptom of emotional origin is the key factor in ineffective performance and no other severe emotional symptoms are evident, it takes a trained specialist to determine that a neurosis is present. Furthermore, the employee will probably be convinced that the symptoms are purely physical and will resist actively any suggestion that an emotional disorder needs treating. Under these circumstances, even if emotional causation is suspected, it is best to have the employee thoroughly checked for physical causation. In some instances, the medical examination will unearth nothing suggesting a physical reason for the condition. This means that the cause is probably emotional. In other instances, a period of extensive and varied medical treatment will have no effect. The person may even have already visited several different physicians with no result. When medical treatment that should have helped has consistently failed, emotional causation may well be involved. In such instances, treatment with psychotherapy or with drugs may be most appropriate.

Problems of Physical Proportions

Perhaps the most obvious relationship between physical characteristics and performance involves bodily proportions. Success in sports is strongly influenced by this factor. A short person can rarely compete effectively at basketball, a big person as a jockey, or a light man at football. Although generally such distinctions are much less important in industry, sometimes a problem will arise because of equipment design. Machinery is constructed to be used by operators with a limited range of physical proportions, and occasionally someone is hired who falls outside this range. Very short people may find it difficult to reach the controls of certain kinds of vehicles. People with very long legs may be so cramped that they cannot get adequate leverage on foot pedals. Usually these problems are easily identified, and transfer to a more physically suitable type of work is the most appropriate solution.

Problems of Physical Attractiveness

The aesthetic qualities of various physical characteristics are unlikely to have any effect on actual performance, outside of a few obvious occupations such as modeling, acting, and similar fields. However, such factors may influence *judgments* of effectiveness. It is easy to assume, almost without thinking, that a physically unattractive person is equally deficient in job-related skills. And some attractive employees have maintained their position because of their contribution to office decor rather than their work performance. It is not always easy to separate such inappropriate criteria from those which are actually related to company objectives.

A particularly good example of the subtle ways in which physical attractiveness may influence decisions is provided by an investigation of college recruiting practices carried out by Professor Stephen Carroll of the University of Maryland. He found that company visits and job offers were much more likely to go to the handsomer students, even though the recruiters were typically unaware of this fact and there was no evidence that would support this criterion as a predictor of performance effectiveness.

Muscular Skill and Strength

A more important physical factor than looks involves the use of various muscles and muscle groups in carrying out work activities. Such characteristics as muscular strength, speed of muscular response, and muscular dexterity vary considerably from person to person and may become sources of failure.

Although there are certainly inherent differences between people in physical speed, strength, and dexterity, training can substantially affect the final skill level achieved. This training tends to be specialized; those who possess one kind of skill do not necessarily possess others. Gross coordination of the arms and legs, the speed of muscular reaction, balance, and various fine dexterities involving the use of the fingers, hands, or arms, are relatively independent skills. They may be developed to a point of minimal proficiency very rapidly, but further training continues to yield increments in improved performance over long periods of time. As a result, extensive practice may be required before a level considered adequate for effective performance on the job is attained. Some people may never reach it.

Actually, when it is said that someone possesses a certain level of manual dexterity or physical agility, this indicates the rate at which that person might be expected to learn new tasks of a related nature and the final level of proficiency likely to be attained. When a person is considered ineffective because of a deficiency in some motor ability which the job requires, this implies that a satisfactory level of proficiency has not been attained after a reasonable amount of adequate training.

Although muscular activity, especially strength, has played an important role in many jobs in the past, the number of positions requiring such skills is steadily decreasing. Machinery, often automated, is taking over from human muscle power and dexterity. Many of the jobs that continue to make demands in this respect are at a relatively low level and may be redesigned in the future to eliminate the physical requirements. In fact, some of these jobs are already in transition, being performed manually in some companies and mechanically in others.

Occupations have not been studied as extensively as they might be in terms of their muscular and dexterity requirements. As a result, managers may not be able to obtain very precise diagnostic information regarding the role of muscular and dexterity factors in failure. Nevertheless, several tests of motor proficiency are available. The standardized tests of typing skills are perhaps the best known, but there are many others. If it is impossible to determine from close observation whether a person's failure is due to problems of physical skill, emotional disruption, or motivational inadequacies, a check with a personnel specialist may be helpful.

Once it has been established that some type of muscular speed, strength, or dexterity is important on the job, and that the employee is failing because of deficiencies in this area, the manager can take appropriate action. If the employee lacks the requisite strength or stamina, this may possibly be gained through physical-fitness training. Often, however, this is either impractical or too time-consuming to provide a solution, in which case transfer to a less physically demanding job is most appropriate. But if the person is already in an unskilled job—and this is likely, since it is mainly laboring jobs that consistently require considerable physical strength—transfer may not be easy. This problem will be taken up shortly in our discussion of older workers.

Where the difficulty involves coordination rather than strength, training may provide a solution. Possibly the employee has not had an adequate opportunity to develop the coordinated movements required, and could attain the necessary skills with more extended learning. If training has been curtailed or was clearly inadequate, this is an obvious answer. But if the employee has completed normal training without achieving the required skills, you must decide whether additional training is practical. There comes a point at which further investment in training is not warranted: even though the employee might eventually achieve acceptable performance, the cost would be prohibitive. In such a case, transfer to some other type of work makes more sense. The new job may involve some physical demands, but it should not impose requirements similar to those of the position in which failure occurred. Since the various physical skills are essentially independent, failure in one indicates little about proficiency in others.

Sensory and Perceptual Deficiencies

Sensory capacities may also influence performance. Among the various senses, only vision and hearing are likely to be crucial. People who suffer from defects of these senses (even when they are not truly handicapped) are frequently placed in jobs where their deficiencies put them at a disadvantage. In part, this is because of inadequate pre-employment testing, in part because of the generally unreliable nature of superficial physical examinations. People with defects sufficient to produce performance failure may well appear in any employee group. Where certain perceptual skills are particularly important in the work, this can be one of the more common causes.

In vision, such defects as far- and near-sightedness are frequent sources of difficulty. The individual may not be able to see clearly because he or she needs glasses, because present glasses are inappropriate, or because the condition cannot be corrected. Such factors can be a major source of errors in many jobs. Under certain conditions, as, for example, when the work requires one to operate a vehicle, other visual factors may become strategic—ability to see at night, peripheral vision, depth perception, color vision. The latter is particularly important when colored signals or safety indicators are involved. Approximately 8 percent of all males (but less than half of 1 percent of all females) have some degree of color blindness; 2 percent are totally unable to tell red from green.

Besides these visual capacities, there is also a skill which has been called perceptual speed. Many jobs require that a person rapidly and accurately identify small differences in visual detail. In one respect, reading demands this ability. Perceptual speed is a major requirement in many clerical occupations where one list must be checked against another or computations compared. Inspection jobs of various types also demand this skill. Often a job requires perceptual speed and motor speed in combination; the employee must quickly note something and then respond with some appropriate action. When a person lacks perceptual speed, the quantity of work produced is likely to be insufficient. Or if the individual is pressured into increasing output, there is often a sharp increase in the number of errors.

Auditory problems are less diverse than visual ones and usually arise from difficulties in hearing sounds of a certain pitch. Often people think they hear one thing and act accordingly, only to learn that they were wrong.

Some partially deaf people go to considerable lengths to conceal their poor hearing by guessing at what others have said. Many times they are right; they combine what they have heard with a knowledge of the context to figure out what they have not heard. On other occasions they are wrong. And if these occasions should consistently involve job assignments and instructions, the resulting errors may be frequent and serious. In addition to problems of hearing the human voice, difficulty in perceiving auditory signals can sometimes be important.

Differences between job conditions and the conditions under which medical and psychological tests of visual and auditory capabilities are administered sometimes make the tests less valuable than they might be. For instance, auditory tests are usually conducted in a noise-free room. But the person who works in a noisy factory must be able to pick out significant words from a mass of background sounds. Even so, a comprehensive examination is the best approach when sensory problems are suspected.

Once deficiences have been identified, they should be handled in the same manner as other handicaps. Various corrective devices such as eyeglasses or hearing aids are, of course, more likely to restore effective performance in these cases than among the severely disabled.

Consequences of Aging

Almost all the muscular and sensory abilities discussed in this chapter tend to decline with age—speed of movement, dexterity and coordination, physical strength, visual and auditory sensitivity, and perceptual speed. In general, the decline starts in the late twenties and is gradual in nature. There are major differences between individuals, however. While some people maintain certain abilities at an almost constant level throughout life, others show a precipitous decline. The result is that the differences in any one of these physical characteristics within a group of people in their sixties will be much greater than those within a group of twenty-year-olds. Thus, although deficiencies of this kind are more likely to cause performance failure as life progresses, physical characteristics do not necessarily contribute to ineffectiveness in an older employee.

In fact, evidence reviewed by Professor Stephen Griew of the University of Dundee in Scotland suggests that the impact of physical decline on actual job performance may often be minimal. Among clerical workers, there are essentially no differences associated with age. In occupations such as typist, and in various clerical jobs involving filing, posting, and sorting activities, older workers are no more likely than younger ones to fall below acceptable levels of performance.

On the other hand, among factory workers there does tend to be a decline in the performance of older employees. The number of poor performers increases steadily above the age of forty-five. Presumably the differences are based on the varying physical demands of the jobs. Strength and stamina are important in factory jobs, and as people get older they are often incapable of maintaining adequate output. Clerical positions, on the other hand, require finer muscular skills, to the extent that they require physical abilities at all. Dexterities of this kind are more likely to be improved by continued practice. This, plus the increases in job-related mental abilities that come with age, presumably serve to counteract any decline in physical competence.

Whether or not older workers will actually perform less effectively, then, depends on the extent to which reduced physical capacities make any difference in the specific work they are doing and on the extent to which they are able to compensate for the physical changes.

Up to a point, most people can make up for physical deficiencies through increased motivation, superior mental abilities, greater job knowledge, and the like. But when the physical demands are primary and the deficiencies marked, performance will suffer. This is much more likely to happen in blue-collar jobs than in clerical and managerial jobs.

Much of this decline in performance is caused by a general slowing down with age. Perceptual and motor speed are markedly affected. Most older workers apparently can perform various job duties just as well as those who are much younger, but they cannot repeat the operations over and over again at the same rate. Even the physical strength that is required for most unskilled positions is entirely within the capabilities of most employees of more advanced age. But the majority cannot maintain the pace. If they are pressed to increase their output, quality will fall off badly. When left to their own devices, most older workers who have experienced some decline in a job-related ability will concentrate on accuracy. Completely eliminating errors is the only way they can approach an adequate overall performance level.

This fact can provide an important clue to the placement of older workers who have failed because of declining physical abilities. The ideal, of course, is to shift the person to a job which does not require any physical characteristics that are lacking. But with many lower-level workers, there is no other position for which they are qualified. The next best alternative is to shift them to positions where accuracy rather than speed is desirable. Placement in assembly-line jobs that require constant repetition of the same physically demanding activities is not likely to restore effective performance. Unskilled work involving continuous digging or loading operations is also of dubious value. Janitorial activities, on the other hand, can be varied at the individual's discretion and may present no difficulties even though the work is occasionally heavy. The important thing is to eliminate any pacing of the work or constant repetition of the same movements.

In many instances, sizable performance improvements can be achieved even within the present position by job redesign. For example, if some very rapid work is required, it might be broken up into small time segments and distributed throughout the day rather than concentrated at one time. That such redesign, or even transfer to another more appropriate position, might require retraining should not be a matter of major concern. It is now clear that under a wide variety of circumstances, older workers can be retrained as effectively as younger ones.

6

Dealing with Family-Related Problems

So far we have discussed the individual characteristics of a subordinate that may contribute to failure: the intellectual, emotional, motivational, and physical factors. We will turn now to group relationships that often can influence job performance. These factors will be treated in ascending order of group size. This and the next chapter will deal with the two smaller groups: the family and the work group.

The Families That Influence Performance

We are using the term *family* in a comprehensive sense. Much of the time we will be talking about the original group into which the employee was born. This includes parents, brothers, sisters, and, on occasion, other relatives. Sometimes, as a result of divorce and remarriage, the family becomes a very complex unit indeed. This group remains important to the individual throughout its existence, although it usually loses some significance in adulthood. In addition, the term *family* will be used to mean the family the individual creates by marriage or by mutual agreement. Customarily, it includes a husband, wife, and children. It may combine to some degree with the parental families of either husband or wife. A third family consisting of the parents of the marital partner may also assume a strategic position under certain circumstances. Sometimes the spouse's parents have a surprisingly strong influence on a person's job performance.

Since the next chapter will be devoted entirely to social relationships on the job, you may wonder at the neglect of other small groups to which an employee may belong—the various friendship groups, clubs, gangs, etc., as well as the bonds formed during engagements or other romantic relationships. The reason for omitting these associations is that they do not appear to have a frequent impact on performance. When they do achieve a strategic position, it is through routes similar to those discussed here. Thus, what is said about the influence of the family can generally be applied equally well to any other small group outside the work situation.

One unique feature is associated with identifying family factors in performance—and it is important primarily because of the opportunities for error it introduces. Events occurring in the parental family during a much earlier period may have considerable impact on the emotional and motivational patterns a person brings to the job. To some extent, intellectual and physical characteristics are similarly affected. Performance failure is often influenced by things that happened many years before, in the so-called formative years. Such early-life factors as mental illness of a parent or sibling, parental separation and divorce, parental conflict, lack of affection in the family, overrestriction of childhood activities, and intense conflict with other family members are much more common among adult neurotics than among those who are well-adjusted. Presumably these experiences contribute to emotional sensitivities that later combine with situational stresses to produce breakdown. Similarly, people who have made poor occupational adjustments, for whatever reason, are more likely to have a pattern of early family problems. Typically they had more conflict with their parents and received less affection. Criminal behavior, emotional disorder, and other deviations were usually more common within their families. In addition, a tendency to lean on parents to an excessive degree may have been actively fostered at home. These relationships were first established some years ago in studies by Jeanette Friend and Ernest Haggard.

Such influences are, however, indirect in that the actual strategic factors are only *conditioned* by family events of years before. Although much of what the manager has to deal with is a result of the employees' childhood experiences, these experiences themselves do not operate directly to create ineffectiveness. For this reason, we will restrict our discussion to family influences that may be present at the time of failure. These may, of course, be continuations or repetitions of influences initiated many years before—but we will not be concerned with the parental family as it contributed to the development of individual characteristics at a much earlier date.

Among the factors that may operate here and now to influence behavior at work are crises in the family, separation from the family, and a variety of demands and events within the home that serve to make work seem distinctly secondary.

What Kinds of Family Crises Can Affect Performance?

The term *crisis* has been applied to a number of different events that may have severely disruptive effects on a family. Sociologists have not always agreed in drawing up lists of these events, but at least three categories seem to be relevant. First among these is economic shock or impoverishment: the sudden loss of savings and income so that the family cannot continue to support itself as a group. Much of the research in this area has dealt with the effects of bank failures and unemployment during periods of economic depression. Although crises of this kind may cause performance failure, this is rather infrequent since usually the loss of employment is part of the crisis. In other cases, the economic factors that affect performance do not involve the family and so fall outside the scope of this chapter. For these reasons, we will not discuss economic crises here, even though from a broader sociological perspective they can have considerable importance.

A second type of event is clearly relevant to our discussion. It involves the actual or imminent disruption of the family by desertion, separation, or divorce. As noted previously, either the parental family or the family formed by the individual's marriage may be strategic in causing poor job performance. Sometimes the disintegration of a person's parental family can be as sharp a blow as the breakup of his or her own marital relationship. The disruption need not actually take place for a crisis to be strategic, but the probability of its occurrence must be high. Infidelity, for instance, may have the same emotional meaning for a spouse as divorce, even though the marriage is not actually dissolved. Both may carry an implication of total rejection and betrayal.

Crises in a third category are even more likely to contribute to deficiencies on the job. These involve the severe illness or death of a family member. Although physical illness with its threat of imminent bereavement is the most common example, emotional disorders of psychotic proportions can have a similar impact. Suicide is probably more apt to have a negative effect on family members than any other single event. To these events should no doubt be added a few instances of increased membership in the family. On occasion, the birth of an unwanted child, whether illegitimate or not, can significantly affect the job performance of a family member.

How Family Crises Cause Ineffectiveness

Family crises most often cause ineffectiveness as a result of the emotional responses to them. What the manager observes directly is a rapid deterioration of performance along the lines described in Chapter 3. There may be even enough stress to provoke a full-scale emotional disorder, although usually it is just the frequent arousal of overpowering emotion that disrupts work. Sometimes the reaction is primarily motivational. The crisis rearranges the individual's hierarchy of motives and introduces new methods of obtaining satisfactions, so that there may be substantially more activity which is unintegrated with the job. Whether the reaction is primarily emotional or motivational, however, the fact of sudden change should suggest to the manager that some kind of family crisis may be involved. The existence of a crisis is particularly likely when a subordinate unexpectedly announces an intention to resign without having formulated any definite plans for the future. Although such resignations occur for many reasons, it often happens when a person who has experienced a severe family crisis attempts to get away from it all and start over again.

We are not saying here that family crises will inevitably result in performance failure. Although most people will be affected emotionally by such events, the majority will not permit their performance to suffer. In other cases, the performance problem will be only temporary. People differ tremendously in their reactions to specific crises.

One particularly important response to family crises is the grief reaction in cases of bereavement. Certain kinds of symptoms have been observed repeatedly among those who become temporarily disturbed after the loss of a loved one. When extended illnesses result from grief, they tend to follow well-defined patterns. Since most managers can expect to handle at least one case of acute grief during their careers, a knowledge of these patterns and their relationships to performance should be helpful. Responses to the loss of a family member for reasons other than death may take a very similar course. Desertion, separation, and divorce (and sometimes the breakup of an engagement or an affair) can provoke grief reactions which are emotionally identical with those precipitated by death, although certain external manifestations may differ.

When the grief reaction is relatively brief, the manifestations are likely to be:

- Tightness in the throat

- Shortness of breath and sighing

- An empty feeling in the stomach

- An overall sense of weakness or exhaustion

- Preoccupation with the image of the deceased person, to the point where it is almost impossible to think about anyone else

- Feelings of guilt, often manifested in self-blame for any unhappiness experienced by the deceased person

- Irritability and anger in dealing with others, often involving total rejection of former friends

- Changes in typical behavior because activities previously shared with the deceased now seem empty and meaningless

- A tendency to assume characteristics of the lost person: mannerisms, hobbies, even symptoms manifested during the terminal illness

As a result of these preoccupations and emotions, a bereaved person may be completely unable to concentrate on work. If the unpleasant feelings are accepted and not avoided, this process should run its course within a reasonable period. Difficulties commonly arise, however, if the person attempts to blot out all memory of the deceased and thus ward off distress. Under these circumstances, there may be practically no expression of unpleasant emotion for a considerable time. Often the individual dives into the job with great gusto. Then, several weeks or even several months later, the depressive feelings may break through in such overwhelming proportions that work becomes totally impossible. At such times there may be almost constant crying.

These more severe emotional responses to loss may occur immediately as well as after a delay. Usually they include exaggerations of the reactions noted previously. The rejection of friends may be complete, and intense hatred of them may even develop. Physical symptoms of emotional origin may be manifested. The person may become indecisive, unable to initiate any activity unless prodded. In the most extreme cases, a depression of psychotic proportions may emerge, with symptoms such as marked tension, constant activity, sleeplessness, feelings of great inadequacy, bitter self-accusations, and an intense desire to be punished for imagined misdeeds. Such people can become suicidal.

The Nature of Separation Anxiety Reactions

In many of these crisis situations, at least part of the distress is precipitated by the threat or actual fact of being separated from an emotionally significant person. Certainly this is true when desertion, divorce, physical illness, or death is involved. In addition, there are many other instances of separation which would not be considered crises except in terms of the individual's reaction to them.

Very young children often become depressed and apathetic when separated from their parents for hospitalization or other reasons, and remain "clingy" and disturbed for some time after returning to the family. Child psychologists are frequently called upon to treat school phobias in youngsters who become terrified each day when it is time to leave home. Later, a child's homesickness may disrupt a stay at summer camp or with relatives. Such reactions are not restricted to the early years. Armies have been plagued throughout history with desertions occasioned by an intense desire to return to the family. This was such a problem to the nationalist Chinese that they adopted a policy of flying all new conscripts to training camps many hundreds of miles away from home. Among prison inmates, separation from the family is a primary source of anxiety.

In the business world, this separation anxiety (or homesickness) can assume importance when the employee must be away from a significant family for considerable periods. It is therefore most likely to be a problem among salespersons, traveling auditors, consultants, and managers whose duties call for frequent trips to company facilities out of town. It can also be troublesome in transportation industries and in companies that make it a policy to send people on extended assignments without their families.

Often, employees perform much less effectively away from home than they do when they can return to their families every evening. Unfortunately, the person who is separated from the family is also often separated from direct supervision. As a result, performance failure does not become evident immediately and may, in fact, never manifest itself clearly unless the individual becomes severely disturbed. Certainly a manager should try to keep a close check on the performance of a young subordinate working away from home for the first time. Once it is clear that separation anxiety is not present, such intensive efforts can be discontinued.

What actually happens in separation anxiety is similar to several processes that we have already described. All of us tend to seek the help and support of certain family members and friends when we are upset about something. We ask others to assist us in making decisions and to cheer us up when we feel dejected. In some people, this response to anxiety and other unpleasant emotions has become a standard defense, an invariable method of reacting to the slightest hint of emotional distress. As long as the need to lean on others can be exercised without disrupting one's other activities, there is no real problem. Once separation occurs, however, the motive cannot be satisfied. Away from the family, an employee with such a motive may lose all sense of security, feel lost and helpless, and eventually become so anxious and depressed that work is almost impossible. Often, this pattern is similar to a grief reaction in that it includes an irritable attitude toward others and an inability to reach decisions or initiate activity. Since those who spend considerable time on the road may well have to meet new people and make important decisions on the spot, this kind of response to separation can have extremely detrimental effects.

Anxiety reactions do not always show up immediately at the time of separation. Many people are able to work effectively away from home for some time before absence from the family begins to have its effect. In these instances, the fears and sense of helplessness are at first counteracted by other strong motives. But finally, the employee is no longer able to compensate in this manner, and despite all efforts the caliber of work falls off.

Some who find separation from their families emotionally difficult avoid it for this reason. But others make a deliberate effort to prove themselves by volunteering for traveling assignments and applying for jobs that keep them away from home. Therefore, employees cannot be counted on to evaluate their own strengths and weaknesses correctly in this respect. The decision on work away from home should be made by managers and should be based on an objective evaluation of the individual. Of course, some people who seek such work do so because they actually want to get away from home. They may even perform more effectively when freed of their intolerable family situation.

In a different form of separation, one family remains intact while the person is separated from another. When a man, his wife, and his children move because he or she has been transferred or taken a job outside the local area, problems may arise because the parental family is being left behind. When the relationship between the two families has been very close and a person has never been separated from his or her parents for any extended period, a move to another part of the country can present a real threat. In spite of the increasing mobility of the "corporate family," this situation remains a potential source of difficulty. Some will refuse to accept a transfer out of the town in which their parents live and, if pressured, will seek employment with another company to ensure against separation. Others will accept or even seek the change only to find themselves incapable of adjusting. They may ask to return to the former position or may resign suddenly to move back to their hometown. Rarely does a person explain any of these actions as a desire to maintain close contact with a parental family. The manager may have to dig under a massive barrage of "rational" explanations to unearth the true cause. The employee may not even be aware of the real motives or real sources of distress.

The potential strength of this type of motivation is perhaps not generally recognized. Although most people who reject jobs requiring separation from their parents and friends would perform effectively if they did make the change, attachments of this kind do often influence important decisions. Many young people will not even consider careers that might force them to leave the area where their parents live. And a major reason why many qualified young people do not attend college is that there are no appropriate opportunities near home.

Other Effects of Separation

Crisis reactions appear to be accentuated by separation under certain circumstances. If an employee is away from home and believes that a wife or husband is unfaithful or contemplating divorce, or that the integrity of the family group is threatened in some other way, the fact of separation may make any crisis reaction much more severe. Being away from the trouble spot produces a sense of helplessness that serves to intensify emotional experiences. Perhaps the person could do nothing to avert the crisis, but separation precludes the possibility of even trying.

Separation may also cause poor job performance in cases where the family has been compensating for an employee's intellectual and physical deficiencies. Away from home, such employees may have to face situations which demand more than they can accomplish alone. For example, many low-intelligence employees are able to maintain adequate performance in unskilled jobs by relying on family members for assistance with personal finances and other matters. Or an employee who does not understand something that develops in connection with the job can sometimes take the problem home and get a solution that can be used in comparable situations that come up. Separation precludes this type of help and may therefore turn a satisfactory worker into an unsatisfactory one.

Somewhat similar is the situation of the individual who has no family or close personal relationships to turn to in time of need. Here it is not separation but a total lack of emotional support that is crucial; social isolation can leave a person extremely vulnerable to emotional breakdown. The presence of other people and the opportunity to talk over problems, as well as the sense of being wanted that goes with being a member of a family or close group, can be very important as a buffer against difficult circumstances. Although isolation is unlikely to be responsible for failure in and of itself, the lack of group ties may serve as a catalyst in the rapid development of debilitating emotional responses under stress conditions.

Dealing with Family Crises and Employment Separation

Family factors contributing to ineffective performance present special managerial problems that are not easily solved. The source of the difficulty is outside the usual orbit of supervisory control, and it is not easy to accomplish a change. When a person has a family crisis and responds with the characteristic grief reaction, practically nothing can be done. However, as long as he or she accepts the pain of loss and expresses sorrow without resorting to extremes, there is little need to take action. Usually performance will suffer for a while, but as the employee's problems are resolved, it will be restored to a satisfactory level. It is important for the manager to refrain from any harsh reactions when the employee cannot maintain adequate performance. At such times, sympathy and understanding are most likely to produce the desired result. If the individual is religious, the manager might recommend a talk with a minister, priest, or rabbi. Above all else, the person must have time to express emotion and work out the problems the crisis has created. Nothing should be done to imply that emotional expression is inappropriate or unacceptable.

When more extreme emotional reactions occur, either delayed or immediately after the crisis, the manager should make every effort to get the person professional help. Psychotherapy can achieve rapid cures in some cases. It is important that treatment be instituted as soon as possible.

If the problem is separation anxiety precipitated by being away from either a spouse and children or the parental family, the most immediately successful approach generally is to end the separation as quickly as possible. It is often striking how merely bringing a person home can raise his or her level of effectiveness. Another possible solution is professional treatment to help adjustment to the new job. However, this requires time and may not be feasible as long as travel continues. Also, there are many cases where performance is affected but the employee is not anxious enough to seek treatment. Then a return to the family is the only really appropriate course.

Unfortunately, transfers home are not always easily accomplished. The employee may have been assigned to the job no more than a month or so before. In addition, the work may be recognized by the company as unpleasant and thus considered to be a test of fortitude. Many traveling jobs are given to new employees with the understanding that as they prove themselves they will become eligible for less arduous assignments. Similarly, assignments in outlying areas or in foreign countries may be rotated with everyone taking a turn. When such placement policies are in force, it is very difficult to bring employees back before they have put in their time, especially when they have failed to meet the implied test of character. Yet this is the action most likely to restore performance and permit effective utilization of their talents within the organization.

However, the greatest managerial problem created by a subordinate who cannot adjust to separation is financial. Employees who must be returned from a foreign assignment with their families represent a sizable monetary loss to the company. So, too, do employees who have received extensive training for their new job. Because of the cost factor, the only really satisfactory solution for separation difficulties is to prevent them by adequate screening. Only people who will probably be able to adapt should be selected for jobs involving extensive travel or assignment away from home. There are several useful guides to effective screening available.

A person's previous employment history and education can yield valuable clues. If the individual has been away from home for military service, college, or prior work and has performed adequately, there is little basis for concern. If there are indications that the person has not done well while separated but has maintained a satisfactory work record when living at home, every effort should be made to obtain detailed information regarding previous failures. Transfers from a college located in another part of the country to one near home, exceptionally short periods of military service, and difficulty in handling sales positions requiring extensive travel often indicate difficulties involving separation.

When people have spent their whole lives in close proximity to their family, however, this type of analysis has limited value, particularly if they are young. There may well have been no special reason for separation to occur. On the other hand, someone in his or her middle thirties who has never married and has continued to live at home quite possibly may have difficulty adjusting to separation. Chances are that this person has had opportunities to live away from home and rejected them. Similarly, people who seem quite resistant to travel or are obviously upset at the prospect of an out-of-town assignment should not be selected. Frequently, they will produce a large number of excuses, none of which is really very convincing. Rarely will they admit even to themselves that the very thought of separation makes them anxious.

What Happens When Family Considerations Take Priority?

The reactions to crises and to separation that we have discussed represent instances where family considerations have taken precedence over job performance. This conflict between family and job can also occur when no direct threat to family unity is involved. In fact, it is often the *presence* of the family that creates the difficulty. Situations of this kind can develop in a number of ways.

One common problem arises when a subordinate is more responsibe to the demands of family members than to those of superiors at work. A spouse may feel lonely and neglected, resenting any intrusion on "our time" occasioned by overtime work, business trips, and the like. A person may even resent the fact that his or her spouse must be at work eight hours a day. Varying work schedules are particularly likely to stir up such reactions. The result may be that the employee refuses to work overtime, or travel, or accept a shift assignment. Absenteeism may become excessive. Whether or not an individual reacts in these ways depends as much on the employee as on the spouse. Many workers are exposed throughout life to a tug of war between family and job demands. Some are able to give priority to the employment relationship when this is necessary to maintain an adequate performance level, while others tend to allow family demands to predominate.

On occasion, family demands of this kind stem from problems created by children. I have dealt with several cases where, when the mother became the least bit ill, the father was expected to stay home from work and take care of the children. If a wife suffers from some physical disorder having primarily emotional causes, this can mean an excessive amount of lost time. In such a case, the husband is often called away from work during the middle of the day to tend his offspring, although he may not describe the situation to his boss in quite these terms.

Problems can also develop when the marital family stays together but is separated from the parental family. In these cases, a nonworking wife may be the one who becomes very upset. This is perhaps most common when the family has been sent to a foreign location. Actually, in any given company, breakdowns attributable to separation and exposure to unfamiliar situations may well be more numerous among wives than among the husbands themselves. This is primarily because the husbands have usually been appraised to determine whether they can be expected to perform effectively in the new assignment, while wives are less often evaluated in this manner. In addition, many women maintain close ties to their parents over a longer period than do their husbands. Since the wife is also likely to be younger than her husband, she may well be leaving home for the first time.

Let us continue to assume a transferred husband and non-working wife (since most transfers involve male employees). What can happen when family problems are caused by a wife's separation reaction? In some cases, she may enter psychiatric treatment. Or she may eventually adjust to the separation. Sometimes she will continue to be upset over an extended period without this reaction affecting her husband's performance. On occasion, more drastic solutions are sought, such as divorce. Or the wife may merely return to her home while the husband continues at work. She may become severely depressed and even commit suicide, although this is rare. When a husband in this situation does place family factors above his job and permits his performance to be drastically affected, he may do so because he believes his family is threatened with disintegration.

In other cases, a failure on the job seems to be only part of a complex pattern of family trouble and emotional upset. It has been long recognized that people treated for emotional disorders in mental hospitals and discharged as cured often become disturbed again shortly after returning to their families. In these cases the family may well actually precipitate or prolong symptoms of emotional disorder, and even though only one member actually becomes ill, the whole group may be basically disturbed. Because of this, psychiatrists and clinical psychologists increasingly carry out treatment in the home with the whole family, rather than in an office with only the person who has sought help.

Disturbing conditions at home may provoke emotional reactions in an employee which, although not indicative of illness, nevertheless disrupt performance. Young employees in their teens and early twenties may have a severe conflict with their parents which carries over into the work situation. These young employees often want to break free of family control but maintain some dependence on their family for financial and other types of assistance. The parents, for their part, may want to retain control over their children's behavior yet expect them to take care of themselves financially, sometimes to the point of contributing to household expenses. Under these conditions, a young employee may confuse supervisory control with parental control and react to a superior's directives with the same emotionality that would be shown toward his or her parents. As a result, such an employee may have a disruptive effect on the performance of the work group. The employee may also do less work out of sheer negativism and may attempt to get even with those seen as responsible for infringing on his or her freedom. The performance of such an employee often improves strikingly once he or she leaves the parental home.

In a different case, the parents may provide so completely for their working children's needs and desires, financial and otherwise, that the children see no necessity for job-integrated behavior. Or siblings who work for the same company may bring their rivalries to the job, with detrimental consequences for performance. Employing several members of the same family need not create difficulties, but if the family situation is disturbed, hiring several members to work in close proximity guarantees the transfer of home problems into the work environment.

The Isolated Employee

A supervisory challenge even greater than the problems caused by separation is the individual who remains isolated, without close family or friendship ties. If the person's performance is adequate, there is no justification for managerial action. In addition, such people may remain equally isolated at work, making it difficult for a superior to find out about their lives off the job. Yet anything that can be done to increase their participation in group activities may pay off. If their vulnerability can be reduced by increasing the opportunities for them to develop personal relationships, they are much less likely to suffer subsequent performance failures. Certainly there are limits to what should be attempted: management should not assume the role of a social introduction service. Anything that might be considered an intrusion into the personal affairs of a satisfactory employee should be avoided. Yet some things can be done, which will be taken up in the next chapter on social factors in the workplace.

The Working Wife

The various sources of difficulty we have discussed can apply to both working husbands and working wives.

Yet certain unique problems appear to emerge when both spouses are working. These problems are becoming more frequent as the number of working wives increases.

The initial impetus to the increased employment of women came during World War II as a result of manpower shortages. Female labor force participation rates have been rising ever since—and women are now 43 percent of the work force. U.S. Department of Labor statistics indicate a steady rise in employment of married women with children since 1950. This increase has been much greater for women with children under eighteen than for those without. However, the most pronounced rise in employment has been among mothers of young children under six; here, the labor force participation rate has quadrupled since 1950. Thus, managers are dealing with more and more subordinates with young children who are not cared for by a spouse at home because both parents are working.

Whatever the advantages of this situation to the individuals involved and to the overall productiveness of our work force, it leaves little margin for error should children need special attention or a parent require care during an illness. The potential for absenteeism because family considerations predominate is increased. Further, it can no longer necessarily be assumed that the wife's performance will be the one affected. Increasingly husbands are being called upon to stay home and deal with crises related to the care of children.

As the female participation rate rises toward 45 percent of the labor force, companies could be faced with more instances of excessive absenteeism occasioned by problems at home. At the same time, managers will be under greater pressure to readjust standards regarding absenteeism to this "new reality." Rather than do this, and accept high absenteeism as inevitable, companies probably would be better off trying to minimize the probability that home problems will interfere with work. Among the alternatives available are the establishment of day-care centers and greater flexibility in scheduling work whenever possible. Even with these approaches, however, managers may frequently be accused of being hardhearted if they refuse to accept the high absenteeism rates tied to the fact that both husband and wife have full-time jobs.

Although absenteeism problems are the most likely performance consequence of the fact that a wife works, one other difficulty deserves mention. A working wife's success at her job may leave her less-successful husband so overcome with shame that his performance is severely impaired. He may be concerned that he is not making an appropriate contribution to the total family income or that his wife has achieved greater recognition and prestige than he. Every time he approaches the work environment, he is reminded of his inadequacy. The result can be an inability to concentrate on job performance and behavior, born out of desperation, that appears to be highly irrational. Efforts to ignore the wife and her accomplishments, or to dominate her, are not uncommon in such instances. At work the individual may overrate his own achievements, make excessive salary demands, and fail to recognize his shortcomings.

What to Do When Family Considerations Predominate

In cases where family demands have become so dominant that job requirements are not fulfilled, the usual approach has been to call the individual in for at least one talk and probably for several. The message delivered by the manager: Devote more time and energy to your job, become more cooperative in accepting extra assignments, and stop running home whenever you receive a call. Although these talks generally do no harm and may be a necessary preliminary to more drastic action, they rarely help for more than a brief period. The reason is that the spouse or other family member responsible for the demands customarily initiates a similar series of talks with a contrary message. The job pressure and family pressure thus cancel each other out, and the situation remains unchanged. Contacting family members directly, in the hope of eliciting a more favorable attitude toward the subordinate's job, rarely accomplishes much either. Unless this is initiated with the assistance and approval of the employee, it may arouse resentment and do more harm than good. Managers are rarely in a position to alter a family situation. As a result, it may be impossible to solve this type of problem, and the person may have to be fired. Transfer to another job will accomplish nothing, since the difficulties stem from factors outside the workplace.

Emotional upsets that result from separation and that occur in family members other than the employee present a different problem. The company should not become directly involved unless the employee has begun to perform ineffectively or has requested a transfer. Under these circumstances psychotherapy and psychiatric treatment are often appropriate, when severe separation reactions occur in other family members. Often company representatives can help in initiating treatment. If treatment is initiated, the very fact that something is being done about the family situation may eliminate any immediate problems on the job. The time required for cure usually has little significance for the employee's performance. Having turned over responsibility for the problem to a qualified practitioner, the employee will usually feel free to concentrate on his or her job. When professional help is not available or feasible and the person's performance is suffering, management will have to decide whether to restore family unity through a transfer. As a rule, if such a change is made, the spouse or other family member will become less disturbed and the resulting performance difficulties will be alleviated.

As with separation problems in employees, the ideal way to handle a separation reaction in another family member is to prevent it through screening. Certainly when a company plans to invest thousands of dollars in moving a family to a foreign country, it is appropriate to take every precaution. Some representative of the company should ascertain the spouse's feelings about the move. Problems of separation should be explored with the spouse, and the company should use any special screening devices it has developed. Such procedures are entirely appropriate, since they relate directly to performance and organizational objectives. Many large corporations continue to lose sizable sums of money year after year because of the need to return employees to their homes from foreign assignments. Contacts with family members should, of course, always be made with the approval and assistance of the employee.

Some have contended that companies engaging in practices such as interviewing spouses are intruding into family affairs and inducing excessive conformity. However, studies conducted by Professor Alfred Stoess at the University of Nevada refute this. The conformity levels of both husbands and wives were found to be almost identical when comparisons were made between companies which did make it a practice to interview spouses and collect information about them for evaluation purposes and companies which did not.

A major difficulty of dealing with ineffective performance based on family factors is that managers may not learn the source of the trouble. Many continuing conflicts and illnesses at home do not become known to superiors for years, if ever. In a typical case, an employee with a lengthy record of job failure remained married to a chronic alcoholic, who over the years was repeatedly hospitalized for her condition. Ashamed of his family problems, the man continued to worry in silence. He retained his job only because his department had a policy that no one should be fired except for disciplinary reasons. Finally, during a recession this policy was reversed, and the man came up for dismissal. Only then was his wife's alcoholism made known to management.

When such problems can be unearthed, it is often possible to take effective action. Subordinates whose performance has been influenced by an emotional disturbance at home can be helped to obtain treatment for the affected person. Young people who have troubles because of conflicts with parents can be offered attractive positions which require them to live away from home. Those whose problems stem from working in close proximity to other family members can be shifted to more distant locations. Striking improvements will almost invariably occur if the diagnosis is correct and if appropriate action is taken soon enough. Such accomplishments can be one of the greatest sources of satisfaction in managerial work.

7

Dealing with Work-Group Problems

Just as a person's various family groups may influence performance on the job, so too may relationships with people at work. For most employees there is only one significant work group, consisting of their co-workers and their supervisor. Within management, however, it is not so simple. Managers are members of several groups. One is the group they supervise. Another is a group consisting of other managers and the superior they report to. Further complexity is added to work groups by staff personnel (who may work closely with a group for periods of time), those with rotating assignments (who may become group members for temporary periods), and project teams (whose members may serve on several teams at once). In addition, organization charts sometimes show either more or fewer levels of supervision than actually exist. A manager may be listed as in charge of a group but the subordinates may actually report directly to the manager's superior. That makes the manager only a particularly well-paid member of a group directed by a higher-level superior. Such situations are common when direct line assistants are employed. They also occur under certain conditions in large staff departments. In production and clerical units, on the other hand, group leaders and others with work-guidance duties may actually constitute a level of supervision, even though it is not formally recognized.

The Nature of Work Groups

Work groups in the business world have certain special characteristics that influence the performance of their members. They are, for one thing, formed primarily on a nonvoluntary basis. It is true that people can resign or sometimes use the threat of resignation to obtain a transfer to another group. But in the initial job placement, other members of the group are rarely asked for their opinion, and the employee, although given information about the job, often knows nothing about the people in the group. Similarly, leadership typically is imposed from outside. The manager is not elected, as in a club or political party, but rather is selected by individuals outside the group. Although these involuntary aspects may well result in a more effective group than otherwise, they can also have some negative effects.

Another characteristic of work groups in business is that the extent of the members' association is limited. In contrast to members of the armed services, for instance, the civilian employee usually remains with the work group for only part of the day and is separated from it over the weekend. Close contact with families tends to be maintained, and other stable social relationships exist as well. Thus, groups at work do not have the crucial significance they might otherwise possess.

These distinctive aspects will show up frequently as we discuss the work-group factors that may cause ineffective performance. One such factor is the degree to which there is a sense of emotional closeness or cohesion. Although lack of unity may introduce managerial problems, its presence can also be a source of trouble. A second factor is the behavior of the manager in charge of the group—a subject on which a considerable body of knowledge has developed. A third factor is the use of inappropriate criteria and standards in reaching decisions on ineffectiveness—that is, the problem of ineffectiveness by managerial definition only. Each of these factors is discussed in greater detail below.

The Group's Sense of Cohesion

Much has been written about the characteristics and functioning of groups. But little of this material is relevant to the study of performance, being concerned with such matters as how groups select their leaders, establish their goals, provide for communication among members, and so forth. A group's sense of unity or cohesion, however, is directly relevant for our purposes.

Groups differ markedly in the degree to which they function as a unit. In some groups, the members want to be with one another. Their sense of emotional closeness makes them stick together even when external pressures are working toward dissolution of the group. In other cases, although a group exists in a formal sense, it is really nothing more than a collection of individuals. There is no particular unity of behavior. The members go their own ways with little sense of pride in their group, little reason to prefer their present associations to others that might become available, and little sense of commitment to group tasks.

Group cohesion need not result from a similarity of motives among the members, but all members must have some desire or need that makes the group attractive. Some may anticipate happiness from the social interaction within the group or may derive a sense of unity from mutual commitment to achieving a given goal, as with an athletic team. Various types of negative motivation may also operate. Attraction to a group can be based on a desire to avoid or reduce fear, or from a wish to share one's own feelings of anxiety in a disturbing situation to see if others feel the same way.

When many members of a group are neither positively nor negatively motivated toward social relationships, cohesion may well be low. Similarly, if the group consistently fails to provide what is desired, it will become unattractive to its members, and only a collection of individuals will exist. A group will not necessarily lack cohesion just because it is geographically dispersed and unable to gather very often. Some sales groups maintain a high degree of unity despite meeting infrequently. The crucial factors are the predominance of certain social motives, the group's capacity to meet the emotional needs of its members, and in some cases the existence of a shared goal.

Advantages of Group Cohesion: From a managerial viewpoint, is this type of closeness and emotional unity desirable? It has often been assumed that too much cohesiveness provides a fertile ground for organizing attempts and union activity. Therefore, it has been argued, individualism rather than group consciousness should be encouraged. This viewpoint appears to be valid under some circumstances. But there is additional evidence suggesting that management may gain some benefits from cohesiveness and a sense of pride in its work groups.

Cohesive groups are by their very nature resistant to disintegration. Because employees in such groups want to be with their co-workers, turnover and absenteeism are likely to be minimal. In contrast, when cohesion is lacking there is a built-in potential for conflict and disruption. Members may bicker, and under extreme conditions there may be almost total dissolution of the group. Although the unit remains on the organization chart, its makeup changes drastically as old members frequently leave and replacements are hired. Sometimes the group does disappear completely as the result of a reorganization. This is most likely to happen with certain specialized staff groups that provide functions for which it is difficult to show a tangible monetary contribution.

Usually, however, a lack of cohesion will lead to group dissolution only when alternative positions are readily available to the members. Units with a high proportion of staff specialists, technicians, and others with transferable, needed skills are particularly vulnerable. University departments are traditionally subject to this tendency. So too are certain research and development groups in industry. In some of these groups, the turnover rates can become very high.

Besides reducing absenteeism and turnover, cohesiveness can also provide a valuable antidote to emotional disturbance. Some employees are able to maintain an adequate emotional adjustment and satisfactory performance level only because of the support they receive from fellow workers. In some cases, group support helps an individual through a crisis situation that might otherwise have been severely disruptive. As noted earlier, the isolated person's vulnerability is eased by close social relationship. Physically handicapped employees or those with intelligence levels below what is really needed for the work may also be helped by fellow members of a cohesive group. Such assistance is generally lacking in a group where everyone operates as an individual with little concern for other members.

In the cohesive group, specialized job knowledge will be shared, and sometimes new members will receive help with their work during the learning period. If the work is emotionally demanding, the support of close group relationships can be crucial for all members. In military combat, for example, buddy and squad ties are often essential in maintaining performance. Similar effects are evident in dangerous industrial work.

A cohesive group also has the potential for responding well to emergency work demands. Some members will work because of pride in their group and other positive motives; others will work because they don't want to be condemned for not doing their share. In groups where unity is lacking, some members will respond to emergency demands but others may not. Group pressures will not operate, and the total effort will be reduced. Thus, the manager who can rely on the unifying effects of group pride and teamwork has a distinct advantage in meeting special production schedules.

Cohesion and Productivity: The relationships between cohesion and the quality and quantity of performance are complex. Certainly a sense of group unity is not always associated with greater output, and even when this is the case, the greater output may well be helping to generate the cohesion more than the reverse. Further, in the case of emergency work demands, a cohesive group may or may not respond with increased output. A manager may push a group to meet emergency requirements only to be faced with a solid front of resistance. For productivity to be affected positively, the group members must have a shared desire to do what higher management wants and thus to pursue company goals.

Group cohesion can well serve to keep productivity at low levels over long periods of time. Enough instances of so-called restriction of output have now been studied to make it clear that employees can band together to keep production down. Through group unity, they apply negative sanctions against wayward members who may try to rise above established standards of output. Very cohesive groups will develop high levels of productivity if increased output becomes a group goal. But if low standards are imposed by the group, output will generally fall off sharply. In noncohesive groups, group-set standards of this kind have no long-term effect at all.

Clearly the cohesive group has a potential for both very high and very low levels of effectiveness. Less cohesive groups will display a much greater range of performance levels, whereas in a cohesive group, outputs will tend to be uniform. The effect of cohesive group pressures and mutual assistance may well be that many employees who might otherwise fail because of individual factors, especially motivational and emotional, are pulled above a minimally satisfactory level. On the other hand, many members may be pushed into ineffectiveness. Performance may also drop to low levels when a cohesive group is not given any reason to set adequate output standards—that is, when a general aura of overpermissiveness permeates the organization.

There is reason to believe that strong cohesiveness and group pride can be deterrents to large-scale ineffectiveness within a group. This is particularly true when members feel a sense of security and trust in the company, have a favorable attitude toward their superiors, and see company representatives rather than the union as the major source of assistance in time of difficulty. Similarly, under these conditions of trust and security, strikes and slowdowns will be at a minimum. It is when group members have a negative attitude toward the company and distrust its representatives that strong cohesion is likely to be coupled with low group performance. It is then that an excessive number of ineffective performers emerge.

Factors Contributing to Cohesion: Certain circumstances tend to foster group cohesiveness, and others almost guarantee that it will be lacking. Many are outside the control of the individual manager. There are real limitations on what can be done to influence the degree of closeness within a group once the membership has been established. British psychiatrist James Brown has suggested several conditions for cohesion, a number of which have been supported by research evidence. One theory is that a group comprised primarily of skilled workers will tend to be cohesive—a proposal that can be generalized to cover occupational prestige as a whole. Generally, the more highly esteemed the jobs within a group, the more probable it is that team spirit and pride will develop.

Cohesion can also be expected when the work is performed in a relatively small and long-established community. Both overall employee satisfaction and the quantity of work produced tend to be higher in small-town locations. By contrast, the heterogeniety of large urban populations seems to reduce the likelihood of cohesion and increase negative attitudes toward the company. When cohesiveness does occur in these groups, it is more likely to be associated with low output standards.

A predominance of casual and part-time workers is also a potential deterrent to emotional closeness. When many employees come and go as a result of seasonal or other demands, group unity is disrupted. Frequent layoffs would appear to have the same effect. Some stability of membership is a necessary condition for cohesion.

Another factor is the number of employees in the group who are married, which can contribute to the closeness of a group. Marriage imposes a certain degree of stability on people because of the increased responsibility and the need for maintaining continued employment. Age does not seem to be a crucial factor, except that older women often form very cohesive groups. In many cases, they are attracted to the work situation by the opportunity for social interaction that is no longer available at home.

When group members are of the same sex and have similar jobs, ethnic affiliations, and social-class backgrounds, conditions are particularly favorable for the formation of a unified group. Another finding is that high group cohesion is not likely among blue-collar workers—except those with dangerous jobs, such as miners. Studies conducted by John Goldthorpe of Cambridge University and by other researchers have revealed very low levels of cohesiveness in blue-collar groups. In part, this was attributable to technology and physical work layouts that kept workers separated, but there was more to it than that. The fact that the workers spent considerable time with their families and belonged to many nonwork groups made them less dependent on the work situation for social relationships. Work was viewed as a means for earning enough money to enjoy those other relationships, not as a means for establishing close personal ties per se. Under such circumstances, strong cohesiveness is unlikely to develop.

How Cohesiveness Can Cause Failure: We have already mentioned that under certain conditions cohesion can contribute to ineffective performance. Unfortunately, this does not complete the story. There are also cases where it is directly responsible for failure. Cohesive groups are capable of rejecting and ostracizing individuals who deviate from their norms. Of course, a rejected person may simply ignore the group and low group standards as well, thus rising to a higher level of productivity, but often the negative impact of ostracism is sizable. Because their strong social motives are suddenly frustrated, ostracized employees either may stop trying to achieve satisfactions through job-integrated means or may respond with emotional reactions that are detrimental to performance. Sometimes they become so worried and upset about their relationship to the group that they cannot concentrate on their work at all. Or they may spend all their time trying to figure out ways of getting group acceptance. Turnover among such people is likely to be high.

The bases for rejection by a group are many. The person may have unpopular opinions or a personality that is not pleasing to the others; may act in ways that go against group norms; may be a known homosexual or have a prison record. Some employees may be ostracized because they come from a different socioeconomic or ethnic background. In one striking example of this, a company experimented with hiring young management trainees for a particular department. The new college graduates were rotated from assignment to assignment so that they could learn various aspects of the business and qualify for promotion into responsible positions. Yet within three years, all but one of the sizable number of trainees had left the company, and that one was working in another department. The trainees had been consistently ostracized by the existing lower- and middle-management organization. Considered a group of young "prima donnas," they were denied access to information and treated much as schoolchildren treat a teacher's pet. Some quit because they realized they were getting nowhere. Others were so upset by the unexpected reception from co-workers that they never did attain acceptable performance levels and eventually were fired.

Actually, something very similar happens whenever new members are introduced into a cohesive work group. There is a period of mutual evaluation during which the new employees, although usually treated cordially, are made to feel very much like outsiders. In most cases, the new employees decide they want to be accepted by the group long before the group comes to a similar conclusion regarding them. The group's need for new members is not nearly as strong as the new employees' need for the group. They may receive help with their work to maintain accepted performance standards, but they will be left out of many other activities. Some people, inexperienced in such matters, never recover from the effects of this initial cold shoulder. Most companies refrain from evaluating new employees on anything but a tentative basis for the first three to six months, because they assume that these employees may require a certain amount of practice to reach a satisfactory performance level. However, this is not the only factor contributing to performance deficiencies in new employees. They are also working under conditions of at least partial ostracism and may be devoting their time and thought to ways of gaining group acceptance. They cannot fully concentrate on their work because their social problems with the group are still unresolved.

Certain firms employ utility workers who are rotated from group to group in accordance with changing workloads, vacation schedules, disability levels, and the like. They never stay in one place very long, and no one expects them to settle into any group on a permanent basis. As a result, they are always "new employees" and subject to ostracism. Some people like the challenge involved and respond well to it. But for those to whom group membership and acceptance are important, it is very disturbing. Some potentially effective workers are incapable of handling rotating assignments for this reason.

Rejection of the Group: Occasionally, the shoe is on the other foot and an employee actively rejects a group of fellow workers. This need not have a negative effect on performance. When it does, however, motivational factors are commonly involved. Usually the employee feels ashamed of associating with the others or considers the group members reprehensible in some respect. The employee wants badly to get away from the whole situation and attempts to deny any relationship with the others. Status considerations often figure strongly in this person's motivational hierarchy.

Rejection of the group deprives the employee of any opportunity for assistance that integration might have provided. In addition, pressures to attain acceptable standards of work output may have no effect on this employee, who may consider good work in such a social context not worth striving for. Such an employee may fail on the job.

Negative Side Effects of Cohesion: Another kind of problem arises not because of rejection, but because of unfortunate side effects of acceptance. A cohesive group is protective of its members and, above all else, loyal. This loyalty may be misplaced from a managerial viewpoint and from the individual's, too. We have already talked about the typical difficulty in identifying alcoholic subordinates. Similar protective efforts may occur in any case where an employee's performance has declined and the group members believe that firing is imminent if the decline is discovered. With the best intentions, co-workers may cover up for someone who is almost incapable of performing the job. They may actually do much of that employee's work themselves. Cases of severe emotional disorder have gone undetected and untreated for this reason. Aside from any disadvantages for the company, this type of misplaced loyalty can mean severe consequences for the protected employee: accidents, unnecessary prolongation of illnesses, suicide, or death due to alcoholism.

Another negative side effect of cohesion is that the group may exert pressure on a manager to place its own objectives above those of the organization. This can lead the manager to become so immersed in protecting certain subordinates that nothing is done to restore them to effective performance. As in all cases of misplaced group loyalty, the group's cohesiveness thus generates pressures that contribute to individual failure. In a less cohesive group, the same manager, free of concerted appeals to group loyalty, might feel able to take appropriate action with failing subordinates.

Can a cohesive work group be compared to a family in the way it affects performance? In some cases the answer is yes, but because groups at work are less close emotionally, these situations are rare. Sometimes, an employee's severe physical illness sets off anxiety reactions among fellow workers. A fatal heart attack is particularly likely to provoke such reactions. Although these emotional reactions often differ in both content and causation from the crisis reactions described in the chapter on family factors, some are very similar. Separation from a work group may also precipitate emotional and motivational disturbances, although this is also rare. Industrial work groups do not ordinarily maintain close associations long enough to be like families. Military groups, on the other hand, with their twenty-four-hour-a-day, seven-day-a-week relationships, often do.

The Dangers of Groupthink: A final source of ineffectiveness related to group cohesion has been explored by Professor Irving Janis of Yale University in his book *Groupthink*. He presents evidence, based on analyses of key policy decisions at the national level, indicating that the more amiable and cohesive the members of an in-group, the greater the probability that independent critical thinking will be suspended in favor of group norms and conviviality. The result is groupthink, which usually results in irrational attacks against out-groups. Here are some symptoms:

1. A sense of invulnerability, which encourages optimism and risk-taking

2. Efforts to rationalize, so that warnings are discounted and assumptions are not questioned

3. A belief in the group's inherent morality, so strong that potential ethical consequences of decisions are ignored

4. A stereotyped view of "the enemy" as evil, weak, or stupid

5. Direct pressure on members not to express arguments against group positions; dissent seen as a sign of disloyalty

6. Self-censorship, so that doubts regarding the wisdom of the group consensus are suppressed

7. A shared sense of unanimity due to self-censorship and the view that other members' silence must mean agreement

8. The emergence of particular members who protect the group from adverse information that might threaten the atmosphere in which rationality is suspended

In this group situation, even people highly capable as individuals can become ineffective performers. Professor Janis has been concerned with high-level policy groups, but the same limitation of individual performance capabilities can occur in any cohesive group at any level. The result may be a major deflection of group effort from organizational goals. Cohesiveness need not have this effect, but the possibility is always there.

Solutions: Inducing a Positive Group Impact: Although lack of cohesiveness is not necessarily detrimental, groups without it are sometimes plagued by bickering, conflict, and excessive turnover. Overall productivity may well be low and the incidence of ineffectiveness (on motivational grounds alone) rather high. Many of the factors that contribute to group cohesiveness are outside managerial control, but some actions may be effective. Low cohesiveness is most easily counteracted by putting together people who are likely to be friendly, who have strong motives leading them to seek social activity, and who are attracted to the specific work group by some characteristic such as high status or challenging work. (Of course, race, sex, age, or ethnic origin should never be considered.)

In addition, reducing the size of the group and treating the membership as a single unit can increase cohesiveness. Meetings, actions regarding pay, and other managerial procedures that are applied only to the individuals in a given group and not to other groups can be used to make the group distinct and more cohesive.

Some of these solutions, such as holding more meetings, can be implemented by the manager. Others require higher-level approval or may not be possible because of other considerations. In many cases, cohesiveness as an objective must take a back seat to these other concerns. Sometimes it is impossible to put together people with the requisite job skills who are also sufficiently alike to guarantee a compatible relationship. If a lack of cohesion leads to constant dissension and if the manager clearly is not directly responsible for this situation, the group may have to be reconstituted through mass shifts of personnel. Reshuffling work associations to put compatible people in the same units has not, to my knowledge, been done extensively in any kind of organization. Yet it does offer a potential solution to the problem of the continually strife-torn group. Many athletic coaches have employed the technique with considerable success.

Cohesion is only half the issue, however. A group may be cohesive, but that doesn't mean it fosters company goals. As noted earlier, some groups set low work standards for their members, who go along because group membership is so important to them. So it is important for the manager to promote not only cohesion, but also as much trust and security in the company as possible. To some extent, again, this may be beyond immediate supervisory control. But a manager can do certain things to minimize opposition to the company. Anything that will convince subordinates that promises will be kept and that they can expect fair treatment, as well as assistance when they need it, will contribute to the goal. As in most situations, actions speak louder than words.

Dealing with Ostracism: When an employee is failing because of ostracism or general isolation, the ideal solution is to help integrate that employee into the work group. Yet the manager cannot force the group to accept a co-worker, and too obvious attempts to foster acceptance will almost invariably be rebuffed. Groups reserve unto themselves the right to make membership decisions, and members usually resent efforts to force this process. However, it may be possible to bring the employee together with some member who is esteemed by the others and then to hope for the best. Team assignments that force the two to work together can be particularly helpful. If the esteemed employee should come to like the other person, this may pave the way for group acceptance. Such procedures are particularly effective in speeding up the integration of new employees.

Don't be overly optimistic about these approaches, though; more often than not, they fail. When this happens, and when the employee is clearly ineffective as a result of rejection, the only answer is transfer to a group where there is more chance of acceptance. The first step is to determine exactly what it is about the individual that has caused the rejection. Then, if possible, a group must be found in which the employee's job skills are applicable and ostracism is unlikely. This may be as simple as taking someone from a rural area out of a group made up entirely of urban employees and finding another group that includes at least some employees with rural backgrounds. Other situations may be more difficult to solve.

Transfer is also the ideal solution for most cases where the employee cannot adapt to rotating job assignments, and for cases where the ineffectiveness is caused by the employee's rejecting the group rather than vice versa. In the latter instance, a strong motive is almost invariably operating vis-à-vis the group factor, and the individual's mere presence in the group frustrates that motive. Since changing the motivational hierarchy is very difficult under such circumstances, it makes more sense to provide the type of associations desired, if at all possible. Similarly, the person who has been unable to achieve compatible working relationships because of rotating job assignments should be placed in a stable group. This should be easy if the employee has been performing different jobs in different groups and has multiple skills to choose from. The fact that the individual has not used any of these skills effectively in the past matters little; if the analysis of the situation is correct, transfer to a stable group should raise the person's performance to an effective level.

When the group is contributing to ineffectiveness through misplaced loyalty among its members, the manager's task is to break through the protective screen and learn what is going on. This is only possible if the gap between leader and subordinates is not excessive. Managers who spend most of their time in their office and rarely talk with their subordinates will not learn about problems in the group that others wish to keep to themselves. Unfortunately, the manager most likely to break through the screen is also most likely to be caught in the cohesive web. This may be the person who avoids the managerial role and frequently works alongside subordinates. If so, knowledge gained by this manager may not result in useful action. The manager, like any other group member, may find it too difficult to go against group norms.

Some managers have worked out a tacit agreement regarding the exchange of information. In any group, certain employees always like to be "in the know," to serve as key links in the grapevine. They will often provide information in exchange for preferred access to data coming down from higher levels. The manager can take advantage of this situation to obtain information necessary for managing effectively. Because unearthing ineffective performance and its possible causes is crucially important, such procedures would seem to be entirely appropriate. If one alcoholic can be identified and helped or one severe neurotic induced to enter treatment, the use of an informal communication source is justified. Unfortunately, however, a manager will need considerable skill to continue to obtain such information for long. The group may soon come to resent this sort of intrusion.

What about crisis and separation reactions related to the group? The appropriate solutions are the same as those for similar reactions related to the family. However, the death of an employee may have a unique impact on someone doing the same kind of work, and a somewhat different approach may be required. In such cases, the feeling that "it might have been me" can precipitate a rapid breakdown which will not necessarily follow the pattern described for grief reactions. To minimize such effects, the manager should especially refrain from saying anything that might suggest the work was responsible for the death. All too frequently someone ventures the opinion that "anyone in that kind of work is bound to end up with a heart attack eventually," and a person in a parallel job is overcome with panic. Often, the anxiety in such instances is so intense that the individual can be induced to seek professional help.

Can Authoritarian Management Cause Employee Failure?

As part of the work group, managers themselves can be the key factor in the performance failure of their subordinates. This means that managers cannot limit their search for the causes of failure to the specific subordinates, their families, and their co-workers, but rather must also look at the nature of their own influence on people under them. Without being aware of it, managers can act in ways that reinforce behaviors by subordinates that are not integrated with the job. A manager may, for instance, want above all else to foster high performance levels in his or her group, but may consistently recommend people for promotion only on the basis of seniority. Subordinates will easily recognize that they can get ahead as fast with poor performance as with superior, but the manager may fail to see the inconsistency between his or her intentions and the subordinates' behavior. Recognizing one's own contributions to ineffectiveness is one of the most difficult aspects of managing.

Early research indicated that managers contribute to the poor performance of subordinates primarily by being too autocratic or authoritarian. According to this view, the democratic, participative, employee-centered, considerate managerial style is most likely to prevent unsatisfactory performance.

It has become increasingly clear in recent years that this view is grossly oversimplified. Serious questions have been raised regarding the interpretation of some of the early research, and new evidence tends to contradict it. Apparently the more democratic style does cause *higher morale* and *greater satisfaction* at work; it probably will reduce turnover, whereas an authoritarian approach may increase it. However, *performance* is another matter. Many studies show no meaningful rise in productivity as a result of introducing a democratic style; a number show an actual decrease. In one such study, Professors Reed Powell and John Schlacter, then at Ohio State University, found little evidence of any change in output when minimal degrees of participation were introduced, but when the group took over all responsibility for work scheduling, output declined sharply.

It now appears that in many of the early studies, the positive performance effects attributed to a democratic managerial style were in fact the result of other factors. Among these factors, all of which are known to have the potential for improving performance, are the following:

1. Setting of definite production goals in the participative situation, whereas such goals did not exist in the more authoritarian situation

2. The fact that there was higher-level management support for specific decisions that the groups arrived at on a participative basis, and the groups knew it

3. The lengthy discussions held in the democratic as opposed to more authoritarian groups, yielding a greater amount of job knowledge that could later be applied to work tasks

4. The existence of incentive pay programs that stimulated productivity and were closely intertwined with the participatory style

An even more important factor has been introduced with the finding that outstanding performance tends to induce more democratic managerial styles. Thus the causal sequence originally assumed may often be just the reverse. Professors Aaron Lowin of Iowa State University and James Craig of Western Kentucky University find that poor performance tends to bring on very close, more authoritarian supervision; there is a great deal of checking and directing, the subordinate's ideas tend to be ignored, and prescribed procedures are consistently enforced. Typically, the poor performers are considered irresponsible and treated rather badly. Professors Barry Goodstadt, David Kipnis, and others at Temple University did a series of studies indicating that when the poor performance is a function of attitude and cooperation, supervisors tend to be very coercive; they may also be more coercive with union members than with non-union workers, and with blacks than whites. In any event, it appears that when a democratic leadership style and good performance are found together, this is often because the manager respects the subordinates for their competence and therefore allows them considerable discretion.

Given what we now know, it is no longer possible to say that an authoritarian managerial style is inevitably bad and a democratic or participative one inevitably good. The tendency now is to judge the desirability of using one style or the other in relation to the specific situation, based on such factors as the supervisor's degree of managerial expertise, the need for subordinate implementation of decisions, the potentiality that problems might arise if subordinates must implement decisions, and the importance of the decisions to be made. Under this view, more authoritarian managing may be entirely appropriate in certain circumstances. It is no longer possible to call this approach a major cause of ineffective performance.

How the Laissez-Faire Manager Can Cause Employee Failure: Given the dead end that the authoritarian-versus-democratic debate appears to have reached insofar as understanding ineffective performance is concerned, can any styles of management be identified that frequently do cause unsatisfactory performance? In all probability, the extremes of both the authoritarian and the democratic approaches do have this effect when they are applied inflexibly. But such extremes are rare in today's business world.

On the other hand, the do-nothing manager who uses a laissez-faire style is a reality; managers of this kind exist in sizable numbers, and they contribute to performance difficulties. Often they do generate a certain degree of job satisfaction among subordinates, but the effect on performance tends to be negative—more so, in fact, than that of any managerial style that has been studied. Such managers neither tell their subordinates what needs to be done, nor establish a participatory process for the decisions to be made.

Managers must assume an active leadership role if they are to have any impact on the productivity of subordinates. If they do not, but rather adopt a passive, laissez-faire attitude, they will be ignored and anything they might do to counteract performance failure will be wasted. Other forces in the group will determine performance levels, and a major influence toward greater effectiveness will be lost.

The manager who does not accept managerial responsibility usually has a poor group. There is little emphasis on following regulations and maintaining standards of performance, and the manager gives the impression of being just another member of the group. He or she does not accept a leadership role, rarely assigning work to anyone or taking a definite position on anything. Planning is neglected, and there is little concern with organizing the work of the group to accomplish company objectives. The manager does not do it, and does not take steps to see that others do.

Although this failure to accept the managerial role can cause subordinates to fall below acceptable quantity and quality standards, the effects on turnover may be favorable. Also, grievances may decrease. Thus, when we say that effectiveness is generally reduced by what is essentialy abdication by the manager, we are talking about a weighted average of all aspects of performance. Some specific aspects may be affected quite differently.

When managers do not accept their role, when they do not organize and coordinate the work of their subordinates, certain consequences almost invariably follow. One is that performance analyses are generally not made and acted upon. This lack of action is particularly unfortunate in cases where motivational factors are responsible for poor performance. In such circumstances, active intervention is usually required to raise performance levels. The manager must take steps to frustrate unintegrated behavior, establish standards, and provide satisfactions within the job context. A group being supervised by someone who does not perform the basic managerial role will usually have a high proportion of people who are failing because of motivational problems.

Another consequence of a manager's abdication of the leadership role is a failure to make decisions on organizing the work of the group. Many such managers feel uncomfortable about reaching conclusions on their own or even pushing others to make decisions. Nor do they want to assume responsibility for errors of judgment. Accordingly they spend much time collecting the opinions of others—and if unanimity cannot be obtained, they put off the decision indefinitely. They want everyone to agree, so that blame for failure can be shared with as many people as possible. The validity of the decision thus becomes distinctly secondary to obtaining agreement.

Because work groups almost always feel the need for direction when their manager abdicates, an informal leader will usually emerge to fill the vacuum. This person may not be capable of leadership, having been selected perhaps for being the oldest or most vociferous. This informal leader will probably not have a strong commitment to organizational goals, will lack access to formal channels of communication, and will find it very difficult to represent the group in interactions with higher-level managers or to exert influence in the larger organization. The result can be chaos, with the whole group falling below acceptable performance standards.

Informal leadership is not always generated by managerial abdication; it can also develop whenever the group's objectives diverge sharply from those of management. The manager who refuses to acknowledge important desires of subordinates, and to try to satisfy them at least partially, risks having to deal with a group member who has been selected to champion those motives.

Informal leadership is unlikely to contribute to increased productivity; more frequently it contributes to lowered output just as the laissez-faire managerial style does.

Artificial Laissez-Faire Management: Informal leadership often fails because its democratic style is not compatible with the organizational climate or value system of the company as a whole. Such leadership lacks a legitimate authority base and thus becomes ultimately meaningless.

In the same way, a mismatch between the organizational culture or climate and the individual style of a manager can cause a major productivity failure in that manager's unit. Thus an artificial laissez-faire situation is created: the manager is viewed as acting in a way which will not be supported at higher levels and which therefore lacks legitimacy. In essence, whatever the manager does will not matter because subordinates do not respond. This is why the term *artificial laissez-faire* is used; the results are the same as under a truly laissez-faire manager.

The best example of this situation is provided in research conducted by Norman Frederiksen and his colleagues at Educational Testing Service. They set up a study wherein managerial productivity could be measured under two completely different organizational climates and, within each, under two different supervisory styles. The organizational climates were:

Innovation: Employees were expected to be creative and original and to invent new and better ways of doing work. Rules existed but they could be disregarded if better ways of accomplishing an objective were found.

Rules: Employees were expected to follow rules and standard operating procedures. Failure to do so would bring disapproval.

Within each of these climates, groups of managers were exposed to two different managerial styles, one compatible with the climate and one not:

Global: Work was assigned with freedom as to how it would be carried out, but still with the expectation that it would be evaluated by the supervisor. This style was compatible with the *innovation* climate, but not with the *rules* climate.

Detailed: The supervisor monitored the performance of subordinates at all times so that mistakes would be prevented before they occurred. This style was compatible with the *rules* climate, but not with the *innovation* climate.

As one might expect, the managers who performed under the innovation climate and the global managerial style were highly productive. But they were *no more so* than the managers under the rules climate and detailed supervision. The key to success was consistency. Organizationally supported authoritarianism was just as effective as organizationally supported participation.

In this study, an innovation climate and detailed supervision proved to be the worst possible combination in terms of productivity, and a rules climate with global supervision, although better, was not nearly as good as the matching conditions. Apparently the non-matching situation makes managers as ineffective as truly laissez-faire managers. Should a manager choose to go his or her own way and utilize a style that is inconsistent with the known expectations of superiors, subordinates will be confused and uncertain, and may seriously question the legitimacy of what their supervisor tells them. The result is an apparent laissez-faire condition that fosters ineffective performance just as much as the actual laissez-faire style.

Failure by Managerial Definition

Since a judgment of ineffectiveness is based on how the manager or the organization defines just what ineffectiveness is, the cause of "failure" may be embedded in the evaluative process. Standards may be set so high that they are almost impossible to achieve. An employee may be expected to complete a report or produce a certain quantity in an unrealistically short time. Similarly, criteria may be employed that have no connection with performance as we have defined it: an employee may be considered unsatisfactory on the basis of evaluations unrelated to organizational objectives. Thus, inappropriate standards or criteria may be used to establish ineffectiveness by definition only.

Inappropriate criteria present the greatest difficulty. Factors such as emotional stability, racial or ethnic background, physical attractiveness, alcoholic consumption, religion, manner of dress, social standing, treatment of wife and children, extent of conformity, and pleasantness of personality are sometimes utilized in making performance evaluations. Some are specifically included in management appraisal forms and guides to employee ratings; other criteria, because of legal and ethical taboos, are unlikely to be stated in writing but nevertheless influence judgments.

The greater the number of factors used to establish

ineffectiveness, the greater the number of employees who will be labeled problem workers. If a firm uses many criteria that have no relation to organizational objectives, the effort, energy, and expense required to deal with the resulting "ineffectiveness" mean that other important managerial functions will be short-changed. A company cannot afford to have a high percentage of management's time devoted to problems of "ineffectiveness" that actually are not associated with profitability.

Furthermore, there is an ethical issue here similar to one raised by William H. Whyte Jr. in his book *The Organization Man.* Our society generally believes that behaviors and thoughts which are unrelated to work performance should not be used to judge a person as an employee. Most people, in fact, feel that such matters are none of the company's business. Consequently, if a firm attempts to utilize these inappropriate criteria, it may well stir up considerable bitterness and anger among employees. Although there may be times when it is necessary to risk precipitating employee discontent, it seems doubtful that introducing inappropriate criteria should be one of them. Most good managers do not take that kind of risk; they have nothing to gain in terms of profitability and everything to lose.

This doesn't mean that a manager should *never* take emotional stability, manner of dress, and similar characteristics into account in reaching decisions on ineffective performance. Such factors may in fact affect an employee's job performance. If so, they are legitimate causal factors contributing to ineffective performance. They become inappropriate only when they have no relationship to actual performance.

This distinction is an important one, since it is easy to fuse the idea of a good person or a friend with that of a good worker, and the idea of a bad person or an enemy with that of a poor worker. People tend to make subjective judgments of this kind unless they train themselves to recognize the differences between their own goals and those of the firm. Managers may dislike a group or a specific person, may wish to have nothing to do with people of a certain kind, or may even wish to harm them in some way. But if they substitute these personal goals for those of the company and, on the basis of nonrelevant factors, define the group or individual as ineffective, they run the risk of becoming considerably less effective themselves. This is not merely a subject for debate on ethical grounds. It is a matter with practical implications for the operation of a business.

It is often difficult to determine whether or not certain criteria are relevant to performance effectiveness. It can be tempting to believe that some behavior or characteristic of a person *might* be related to performance, or that it *could* have a negative effect on the firm. But there are resources the manager can use in making valid decisions concerning these questions. For one thing, the manager can profit from the results of research. Evidence indicates, for instance, that emotional instability or disturbance does not necessarily produce ineffective performance. The manager who has a personal distaste for unstable people can use this evidence to keep subjective preferences from dominating decisions on such a subordinate.

For another thing, the manager's experience over the years can produce common-sense solutions to problems of performance criteria. If an employee makes derogatory statements about the company to a group of co-workers, for example, it's probably a case of old-fashioned griping—the employee usually neither intends, nor has, a negative effect on the company. Experienced managers know that this kind of "disloyalty" is rarely related to performance. Under some circumstances it *might* be, and could even be an appropriate basis for considering an employee totally ineffective, but these would be exceptions rather than the rule. The individual's superior may be angered by the derogatory statements and may even develop an intense dislike as a result. In such cases, however, the anger and dislike are usually precipitated by the employee's failure to behave according to the superior's personal attitudes. This differs considerably from a failure to behave according to organizational goals. The key question remains: Has the behavior had sufficient negative impact on performance to justify labeling the person a failure?

To take an example in which behavior does affect performance, suppose that an employee engaged in the production of delicate instruments has a high breakage rate and a poor record of quality. If investigation reveals that the periods of poor performance coincide with periods of drinking on the job, alcoholic consumption might legitimately be viewed as a contributory factor in the failure, even though the employee never becomes intoxicated. Management is generally considered justified in forbidding employees to bring liquor onto company property because of just such possibilities. On the other hand, if an employee were to get drunk at a private party attended by several other employees of the company, there is little justification for relating alcoholic consumption to job performance.

Inappropriate Criteria in Promotion and Hiring: Individual characteristics and behavior that have no real relation to performance often play a part in promotion, as well as in performance evaluation. Either the employee is not promoted because of some such factor, or is told to change in order to get a promotion. Again, this is appropriate if there is a relationship to performance. But there is no good reason why an organization should promote people into responsible positions on any basis other than their contribution to company objectives. Correspondingly, it is inappropriate to refuse promotion to a competent person on the basis of irrelevant criteria. Yet sometimes such decisions are made. In one case, a man resigned from his job when he was led to believe that he could never progress in his company because of his religion. Subsequently, after a long and distinguished career in government, he was rehired at a high fee to be the same company's major consultant on industry problems. There seems little question that if actual performance had been the sole criterion, this man would have risen to a high level in the company and made a major contribution to its success.

Although many different factors irrelevant to performance may be applied in making promotions, the worst offender is probably seniority. Union contracts usually require that represented employees be promoted according to length of service. Although this may be consistent with union goals, it does not necessarily help achieve company goals. If promotions are consistently based on length of service, profitability will inevitably be reduced from what it might have been with performance potential as the criterion. A larger number of ineffective performers will be placed in the more responsible positions.

Although promotion by seniority may be unavoidable today in jobs under union jurisdiction, this is only part of the problem. Many firms also apply the criterion of seniority in promoting nonrepresented employees and even those well up into management. In doing so, a company not only ensures an unnecessarily high incidence of ineffectiveness, but also discourages younger employees who believe themselves capable of progressing more rapidly than seniority would permit.

Just as the use of inappropriate criteria bars some people from promotion and defines others as ineffective, it excludes still others from employment entirely. Sex, race, nationality, religion, age, and other inappropriate factors are sometimes used to screen out job applicants in spite of laws forbidding such practices. Physical characteristics and idiosyncrasies of grooming and dress often receive undue emphasis. The use of inappropriate criteria in hiring unnecessarily restricts the size of the labor force from which a company must select employees. It is usually difficult enough to find potentially effective employees without eliminating many of them at the outset by using inappropriate criteria. In addition, fair employment practice laws make discrimination in employment a real and costly risk.

Dealing with Oneself as Manager: When managers themselves are responsible for the failure of their subordinates, the ideal solution is a change in managerial behavior. Such managers must come to recognize what they are doing and gain sufficient understanding of their own feelings and motives to permit change. This is as true with artificial laissez-faire management as with the laissez-faire style itself. The same prescription for change holds when the manager is using inappropriate standards or criteria. Managers must learn to discriminate between personal feelings toward a subordinate and evaluations of that person's work effectiveness. This requires considerable self-understanding and the ability to act on the basis of such insight.

Basically, these managers must bring about a shift in their own hierarchy of motives. As noted earlier, it is very difficult to induce such changes in subordinates. It is no easier when managers themselves must change. In fact, outside assistance may be required to bring about more than superficial changes. Sessions with a qualified clinical psychologist or psychiatrist can contribute much to self-understanding and ultimately to managerial effectiveness. Although managers do not usually seek this kind of assistance, many mental health workers in training do undergo psychotherapy as part of their professional preparation. From this experience, it would appear that reasonably well-adjusted people, who are by no means emotionally ill, can still improve their effectiveness as a result of exposure to psychotherapy.

However, managers can also change without such individual counseling. I have conducted several management development programs that have had a positive effect on many of the participants. Similar results have been obtained by Professor Robert Bowin at San Bernardino State College in California. In these programs, managers and managers-to-be shifted their motivational hierarchies so that motivation to manage assumed a more dominant position. Adopting a laissez-faire style became less desirable to these participants because they came to really want to manage and so would derive much satisfaction from doing so.

Managers can also bring about the same kinds of changes by themselves if they really want this to happen. This book is intended to provide insights that can facilitate such changes. Chapter 12, particularly, can help you to understand the motivational factors involved in managerial success and failure.

What if you are a manager with a subordinate manager who is responsible for employee failures—and there have been no results from counseling, management development programs, or attempts at self-change? To be realistic, we must recognize that not all managers will want to change or are capable of it. And certain employees clearly possess emotional reactions and motives that inevitably will cause them to fail under certain kinds of managers. Where these managers are equally lacking in flexibility, the only solution is a change in supervision.

This can be accomplished by replacing the manager in charge or by transferring the subordinates to another group under a different kind of supervision. If many employees are involved, it may be best to replace the manager. If there are only a few, transferring them into groups under more suitable supervision may be sufficient to correct the situation.

8

Dealing with Organizational Problems

We have discussed the various small groups, including families and work groups, that may influence performance. Now we turn to the next larger social unit: the organization as a whole. Many decisions are made at the higher managerial levels of a firm with no direct personal knowledge of the individuals who may be affected. Yet these decisions take on increasing significance for specific employees as they are applied at lower levels.

Such higher-level decisions establish policies in all areas of company operations—sales, purchasing, production, finance, personnel, and so on. Decisions concerning personnel are the most relevant here, since they tend to affect individual performance the most. Such policies deal with promotion, wage and salary administration, employee benefits, leaves for military service and illness, retirement plans, labor relations, and many other matters. They are formulated to apply to all the employees of the company or, on occasion, to specific groups, and they indicate what actions should be taken under specific circumstances. They tend, therefore, to limit the discretion of individual managers and to serve as commands that are invoked when these circumstances arise.

Actions at the Top—And the Manager Below

The results of high-level decisions are usually evaluated in terms of their overall impact on company objectives. But questions may also be raised about the effects on specific employees, because a policy that is generally beneficial can still have negative consequences for a given individual. Example: A policy of promotion from within can prove very successful and yet contribute to failure when the only possible candidate inside the organization is promoted and becomes ineffective in the new position.

In addition to unintended consequences of organizational policymaking, there are also cases where individual decisions at the organizational level are instrumental in failure. Such decisions are typically made either by company officers or by the specific individuals to whom such decision-making powers have been delegated. They deal with matters not covered by policy that arise in the normal course of events and require action at a level above that of the immediate superior. As with policies, these decisions may have either positive or negative consequences in terms of performance. They may also, over time, accumulate to form what amounts to policy by precedent. It is in these cases, where a series of individual decisions have coalesced into organizational policy without consideration of broader consequences, that ineffective performance is most likely to result.

Note that although the negative consequences of organizational action are being emphasized, the discussion here is not meant to imply that a policy or decision with some adverse effects is necessarily poor. In evaluating such actions, many more things must be considered than the performance failure of a single individual. High-level directives apply to large groups, so their success must be evaluated according to the results on balance. Only when negative consequences, such as performance failures, become too widespread or when more effective policies are available can policy decisions be faulted. Many top-management decisions have a positive overall effect on the attainment of company objectives. In addition, it is a rare company indeed whose policies produce all the negative effects noted. Some generally occur in one type of firm, some in another. The points being made here represent a distillation from many sources.

How much the individual manager can do to remove these causes of ineffective performance varies considerably. The manager in a position to make policy or exert direct influence on its formulation may well initiate corrective action. Managers at lower levels, however, are relatively powerless when organizational factors are responsible for subordinate failure. The most they can do is bring the negative effects of a policy or higher-level decision to the attention of their superiors. This may or may not bring about a change, depending on many factors. Nevertheless, to further organizational objectives, managers should provide such feedback. Senior management must get information on the impact of its policies in order to evaluate them properly. Only if managers who are in a position to observe these effects send their impressions back up the line can appropriate revisions be made. However, in many companies feedback is not forthcoming, usually because managers consider it suicidal to criticize the actions of those responsible for their future career. Studies by

Professor John Athanassiades of Georgia State University and by Professors Karlene Roberts and Charles O'Reilly of the University of California at Berkeley indicate that one of the most significant blocks to effective corporate functioning is the withholding and distortion of upward communication.

Obviously, when organizational factors are involved, the role of the manager below the top level is advisory at best. So why should this manager bother to identify such factors at all? One answer is that he or she cannot provide meaningful feedback without detailed knowledge of the consequences of higher-level actions. Secondly, knowing that the causes of a subordinate's failure are organizational and beyond the manager's control can make the managerial job considerably easier. Once this fact has been clearly established, the manager's energies can be devoted to problems more amenable to solution. As most managers are well aware, some things cannot be changed. So in discussing various company policies and high-level decisions that may assume a key role in subordinate failure, we will give only limited attention to corrective action. When implications for policy change and decision making at higher levels in the company are mentioned, it is with full realization that such changes may not be available or desirable as immediate solutions to problems of ineffectiveness.

Policies That Allow Employees to Fail: Ineffective performance may occur because the company does not take the action necessary to eliminate the causes of failure. Ironically, this may be a matter of deliberate choice: decisions that allow employees to fail may have been reached after extensive study. An example would be a company decision not to invest in training. Most firms make it a practice to hire people who are already fully educated or trained for their jobs. They decide not to invest in certain types of development activities or provide internal training facilities. Nor do they make outside resources available at company expense. As a result, an employee may be permitted to fail because of inadequate training without any corrective action being taken.

For example, firms do not normally invest in stenographic and typing training for secretarial and clerical personnel. Should an employee fail as a result of inadequate preparation in these areas, rectifying the situation is assumed to be entirely up to the employee. Similarly, illiterates are rarely taught to read and write even though such knowledge is essential to almost all industrial employment.

Advanced training in job-related technical specialties is sometimes provided at company expense, but this is not universally true. Many companies will pay for courses taken in local universities, although the payments may depend on the attainment of certain grades. But many other companies will not reimburse employees at all. They will permit employees to fail from lack of required technical knowledge rather than supply it at company expense.

Often, similar decisions not to invest in an employee are made with regard to the treatment of physical and emotional disorders. Some firms will provide treatment in company-operated dispensaries or even hospitals. Others contribute extensively to union medical facilties or to comprehensive insurance plans. Yet, many firms operate on the assumption that certain types of treatment should be left to the individual. As a result, no company expenditures are allotted when an employee fails due to inadequate treatment of an illness. The employee who does not seek help or who turns to quacks is left to his or her own devices.

In these and other instances that might be cited, the employee is permitted to fail without direct action being taken that would involve a cost to the company. Sometimes the firm may arrange for a transfer or a new placement to overcome the deficiency, but such a transfer may be carried out without sufficient investment in training or effective placement procedures to provide any chance of success in the new position. Some companies maintain only skeletal personnel departments and take the risk that employees may be inappropriately assigned. This policy decision makes a number of failures inevitable. Organizational-action failures of this kind will be taken up in greater detail shortly.

In reaching such policy decisions, most companies take a variety of factors into account. A primary consideration, of course, is cost. Some investments are viewed as too expensive even to think about or they involve an initial outlay too large to ever be recovered. Extensive training or medical treatment, for instance, may cost more than seems warranted by the apparent gains. These services can be very expensive—in part because physicians, psychologists, and educators may be in short supply.

The second major factor is time. Will the investment, even if successful in restoring effective performance, achieve its goal rapidly enough? There may not be sufficient time available to await the results of long training or treatment. For example, an experienced personnel manager with a bachelor's degree in psychology might be given responsibility for developing an extensive psychological testing program within the company. After a while, it may become clear that this manager lacks the necessary knowledge to do the job effectively. The company must then decide whether it should invest in the required two or three years of graduate study. If the testing program is urgently needed, the investment would presumably not be made. The personnel manager would be permitted to fail, at least in developing the testing program, and someone more qualified would be hired from the outside to undertake the project immediately. Time considerations would preclude investment in corrective action.

Another important factor is the availability of suitable replacements. Are there people in the labor market who can take over the job and perform effectively, if an investment is not made in the incumbent? In the preceding example, for instance, the company would have been forced to provide graduate training for its own manager if it had been unable to recruit a qualified psychologist or a consultant. Similarly, most companies would invest in typing and stenographic training for secretaries if not enough pretrained people were available.

Finally, in making such decisions a company must consider whether corrective action will achieve the desired results at all. What are the risks involved? The personnel manager with the psychological testing project might succeed as a graduate student—or then again, might not. There is little point in a company spending large sums if there is only slight chance that this will bring about effective performance.

Failures to Implement Policies: Considerations of cost, time, availability of replacements, and risk may, then, lead to a decision which, in fact, allows certain employees to fail. They are permitted to fail somewhat in the same way that machines are allowed to break down under a deferred-maintenance plan. But this lack of corrective action is not always based on a conscious policy decision. In many cases, the company omits special services or conditions of employment for reasons having nothing to do with investment considerations. There may be deficiencies and conflicts in personnel policy formulation and planning which necessitate considerable improvisation at lower levels. Such improvisations may, on occasion, be totally inadequate to the task of maintaining effective performance levels.

At other times, policies may have been formulated only to fail in implementation. A person hired with the understanding that the company will take certain actions or provide certain conditions to facilitate satisfactory performance may later be denied them. Across-the-board cuts in department budgets during rough times can often produce such results. The implementation of policy may give way before the practical reality of available financial resources, even though top management never intended that this should be the consequence of the budget cuts.

Similarly, an individual may have a physical or emotional condition that limits his or her employment to a certain type of job. A physical handicap, for instance, may be noted during the pre-employment physical examination. Yet for some reason this person may not be put in a suitable job and may thus be permitted to fail. Or a company may have an active safety program with specific regulations concerning the use of protective devices. Yet delays in purchasing may produce a temporary shortage of goggles, and perhaps as a result an employee is severely injured. It may also be that the company, although generally interested in reducing accidents, does less than it should to study jobs for potential hazards or establish uniform safety rules. As a result, some actions taken at lower levels may be haphazard and totally inadequate. Such failures of company action can result in serious injuries that are not only personally catastrophic for the employees but hurt the company as well.

Often companies hire employees who lack job knowledge with the understanding that they will get training after employment. Many management trainees, including most liberal arts graduates, initially have few usable job skills. These are to be developed through training programs, job rotation, and the like. Sometimes, however, things do not work out as intended. The person misses instruction because of illness, or is considered too good to require the usual training, or the program is not set up as planned. Occasionally, the need for productive workers becomes so acute that development efforts are curtailed and people are given full job responsibilities long before they should be. For whatever reason, the company unintentionally deprives the individual of the preparation that is essential for success.

How Poor Job Placement Can Cause Failure

As we have noted, placement decisions may contribute to ineffective performance when a company decides to limit investment in this area. In such cases, little effort is made to identify the demands of specific jobs, and people are assigned with minimal information on their abilities, emotional patterns, motives and physical characteristics. Sometimes placements are made almost at random, depending on the immediate availability of people and the existence of openings.

Poor placement decisions do not always stem from limited investment in the personnel function, however. Some companies have policies that simply eliminate the process of careful placement. For example, a company may have an across-the-board policy that every new hire must start at the bottom in any entry-level job and then work up through the department.

Placement decisions need not even be organizational in nature. They are not always made from a separate personnel department that has been delegated authority in this area. Although the closed shop has been outlawed, there are still many situations in which people are assigned to work largely at the discretion of the union. Or sometimes the individual hiring manager has complete authority over placing the new employee.

It is more usual, however, for applicants to be screened in the personnel office. Then only those considered capable of performing a certain job are sent to an individual manager for consideration. Thus, the personnel or industrial relations group typically plays a major role in the final placement decision. As the tools and procedures required for the study of jobs and individuals have become increasingly complex, this role has expanded. In many large corporations, placement has become primarily a special staff function, and smaller companies are shifting in this direction as well. In these firms, placement errors must be considered organizational in nature.

There are many ways in which people may be incorrectly placed, some of which we have already discussed. People may be assigned at too high a level for their verbal ability, or may lack the special abilities (numerical, mechanical, etc.) demanded by the work. There may be job knowledge deficiencies of a specific kind. Emotions such as anxiety, depression, guilt, and anger may be persistently aroused in a certain job and contribute to failure. Neurotic symptoms are particularly likely to have detrimental effects when the placement is at a relatively high level. Dominant types of motivation may be continually frustrated by a specific kind of work—certain jobs just do not permit the satisfaction of important positive motives or the avoidance of major sources of distress. Specific occupational interests may be inappropriate for the particular position.

Equally detrimental consequences may come from errors in fitting physical characteristics to job demands. Various handicaps may interfere with performance. A person with brain damage may be assigned to a job that requires greater intellectual and perceptual capability than are available. Physical proportions such as size and weight may be inappropriate for performance requirements. Strength, stamina, muscular speed, and coordination, as well as other more specific muscular skills and competencies, may be inadequate. Vision and hearing, including depth perception, color vision, and other factors, may not be sufficient for job demands. Speed of perceptual response may be below what is required.

Placement errors involving the individual's intellectual, emotional, motivational, or physical functioning may also involve certain social or group factors. Thus, some people fail because they have been assigned to work requiring constant separation from an important family group. For example, a wife may be separated from her parents by a foreign assigment. Or an employee may fail because his or her work created certain family problems that in turn interfere with effectiveness.

Work-group factors may also operate. The group may lack the cohesiveness a specific individual needs for effective performance. Or its cohesiveness may be based on characteristics which the person lacks, so that ostracism results. The supervision available may be totally inadequate to an individual's needs. For example, a person may have motivational problems that require firm direction and the establishment of high standards, but may belong to a group that is in essence leaderless.

As will be seen in the following chapters, placement errors may also be associated with societal and situational factors.

 The Varieties of Placement Error: Two of the most important types of placement error are those of over- and underplacement. People may be put in jobs that demand more of them intellectually than they are capable of producing. They may also be assigned "over their heads" in an emotional sense: symptoms may be precipitated by the specific situational stresses inherent in higher-level positions. Many people do not want the responsibility inherent in managerial work. Such a job produces an anticipation of anxiety that leads them to avoid job duties. When pushed or pulled into such positions by threats or offers of large incomes, they will probably fail. Furthermore, overplaced individuals often create difficulties for those under them. Many problems develop when a person is put in charge of others who are clearly more competent.

Underplacement, on the other hand, does not cause that much ineffective performance. Although there is undoubtedly a tremendous waste of developed intelligence in this country, it is unlikely that the majority of underplaced people are ineffective performers. Many people are not frustrated by jobs that are, in a sense, beneath them. Their motivation remains entirely satisfactory.

This is not invariably the case, however. In one study I conducted for a company, performance failures were found to be unusually frequent among very intelligent female employees working in skilled positions. The company, like many others at that time, had very few women in managerial and professional jobs. As a result, those who had reached the more responsible secretarial positions or something comparable were unlikely to progress further. For many of the most intelligent, this situation apparently became intolerable, and either the quality of their work fell off badly or they began to have a negative impact on the work of others because of constant bickering. Similar effects may occur in other situations. In short, underplacement can be strategic for performance failure, but unlike overplacement, it need not always be so. When underplacement does assume a causal role, the solution can often be promotion.

Although the personnel placement process is most likely to contribute to failure by putting a square peg in a round hole, there is another way in which it can be strategic. Occasionally, for training purposes or other reasons, people are transferred to a number of different jobs in rapid succession. As discussed earlier, they are often faced with initial ostracism from each new group and repeatedly must gain acceptance. For some individuals, this may be so difficult that effective work becomes almost impossible. Thus, although transfer has been recommended as a solution to many instances of ineffectiveness, there is such a thing as excessive transfer. Certainly such shifts should be undertaken with a specific objective in mind and with some reason to believe that this objective will be achieved. The random shuffling of personnel that some companies go in for is likely to have negative consequences in the long run.

Sometimes placement considerations have to be subordinated to other considerations, as when a company must assign large groups of employees to a new type of work. Then it is not always possible to take time to work out appropriate placements. Conversion to new equipment may require this action. So too may the discontinuance of a product line, coupled with high demand for other products. Or a large order may have to be filled on a rush basis. Under such circumstances, an increase in ineffective performers is to be expected, but the risk must be taken in order to meet production requirements.

When urgent problems like this arise, there are bound to be placement errors. Sudden job changes give employees little time to learn new work procedures and can create resentment leading to poor performance. Such resentment can be minimized by providing employees with detailed information and allowing them as much freedom as possible in adjusting to change. This approach can make mass transfers more peaceful and reduce ineffectiveness.

How Can Placement Errors Be Minimized?

What is the best way to avoid placement errors that cause ineffective performance? The answer would seem to be a flexible personnel placement policy that emphasizes individual differences and varying job demands.

More rigid policies, although they may yield other advantages, seem to produce more than their share of failures. Many such policies derive from an earlier time when human resources were more expendable and firing relatively easy. Nowadays, a policy of starting all new employees at the bottom, irrespective of their final destinations, may result in many failures and disrupted careers among those who would otherwise have made good managers. Rotating all line managers through staff assignments or administrative-assistant positions can have similar effects. So too may the requirement that all must take a turn in traveling jobs or at a foreign installation. In all these cases, although the diversified experience may be broadening for some, it may produce nothing but failure and anxiety for others. Ideally, only those who are likely to benefit from such experiences should be exposed to them. Placing people in positions in which they will ultimately fail is helpful neither to them nor to the company. Even though techniques for making sound placements are imperfect, they will produce fewer failures than rigid enforcement of a single rotation policy that does not consider the differences among individuals.

Organizational Overpermissiveness

Just as a manager may fail to assume leadership, so too may a company become overly easygoing and permissive, both in its policymaking and its high-level decision making. This has a detrimental effect on employee motivation. There are numerous ways in which company policies may thus fail to reflect organizational performance objectives. Here are some examples:

Employee Discipline: If there is no provision for disciplinary action when company regulations are flagrantly violated, chances are good that at least some employees will get into trouble who would not otherwise do so. True, some people may be unaffected by the deterrent power of disciplinary actions such as suspension without pay—but others will scrupulously avoid behavior that they believe will bring such discipline. If there is no operational disciplinary machinery, they may be tempted into harmful behavior. For example, theft of company property may be a major problem unless it is company policy to call in the police when it occurs.

Recruiting and Training: Some employers recruit young college graduates by offering extensive training programs, which tend to become longer and longer as companies bid against one another for the best potential employees. Often, the recruiting brochures give the impression that the young people will be given a year or two of vacation rather than an intensive educational experience. This attracts those graduates who least anticipate taking pleasure in actual work.

Sometimes, the training turns out to be just as undemanding as was originally implied. This simply perpetuates the deficiencies in work motivation that existed at hiring. Once a permanent placement is made, failure generally occurs because the employee has come to believe that job-integrated work effort is unnecessary.

Of course, there is nothing wrong with using training programs to attract high-quality employees. But this approach defeats its purpose when the employer implies that hard work is not a requisite for success in the organization.

Grievance Procedures: In some companies, higher-level managers frequently fail to support their first-line supervisors in grievance situations. Not being personally involved in the situation, these managers find it tempting to portray the company as an understanding organization that is willing to forgive and forget. The unintended consequence is that supervisors do not discipline their subordinates, because they fear that the result will be a grievance that is eventually settled against them.

Naturally, some reversals at higher levels are inevitable—and justified. But when these reversals are so frequent that supervisors doubt that they will get company support for their disciplinary actions, performance is likely to suffer.

Sick-leave Policies: When an employer provides sick leave with pay, absences should be carefully monitored to make sure the program is not being abused. If there is any implication that sick-leave time is an employee right comparable to a vacation, absenteeism may rise substantially. Although policies vary widely, some firms pay full salary over long periods without checking to make sure that the claims of illness are valid. Most employees will not take advantage of this, but some will use up their allotted sick leave year after year, and then take more time off for real illnesses.

Transfers: Some companies have policies that make transfers absurdly easy. As a result, managers are encouraged to shift employees to other groups as soon as performance problems show up, rather than analyze the situation and apply solutions that might be more appropriate. The failing employee may go from one group to another and another and another in rapid succession—and in the process lose any chance of being restored to an effective level.

This does not mean that transfers should be made difficult, since transfer is sometimes the best answer to a performance problem. But overly easy transfers encourage managers to get rid of their problem employees rather than try to solve the problem.

Excessive Spans of Control

Business literature has had a lot to say about span of control. Generally, this literature has emphasized the ideal span: a group of the size that can be effectively supervised by a single manager. Our concern, although similar, has a somewhat different orientation. If a company is organized so that managers are responsible for large groups of subordinates, the sheer numbers involved may preclude adequate analysis and solution of subordinate problems. Thus, the size of the group in itself can be a key contributor to performance failure. In a smaller unit, the ineffective employee could have been given the attention required to attain an acceptable performance level.

Work-group sizes are typically determined by higher management, often in conjunction with an organization planning unit, not by the groups themselves or even the manager in charge of each group. Since larger spans of control throughout an organization require fewer managers, and managers are expensive, most top managers prefer to see that each manager supervises as many people as possible. In this respect, the span-of-control problem is identical with the other policy-based problems considered in this chapter. Because excessive-span-of-control problems originate in company policies and higher-level decisions, solutions can only come from top-management action.

Despite this, when an excessive span of control causes unsatisfactory performance by one or more subordinates, the problem superficially appears to be ineffective supervision. It appears that the manager is abdicating the managerial role by not dealing with motivational or other problems of subordinates. The manager may even believe this. But on closer observation, it becomes evident that the manager cannot possibly handle all problems of performance failure with such a large number of subordinates. Thus the problem emerges as one of company policy—of decisions regarding staffing and the organization of work—rather than of leadership within the group.

The question remains: What size group should a manager have if this problem is to be eliminated? There was some agreement in the early literature that the ideal number is from three to nine at the upper levels of the organization and between twenty and thirty at the lowest level. However, when these figures are set against those found in actual practice, marked disparities emerge. Production groups may range up to 150. Spans at the top as large as twenty-five are not unheard of.

The impression that many companies do have excessive spans is reinforced by two analyses of research on how group size affects output and productivity. The first is by Professor Ivan Steiner of the University of Massachusetts; the second by Professor Robert House of the University of Toronto and myself. The conclusion is clear that the optimal span is in the range of five to ten. The larger spans within this range, say eight to ten, appear to be most appropriate at higher levels, where greater resources for diverse decision making are most likely to be needed. In a situation where large numbers of production workers are employed, it may not be economically feasible to have a supervisor for each group of six or seven workers, even though this would be desirable. Nevertheless, at the lowest levels, the ideal numbers are so frequently exceeded by large amounts that a widespread problem obviously exists.

Presumably, a major factor in the superiority of smaller units is the greater opportunity for adequate handling of performance failure. The increased cohesiveness that is likely to develop may also contribute in some instances. Clearly, groups should be made as small as possible within the limits set by cost considerations, the inherent organization of work, and the availability of competent supervision. If enough effective managers cannot be obtained, of course, group size will have to be increased. The extent of this increase should be based, at least in part, on the trained competence of the workers. "Green" employees will require more attention than experienced ones, and thus the number a manager can handle effectively is considerably less. This is in accordance with the general proposition that the span of control should be established according to the probable incidence of ineffectiveness. The importance of keeping a group small increases when people are inexperienced, turnover is high, and certain conditions predispose toward a high incidence of performance failure.

When the span-of-control problem is placed in its organizational context, we also have the question of how many managerial levels are desirable. For maximum performance effectiveness, a minimum number of steps in the hierarchy seems preferable. Communication and implementation of policy are facilitated in the "flat" organization, and there's more likely to be feedback from lower levels. This conclusion doesn't necessarily conflict with that regarding group size. The higher a position, the greater effort most organizations devote to screening and selection, and the more experienced and intelligent the incumbents. This reduces the probability of performance failure considerably above the first level of supervision, and indicates that the span of control toward the top might well be broadened relative to that at the lowest level. If groups within the company were established on this basis, there would be less difficulty in maintaining a relatively flat organization. It is the telescoping of group size as the hierarchy is ascended that contributes most to the proliferation of levels.

These conclusions must be qualified by one factor: the extent of managerial activity required in addition to that of a basically supervisory nature. Many company presidents, for instance, must devote most of their time to representing the company personally with outside organizations and groups. This public relations function may preclude giving much attention to the performance of subordinates. Similarly, an industrial relations manager may have to spend many hours in negotiations with union representatives and in efforts to settle disputes or ward off organizing attempts. Here an unusually small span of control may still be too large and may contribute to the failure of an individual subordinate. Probably the best solution in such cases is to employ a direct line assistant to handle more strictly supervisory matters. Often executive vice presidents or group vice presidents perform this role for the company president. Certainly the extent to which a manager must carry out specialized work functions, in addition to directing the performance of others, must be taken into account in deciding whether a performance failure is attributable to an excessive span of control.

Inappropriate Organizational Standards and Criteria

Just as a manager may establish performance standards that make an employee ineffective by definition only, so too may the organization as a whole introduce standards and criteria that are inappropriate. In general, inappropriate factors are somewhat less likely to be found at the organizational level than at the level of immediate supervision. Policymakers are usually intimately and personally concerned with the attainment of company goals and thus are less likely to let irrelevant factors intrude. Yet such problems do sometimes crop up. Example: An employee is defined as ineffective and dismissed because a relative of a high-ranking company official desires the position. Or prevailing prejudices become institutionalized as part of the company's selection and promotion policies. It is possible for any of the inappropriate factors noted previously to become strategic at the organizational level.

One of the primary ways in which the company may create performance failure by definition has to do with the control process. Control requires that performance standards be established—usually but not necessarily in budgetary terms—and actual performance compared with the ideal. Generally, it is assumed that remedial action will be taken if the two consistently differ. Performance standards set at the organizational level can be inappropriately high, as when an inadequate budget is allocated to an unpopular manager to ensure failure. A company may also introduce criteria having no direct relationship to performance. A manager may, for instance, be expected to achieve election to a certain club before being considered effective in a job. Such inappropriate factors in carrying out evaluations for control or other purposes are presumably rare, but they sometimes exist.

When Forced Retirement May Be Inappropriate

Age is one inappropriate employment criterion that is extensively applied at the organizational level. Most employers are forbidden by the Age Discrimination Act to forcibly retire employees before age seventy (with exceptions allowed in the case of executives). However, employers can still force retirement at age seventy— and many do, without considering the performance level of the individual employee.

This use of age would seem to qualify as an inappropriate criterion, since people are being defined as ineffective on a basis not related to organizational goals. Of course, if a person actually wishes to stop work, this is a different matter. Clearly, however, some people do not wish to retire but are forced out by compulsory provisions. Many still are capable of an extended period of effective performance.

The evidence on changes in skills and abilities throughout life shows that job-related intellectual abilities are not likely to decline in the sixties and early seventies unless a brain disorder develops, and this happens in only a small percentage of cases. Physical illnesses generally are more frequent in older employees and may result in extensive absence from work, although this problem is not heavily concentrated in any specific age range. Muscular and sensory skills and speed will probably decline. Clerical, sales, and managerial tasks do not seem to be affected by these physical changes, but performance in certain kinds of heavy work can be. However, in many cases a job change will solve the problem.

These findings suggest that specifying a fixed retirement age is often inappropriate. Many people who are performing effectively by most standards and who wish to continue are forced out of their jobs by compulsory retirement. A flexible retirement policy more closely tied to actual performance is more consistent with the objectives of a business enterprise.

Since retiring employees prematurely on pension is costly and the firm loses significant skills and knowledge, especially at the managerial level, why do so many companies have a mandatory retirement system? The major argument appears to be that the procedure is simple, orderly, and impartial. Furthermore, promotional opportunities for younger employees become available more frequently and on a predictable basis.

Many firms believe that compulsory retirement can reduce jealousy and conflict. If everyone is separated at the same age, the system seems inherently fair and no one is likely to resent being retired while another person is not. The system makes it unnecessary to tell an individual directly that he or she is too old to continue to work. Also, it serves as a partial control on the ambitions of people in lower-level positions, since they know the specific date when an opening will occur and consequently are likely to hold back on their upward pressures until the appropriate time.

Nevertheless, many companies have utilized flexible procedures and established early retirement programs of a largely voluntary nature. These programs also minimize conflict and, to the degree that they are voluntary, do not introduce the problem of inappropriate criteria. On balance, the more flexible approaches, to the extent they retain effective employees, seem preferable. No firm can afford to throw away competent, experienced personnel. Using age alone to define ineffectiveness, like using any other inappropriate criterion, should be avoided.

Exceptions to Policy

A policy can contribute to ineffective performance either because it is poorly thought out or because it has a negative impact on a specific individual in a given situation. Although lower-level managers may help to change such policies, this takes time and often is neither feasible nor appropriate. The best way to deal with an individual case, therefore, is to try for an exception to policy.

Such exceptions to policy can help to remedy a relatively unusual instance of unsatisfactory performance while leaving the overall policy structure intact. However, exceptions to policy should be kept to a minimum and made only when there is convincing evidence that an exception will yield an improvement in performance. Exceptions should be made only at the highest levels, or by units or committees to which such powers have been delegated. They should be recorded, because if a number of exceptions are required in a given area, there will be documented evidence that the policy itself may need revision.

It is particularly important to have established procedures for making policy exceptions. In many companies, such procedures exist in certain areas but not others. Thus, it is typical to have wage and salary committees that can certify "red circle" rates permitting an individual to be paid above the existing maximum for the job for various reasons. However, there are often no procedures for making exceptions to standardized training procedures for management trainees or for reducing the span of control in a particular group because large numbers of poor performers require individual attention. Companies should identify those policy areas that are susceptible to performance deficiencies and establish mechanisms for granting exceptions. These mechanisms must then be brought to the attention of individual managers, so they can be used. Such an approach provides not only for individual performance change, but for feedback on existing policies so that they may be modified as needed.

9

Dealing with Society-Related Problems

Now we come to the largest social unit that may affect performance: the society of which the person is a member. Various cultural influences can be strategic factors in failure. By a culture, we mean the total way of life of a people, the modes of behavior and thought that are transmitted from generation to generation. For purposes of understanding performance, the crucial factors are the cultural values—the concepts of right and wrong, good and bad—which constitute the ethical precepts, aspirations, and ideals of most members of society.

More specifically, cultural values are the widely accepted directives that establish modes of social relations, achievement or performance patterns, goals, approved types of gratification, and social ideals for a society. Examples are human dignity, patriotism, sexual morality, respect for private property, religious beliefs, honesty, heroism, democracy, respectability, fair play, cleanliness, equal opportunity, success, and individual freedom.

These generally accepted concepts of right and wrong serve to direct the behavior of many of society's members. They are thus instrumental in much of human motivation, indicating acceptable means of achieving positive emotional experiences and of avoiding negative ones. These values are very similar to the individual motives discussed previously. But here the emphasis is on cultural rather than individual motivation—on the things which, as members of our particular society, we have learned to believe *should* be done. Although these values exist in specific individuals, they derive from society as a whole. The distinction between individual and cultural motivation may seem unimportant at this point; after all, motives are motives. As will be seen, however, whether a motive is unique to the person or is derived from that person's culture can have considerable significance for reducing ineffectiveness. Because cultural values are embedded in a sizable social context, they are much more difficult for an organization to change than individual motives.

The Nature of Cultural Values

Cultural values provide individual members of a society with explicit guidelines for their behavior. There is no need to think about alternatives; as long as one's actions are in accord with these directives, one cannot be judged wrong by the majority. Thus society makes available to its members an automatic, silent mechanism for the selection and channeling of behavior. We become particularly sensitive to things that are positively valued, while our perception of that which is negatively valued is often delayed.

The methods employed to perpetuate a culture are complex. Basically, a cultural heritage is transmitted from one generation to another through the actions and words of parents, peers, and other associates. The same things are said and taught over and over again in homes and schools throughout the country, and thus a uniformity of behavior and thought is created. If a child acts in a manner that is inconsistent with accepted values (perhaps by being dishonest or impolite), his or her parents will probably feel acutely uncomfortable and seek to reduce their distress by forcing the child to do what is culturally defined as right. Punishments may be invoked. Eventually the child comes to accept the values as guides to behavior, having learned that only in this way is it possible to escape the unpleasant emotions that so often accompany deviance. The values become part of the individual's motivational hierarchy.

Like individual motives, cultural values are closely allied to the emotions. Actions or impulses that deviate from established values may provoke intense feelings. A person may experience considerable guilt if he or she deviates. Or, a person who is treated in unacceptable ways by others may react with rage and resentment. Parents tend to pass on the values of their culture because they feel they must. Should they fail to do so, they often have strong feelings of guilt and shame. Thus, the culture imposes its control over individual motives that might be detrimental to its perpetuation.

By definition, cultural values are widely accepted and generally govern behavior. But they are neither universal nor universally acted upon within a society. There are numerous exceptions. Other motives may be more dominant and therefore determine behavior when a conflict arises. The individual may experience guilt, yet still overrule a value. On occasion, people hold conflicting values. Many believe in individualism and the survival of the fittest, at least in an economic sense, while at the same time espousing group loyalty and patriotism. Others laud democracy as a basis for social organization while pointing out that no business could operate effectively without a firm hand at the top. Clearly, values may be established at different levels in the motivational hierarchies of different individuals and thus may influence behavior to different degrees. We are not all subjected to identical cultural learning experiences.

Moreover, cultures tend to change their values. The process is gradual and the conditions that foster it are not precisely known. It is known, however, that some individuals accept new values before others, so that a culture in transition can hold values that are sharply at variance. Some people have already adopted the new; others retain the old.

Finally, there are within each culture various subcultures associated with classes, castes, ethnic groups, geographical groupings, and so forth. Each holds its own set of values, which may or may not coincide exactly with those of the larger unit.

Changing Values in the United States

It will not come as a surprise to anyone that values in this country have undergone some major changes in recent years. Many of these changes became widespread during the middle 1960s and were concentrated among the young. As a result, a generation gap has developed, at least to the extent that the younger and older members of society are likely to hold somewhat disparate values. This disparity has importance for understanding performance problems for two reasons: it means that younger employees may be guided in their work behavior by forces that their older superiors neither understand fully nor appreciate, and that the older superiors may evaluate their younger subordinates on the basis of values that the latter do not share. This disparity creates considerable potential for an apparent increase in ineffective performance. At least part of the increase can be blamed on managerial and organizational *definitions* of poor performance. These definitions may include largely inappropriate criteria such as unconventional hairstyles, short skirts, the playing of radios at work, and so forth.

There is wide documentation of younger people's changing values relating to work, efficiency, bureaucracy, affluence, and the like. Two prominent reports are *Work in America*, prepared by a special task force to the Secretary of Health, Education, and Welfare, and *The Worker and the Job: Coping with Change*, edited by Jerome Rasow. Writing in the latter, Daniel Yankelovich notes four major values of our society that historically have played important roles in society:

- Paid work is good because it means independence.
- The working male is valued as a good provider and a real man.
- Hard work is good in its own right; it is a source of self-respect and a sense of dignity.
- Hard work pays off in terms of economic success and security.

A number of studies indicate that all of these values now have changed or taken on new meanings among younger people. The "paid work is good" value thrives, but now much more as applied to females; it is closely allied to the new value placed on the independence of women. The "working male as provider" value is correspondingly in eclipse and may be disappearing altogether. The "hard work is good" value applies only to work regarded as meaningful, such as that of a professional nature. Furthermore, the payoff of hard work in terms of substantial economic success is not as highly valued as it used to be.

All this certainly does mean a changing work ethic. It also means that increasing numbers of young employees, especially males, are likely to be viewed by older superiors as *lazy* and unambitious when assigned to certain types of work. Appeals to self-respect, manhood, and the prospect of future economic success will often go unheeded.

Information on these and other values of younger people is provided in my earlier book *The Human Constraint* and in articles by Ann Howard and Douglas Bray of the A.T.&T personnel staff, as well as in articles I have published recently. Some of these new values are relevant to the world of work and to performance. For instance, values placed on authority have shifted sharply in a negative direction. Authority and authoritarianism are viewed more negatively, everyone should be free to do his or her own thing as long as others are not harmed. Confronting problems, being open in expressing feelings, and saying what one feels are good; holding in emotions is bad. Groups, group decisions, and group action are good; individual competitiveness is bad. The values of managers, bureaucracies, and large organizations with long-standing traditions are far less attractive than those of the professions.

All this presents the manager with many new problems. Such values cannot be expected to reverse themselves in the near future. Many traditional appeals will have less effect, because the values and motives that made them work in the past are no longer there. Appeals based on the authority of one's managerial position may simply be ignored. Insubordination may manifest itself in many forms, often quite openly. Attracting qualified employees, and especially managers, will be an increasing problem. All in all, changing values present managers with a major challenge to their ingenuity and stamina. The managerial job is going to be an exciting place to be in the years to come, but it will not be a place for the fainthearted or for those who want to rely on tried-and-true approaches.

Failure Associated with Legal Sanctions

The extent to which different kinds of sanctions are invoked to enforce society's values varies considerably. Some values have been converted into formal statutes and thus receive the support of the whole legal system. Others are perpetuated by informal social pressures and the prospect of ostracism. In general, the distinction between these two types seems to be based on the degree of potential threat to the survival of society. Lying is, in itself, not normally punishable through legal action, but when it occurs in court under oath it is defined as perjury. Since overt aggression and uncontrolled conflict between members are most likely to result in the eventual dissolution of any social unit (a country as well as a company), legal sanctions are particularly prevalent in this area. Conflicts can easily develop over private property and relationships between the sexes, and for this reason, laws regulating such matters are numerous. Similarly, any kind of physical attack on another member of society tends to be rigidly proscribed.

How can this affect performance at work? Fines do not necessarily have any direct impact on a person's work, but extended imprisonment removes that person from the employment situation entirely. In addition, the mere fact of a past conviction may serve to make a person ineffective in certain types of work. A sales representative may lose many customers if they learn of the conviction, or an individual whose job requires bonding may not be able to meet the conditions. In such cases, members of society impose sanctions beyond those imposed by the courts. Probably the people most vulnerable to the societal pressure are those at the highest levels. Should the financial community lose confidence in the top management of a company because some members have failed to meet cultural values as interpreted in the law, the company may be unable to obtain financing that is necessary to its growth or survival.

Values as Inappropirate Criteria

It is true that in some cases, a conflict in values can produce actual ineffective performance. A salesman may be boycotted by customers because he is disregarding one of society's values, by dressing outlandishly, for example. In this instance, the employee is clearly ineffective, and appropriate criteria are involved. The solution might be to transfer the employee to a position where he will be less vulnerable to public action and censure. Whether this would work depends largely on whether the employee would be accepted by co-workers and supervisors in the new job, or could withstand ostracism if it were imposed. Normally, successful transfers of this kind are more easily accomplished with lower-level personnel like the salesman than with those in top positions. Most jobs in the upper echelons have a high degree of public visibility.

But what if this particular salesman were doing well with customers and yet was defined as ineffective by management purely because his behavior conflicted with social values? Clearly, that would constitute use of an inappropriate criterion for defining poor performance.

The point is that the values of the larger society and the requirements for organizational effectiveness do not always coincide. Something can be good or bad in terms of the culture as a whole without having the same implications for achievement of company objectives. A person can be guilty of conduct that deviates from cultural values but may continue to make a distinct contribution as an employee. Therefore, when values are invoked as if they were performance criteria, ineffectiveness by definition will result. In such cases, the culture itself plays a strategic role in the failure. And the company may find itself performing in a quasi-legal capacity in direct opposition to its role as a business organization.

This is not to say that cultural values and the goals of business enterprises are necessarily conflicting, or that companies do not have to live within the constraints imposed by the legal and ethical system of the larger society. Clearly, many values tend to reinforce employee motivation and this contributes to a firm's profitability. And society proscribes many actions while at the same time indicating the appropriate scope of the economic function. It is society which establishes the rules of the game. Nevertheless, a firm need not go *beyond* societal legal sanctions to impose punishments or enforce values in a manner detrimental to organizational goals and individual welfare.

It is, of course, very difficult for many people even to imagine establishing policies which might seem to condone behavior that they consider bad. Some managers may react to instances of homosexuality, adultery, atheism, and the like with distaste, and want to get the person as far away from them as possible. Yet if they act on this impulse and terminate employment, they permit their values to assume a strategic role, and performance failure becomes a matter of definition only. The fact that companies and individual managers often do this indicates the great significance that values hold in motivation.

One factor contributing to such decisions, either at the corporate level or the level of the individual manager, is the diversity within the larger culture. Worker and superior may well come from different ethnic and socioeconomic groups. Their conceptions of right and wrong may be sufficiently far apart so that it is almost impossible for one to understand the other's actions. The occasional clash between black and white subcultures at work provides an example of this kind. As a

result of misunderstandings, managers may apply performance criteria that have little relationship to company objectives. The situation is not unlike that
between an older manager and younger subordinate. In
fact, the current "generation gap" might be interpreted
as a special case of subcultural variation.

When cultural values are involved in this way in
cases of failure by definition, the solutions are similar
to those that should be used with any other inappropriate criteria for job performance. The only difference
is that inappropriate criteria—whether introduced at
the organizational level or by the immediate superior—
are particularly resistant to change if they derive from
cultural values. Managerial actions based on these criteria may be widely supported. A manager who fires an
employee for immorality may become a hero. Pressure
will rarely be exerted to produce a change in inappropriate criteria that are based on value considerations, if
the values in question are held by the majority of
employees. As a result, the possibilities for change are
drastically reduced. The same conclusion holds for
ostracism by a group. It is very hard to change individuals or groups when a hundred others will applaud
them.

Conflicts Between Job Demands and Cultural Values

A major source of difficulty can be the influence of cultural values on the specific actions of employees who
fail. People may become ineffective because their cultural values lead them to act in ways that are inconsistent with job demands. If a conflict develops between
cultural directives and work requirements, the values
often win out and the employee may fail on the job. Or
the employee may attempt to overcome these cultural
imperatives and comply with the demands of the posi-

tion, only to experience considerable guilt and shame. Probably the most common reaction involves both kinds of behavior. The individual gets very upset and finds it impossible to concentrate on work, and at the same time tries to reduce emotional distress by avoiding certain job activities considered particularly bad according to his or her cultural values. Prolonged stress of this kind can contribute to emotional disorder.

Suppose that a male employee, because of his cultural origins, has long accepted the dictate that males should demand obedience of "the weaker sex." Unexpectedly, he finds himself reporting to a female boss. He believes it is bad to permit a woman to direct his activities, just as some young sons may consider obedience to their mothers a sign of weakness and inferiority. But at the same time he wants to progress in his work and do a good job. The outcome might be a series of outbursts directed at his new boss. On the other hand, he might attempt to adopt a more subservient attitude, only to find himself so overcome with shame that he cannot keep his mind on his work. Perhaps he would alternate between attempts to demonstrate his superiority and periods of submission during which frequent errors occur in his work. In cases like this, conflicts between job requirements and values are primary causes of failure.

It is not easy for the manager to change employees who are experiencing such a conflict. A very strong motive is involved in such cases—one dominant enough, in fact, to win over all other motives that might work *against* ineffective performance. Furthermore, this motive may have widespread public support. The two factors combined make it very difficult, if not impossible, to change cultural values once they have been identified as a cause of failure on the job. Individuals' values do change, of course, but this would probably have happened long before performance was so drastically affected if it were going to occur at all. Thus the mere presence of unsatisfactory performance attributable to a value problem should usually be interpreted as convincing evidence that the person is not going to change.

This means that any change which is to produce adequate performance will have to be made in the job, rather than in the individual. Usually this involves transfer to some other kind of work where the specific values responsible for failure will not be activated. In some cases, a change in the conditions of the present job may be possible.

Unfortunately, many value-based responses involve factors that are almost universal within a firm and cannot be changed. The individual whose liberal, anticapitalistic values are strategic for failure will benefit little from transfer to some other job in most companies. Similarly, the scientist who requires an environment where there is great respect for individual freedom is unlikely to find it anywhere else in the organization if it does not exist in the research division. Problems involving moral values can normally be handled by transfer, but not always. Salespeople who cannot live with their own "dishonesty" will usually improve if shifted to a position far removed from sales. And the person who is disturbed by the sexual immorality of fellow workers can usually be placed where such circumstances do not exist or are minimized. But those who work for a military contractor may not be able to erase a negative image of the firm and of their own job no matter what the specific assignment. Many cases in which value factors are strategic are best handled by dismissal or by trying to induce the employee to resign.

Job/Value Conflicts Involving Equity and Fairness: One factor that appears frequently in job/value conflicts is the value placed on equity or fair play. Parents characteristically teach their children this concept at an early age, although they often come to regret it when they are subsequently besieged with appeals to their own sense of fairness. Children are taught that it is unfair for one child to get something that another does not get; for someone to break a promise, whether implied or stated; for their parents to require something of them that other parents do not require. The examples can be multiplied many times for both children and adults.

At work, difficulties frequently arise when an immediate superior or higher-level manager acts in a way that makes an employee feel victimized by unjust treatment. This could be a case of the employee blaming others for his or her own shortcomings, but that situation would not involve cultural values. Efforts to find a scapegoat often look very much like value problems, but they are not. It is when the person is convinced that treatment has been unfair, *and* most people who share that person's cultural background agree with this interpretation, that the issue relates to the value of fair play.

It is important to emphasize that infringement of the sense of fair play need not have an impact on performance. Many people who experience numerous inequities do not decline in effectiveness, even if they are quite upset about the wrongs done them. But in some cases, the value of fairness is held with such intensity or the provocation is so flagrant that performance failure does occur. The person feels justified in expressing dissatisfaction, or even feels an obligation to do so. As a result, this person may stir up other employees, refuse to perform job duties, or in general become uncooperative and difficult to deal with.

The potential causes of such reactions are many: unfulfilled promises concerning conditions of employment, promotion of a person with considerably less seniority, discriminatory treatment because of sex or race, insufficient recognition for services performed, inequities in payment, and so on. Among union-represented employees, the grievance system provides a sanctioned outlet for the resentment, and a flood of formal complaints may be made when inequitable conditions are believed to exist. Some management groups tend to blame these high grievance rates on union pressure tactics having little relationship to actual employee feelings. This, of course, can be entirely correct. But value problems, and in particular, violations of the sense of fair play, represent a common cause too. One inequity perpetrated against a single employee can produce a whole series of grievances of even an extensive work stoppage. Others who hold the same values as the aggrieved individual may react just as emotionally and may well take up the employee's cause.

When a subordinate reacts to what he or she considers unfair treatment by sulking, expressing resentment, and working less efficiently, the manager should generally bring the problem into the open. A lengthy discussion may not solve the problem, but a solution is unlikely to be found without it. This discussion gives the manager an opportunity to present a detailed, logical explanation of why the resented action was taken. This need not be done apologetically—some inequities or seeming inequities are inevitable, and others, like promotion on the basis of merit rather than length of service, are actually desirable from a managerial viewpoint. Most employees will appreciate an explanation, however, and will at least partially accept a logical analysis. Certainly this is more likely to minimize future trouble and ineffective performance than a rigid insistence on managerial prerogatives.

If the logical explanation is not accepted and the resentment continues or even grows, there could be a number of reasons. One is that the action was in fact unfair, and that is why the attempted explanation fell flat. If so, every effort should be made to rectify the situation. It may also be that the matter is more emotional than cultural in nature. The employee may feel unjustly persecuted and may be unwilling to approach the problem in a rational manner. In such cases, a discussion may not do much to solve the difficulty, but it can bring out information that makes it easier for the manager to distinguish between emotional and cultural causes. Another possibility is that the values of the manager and the subordinate are so far apart that there is no common ground on which a solution can be built. Transfer is appropriate in this situation. If a person can become effective by being assigned to a manager with more compatible values, then the change should certainly be made.

Job/Value Conflicts Involving Individual Freedom:
Another value that appears to have major implications for performance is individual freedom. In the United States, it is widely held that people should, within certain limitations, be permitted as much freedom as possible to live in accordance with their own desires. This value, in fact, is codified in the Bill of Rights. Yet studies such as those by Morris Rosenberg indicate that people entering upon different careers differ greatly in the importance they attach to this value. Architecture, journalism, drama, art, the natural and social sciences, advertising, public relations, engineering, and teaching seem to attract those who value freedom highly. Sales promotion, hotel management, real estate, finance, personnel, government service, and general business do so to a much lesser extent. Furthermore, the value of individual freedom is apparently more strongly held among those employed on university faculties than in most other segments of society. Academic freedom is without question a potent factor on the campus. It is frequently employed as a guide to decision making and policy formulation within the university community, and it is defended vigorously.

In the business world, emphasis on individual freedom is probably most pronounced among physical scientists engaged in research and development activities. It is marked in a number of other business occupations as well, but scientists appear to represent the largest group. Most have been exposed to long periods of university training as undergraduate and graduate students. A number have been employed on college faculties at one time or another. In addition, much of the work is creative and intellectual, and it is among intellectuals that freedom appears to be valued most highly in U.S. society. An especially strong commitment to freedom might be considered characteristic of the whole scientific subculture.

This value clearly has functional importance for the work of the industrial scientist. To be maximally effective, the scientist must be free to investigate problems even though they may appear to have been solved already, and in spite of the apparent lack of immediate applications. For creative scientific ideas to be developed, a number of conditions appear to be necessary. There must be strong motivation in the area of learning and ideas. This must be wedded to a certain excitement, which is anticipated and experienced when creative effort is in progress. Excitement of this kind appears to be the crucial emotional factor in motivating people to do creative work, leading the scientist to return again and again to a problem in the manner of someone with a sizable stubborn streak. To this must be added a quality which no doubt strikes many people as a sort of conceited negativism—the capacity to consistently reject or ignore the directives and conclusions of others. The result may be that the most creative scientists are likely to adversely affect the work of their associates. Skepticism concerning the ideas of others and singleness of purpose appear to be essential conditions for the pursuit of new solutions, but they do not always make for close friendships or serve to encourage collaborative scientific efforts.

Thus, creative and effective scientific performance is likely to occur in conjunction with intellectual preoccupation, intense excitement, stubbornness, skepticism, conceit, a contentious and perhaps domineering attitude, deviance, a dislike for the orderly and correct, freedom of emotional expression, and a tendency to live in the future. Many of these qualities suggest an individual who is not always easy to get along with. Yet most of them appear to be essential to really effective performance in research positions. An environment that restricts or suppresses these tendencies would eliminate creativity at the same time. It is not surprising, therefore, that scientists value individual freedom so highly.

How, then, might a strong concern for freedom contribute to ineffective performance? As we have noted, the creative scientist can have a negative impact on the work of others. The quantity and quality of work may be outstanding, and at the same time a scientist can stir up all kinds of dissension in the laboratory. A constant stream of new ideas from the scientist may be matched by a complete lack of creative accomplishment among colleagues. The scientist's hostility to divergent proposals may have a stifling effect on younger and less experienced scientists. In spite of their emphasis on individual freedom, creative people may not show much tolerance of others, at least in the realm of ideas. Secondly, the concern with freedom, together with the personality characteristics which this releases and fosters, may conflict with job demands not related to creative production. Any company requires a degree of cooperation among employees in order to survive. Loyalty and a willingness to abide by the decisions of others are essential to this kind of cooperative effort. These factors assume particular importance in research establishments, because the people employed there often possess knowledge which, if it became available to competitors, could adversely affect company profits. The generally high turnover among scientific personnel accentuates this problem. Thus the loyalty of research scientists is a constant source of concern to industrial managers. Multiple controls are often installed to prevent a breakdown of cooperative effort. Sometimes rewards are bestowed for long service, obedience to authority, friendliness, and conformity rather than creative research. The danger of this approach is that success as defined by the company becomes available only to those who are really less effective—to those who have given up their values and their creativity.

This conflict between the scientific role, with its high valuation of freedom and creativity, and the role of a company member with its emphasis on cooperation and loyalty, is usually felt most intensely by younger scientists. Some may resolve the conflict by what may strike others as an extreme devotion to freedom and nonconformity. Some may resolve it by leaving the company. Others may not really resolve it at all, and may experience intense and continuing emotions that make effective work difficult. In such people, guilt and anxiety tend to predominate, but intense outbursts of anger may also occur.

Job/Value Conflicts Involving Moral and Religious Values: In addition to equity and freedom, other moral values can affect performance. Often these have roots in early religious training. An extreme example would be the proscription against killing. Many people in the armed services during wartime develop severe emotional disorders when caught between the demands of combat assignments and their cultural values. Many more either do not fire their weapons or deliberately miss. Conscientious objectors avoid conflict and guilt when they are permitted to follow their religious teachings by serving entirely outside the armed forces. In all these cases, the individuals find it impossible to suspend their moral principles during wartime.

Similar job/value conflicts can arise in the manufacture of products that might be used either to fight a war or that represent a possible threat to human life under any other circumstances (such as the manufacture of certain chemicals). Those who hold strong values regarding killing may well refuse to do certain kinds of work which they consider bad. Since they may be reticent regarding the cause of refusal, their reaction can appear quite irrational. Or they may attempt to continue in work of this kind despite their values, in which case they may well fail. The guilt aroused by continued exposure to a situation that they view as wrong or sinful tends to make effective performance very difficult. Sporadic attempts at escape from the situation may also result in considerable absenteeism.

Performance can be affected even when the work's relationship to killing seems quite indirect to other people. I know of instances where young men employed in research projects on military screening and placement have not been able to do the work because of strongly held values. All were competent individuals with outstanding academic records and histories of satisfactory employment. But while working on the military research, they felt that they were contributing to the development of personnel procedures that could indirectly serve to perfect the art of killing on a grand scale. As a result, they became preoccupied with guilt, to the point where one man with advanced training in mathematics failed over and over in attempting to add a column of figures on a calculator.

Values in the area of sexual morality may operate in a similar manner. In some work environments, four-letter words are heard rather frequently, and there is a good deal of joking along sexual lines. To certain people with strong feelings about such matters, this can represent a major source of distress. The result may be a deterioration of performance because the person feels guilt by association. More frequently such employees will become irritable, argumentative, and critical of their fellow workers. On occasion, they may berate the group en masse, with a generally disruptive effect. Eventually, they may be expected to resign, but not before heaping condemnation on everyone around.

There may also be value conflicts associated with feelings about honesty. No doubt some jobs encourage their incumbents to engage in questionable practices, to lie, and perhaps even to behave in ways that are clearly illegal. But these instances are presumably rare. It is more common for a person to *view* a job as basically dishonest and thus to either avoid certain aspects of it or experience guilt while performing it. The borderline between good and bad is often hard to establish precisely, and those with strong values can easily accentuate things which to others might appear quite appropriate. This is a common problem among salespeople. For some individuals, the whole selling and advertising process represents a colossal racket, an attempt to steal the money of others by forcing them to buy a worthless product which they do not want and cannot use. Such people usually have strong values regarding honesty and humanitarian behavior. Should they find themselves in a sales position, they may well become obsessed by guilt. The resulting impact on their performance is not entirely predictable, but it is unlikely to be positive. They may fail to carry out those duties which they consider dishonest. They may quit. Their guilt may interfere directly with their work, even to the point where they fail deliberately in order to expiate their sin. Or they may condemn the company to their customers and point out various defects in the products they are supposed to be selling without being aware of what they are doing.

Something similar can occur simply because someone is employed in a competitive, profit-making organization. Many people whose values lead them to consider the business world reprehensible avoid such employment. But some are attracted by money or other factors and deliberately enter a work environment in which they are likely to fail. Someone who holds strong liberal values can face considerable difficulty in an organization that epitomizes capitalism and private investment for profit. Many people who begin college intending to prepare for business, and who have a value conflict in this area, subsequently change their minds and enter some other type of occupation. Other people follow through on their original plans and adapt their values to fit the new environment. Where neither of these situations occurs, the probability of performance failure is high. Problems of this kind seem to be growing in frequency as new values come in conflict with the realities of the existing business system.

Job/Value Conflicts—Are There Any Solutions?
We have noted that people sometimes modify their value systems to be more in tune with vocational aspirations and actualities. This is a much less common response to value conflict than a shift in occupational choice, but it does happen—usually when the person has a motive of greater personal importance than the original value. This makes the change largely a matter of expediency. Typically such people hold strong liberal values but also want the money or prestige which they believe is only available in a business career. To resolve this conflict, they will adjust their beliefs.

The same thing can happen in society as a whole. During wars and economic depressions, we may change many values that seem to conflict with our immediate needs. Some of the changes are merely temporary; others are permanent. The idea that a woman's place is in the home began its decline with World War II. The number of women holding full-time positions increased markedly in response to the requirements of war, and today the figure is higher still. Value change, in the individual and in the society, seems often to be a matter of expediency—a mechanism adopted in order to satisfy more pressing needs or motives.

This, or course, does not give a manager much to work with. Problems created by value conflicts are among the most difficult that managers face. Many are beyond their power to solve. Any manager who tries to change an employee's values will find it much harder than changing motives, because of the strong societal support for these values. The only way to change an individual's values might be to change the society's values—obviously, not feasible. Sometimes the only possibility would be to change the employee's subcultural identification—also unrealistic, since it would be time-consuming and require resources unavailable to the manager.

Beyond that, there's the question of whether a manager *should* try to change an employee's values. This is a value question in itself, and just makes the value-change approach even more unattractive.

The unsolvable nature of conflicts between a job and an employee's values makes it important for the manager to distinguish between individual *motives* and cultural *values.* Individual counseling and management development programs can change attitudes and motives—but if the problem involves values, these approaches would be ineffective.

10

Dealing with Problems Related to the Work Situation

We first considered performance difficulties that originate with the individual employee. We then discussed the effects on performance of various groups of which the employee is a member: family, work group, organization, and society. Now we will look at another set of influential factors that a manager should consider in trying to determine why a performance problem has arisen. These factors are part of the work situation and the work itself.

Key Situational Factors in Performance Failure

There is a wide range of situational forces; however, only a limited number seem to contribute to performance difficulties.

Some key situational forces are basically economic. They include the labor market as it affects the availability of jobs, the impact of competing firms on the performance of specific individuals, and other forces with economic implications such as actions taken by foreign governments. They also include union policies and decisions made at the level of the international union or of the labor movement as a whole, or perhaps even at the local level.

A second group of key situational forces is primarily geographic. Climate and topography can combine with emotional or physical factors to influence performance in important ways. So too can the isolation of the environment in which the work is carried out and the novelty or strangeness which the situation presents. The factor of strangeness is allied to that of separation, which was discussed previously. For some people it is not so much the separation from loved ones that produces performance failure after reassignment, but the threat of the new and unknown itself.

There are also the various physical conditions which may exist in the workplace itself. Noise, lighting, and temperature are particularly important. Also significant in many jobs are the design and operating condition of equipment used in the work.

The degree of danger on the job—whether it actually exists or is merely perceived by the worker—can be a key factor in performance. Accident causation, safety management, and accident-proneness are all involved here. Perceived danger influences work effectiveness primarily through the emotions and motives aroused. Unconscious motives may contribute to fear reactions on the job and may thus play an important role in job difficulties.

Finally, there is the work itself. Clearly, people sometimes fail because they simply cannot do what has to be done. When this happens, individual capabilities of the employee may be involved, as well as the organization's structure and the decisions made by managers who define the jobs and assign people to them. But beyond this is something more: the overall work to be done as a result of top-level decisions regarding missions and strategies. The work may be carved up and divided in many ways, but it is still there. Since work differs from one industry to another, this factor is a function of the nature of the business, but at the individual level it is translated into the nature of the work itself.

How Economic Forces Affect Employee Performance

How, specifically, do factors in the economic environment affect individual performance? One such factor, the existing level of employment, affects primarily how performance standards are established. Under tight labor-force conditions, standards may be adjusted downward to ensure that people will be available to fill essential positions. Under the opposite conditions, standards may be shifted up. When it is easy to hire satisfactory replacements, companies tend to tighten up on current employees and expect more of them. Companies are also more likely to consider dismissal as a solution to ineffective performance. In fact, standards of performance may be raised as a preliminary to dismissal or demotion, on the assumption that the job can easily be filled from among the unemployed. This practice usually affects less well-educated employees and those with minimal or obsolescent skills, among whom unemployment strikes hardest. Occupational surpluses in highly skilled, managerial, and professional jobs are less frequent. Thus, this situational factor exists mainly when the subordinate is at the bottom of the job hierarchy and when the particular position is on the verge of extinction.

Depressed economic conditions may also operate directly to produce a change in performance. In territories where unemployment is high and income levels low, salespeople can often become so disillusioned and upset that they are unable to regain their former effectiveness when economic improvements do occur. In the Pittsburgh area, for instance, retail purchases drop sharply whenever there is a steel industry strike. The impact on sales and salespeople can be serious, even when managerial expectations are adjusted to existing conditions. Many young and inexperienced salespeople intent on setting the world on fire see their declining figures as a reflection on their own competence and become very disturbed. Unable to meet their own standards, they either quit prematurely or adopt a fatalistic helplessness; a few become really emotionally ill. Depressed areas have ruined many a promising sales career, and even the experienced are not entirely immune. A continued inability to make sales is likely to be viewed as a personal defeat by any salesperson, although rationally it is clear that nothing more could be done under the circumstances.

Something very similar may also occur at the top levels of a company. The officers may be at the mercy of situational influences and thus unable to return a profit. The emotional impact of these economic conditions, over which they have no control, may be enough to practically incapacitate them. A few may resort to dishonest and illegal actions; many more may fail because their emotional state has adversely affected their performance. The suicides and emotional breakdowns attributable to the 1929 stock market crash provide an extreme example of this phenomenon.

At these higher levels, there is less tendency to adjust standards to existing conditions. Company officers, like football or baseball coaches, may be held accountable for losses irrespective of their actual control over the situation. Thus, many an outstanding executive has been dismissed during economic recession because standards were not adjusted to reflect the possible.

These effects are not limited to general economic conditions, however. Individual competitors may break through and take away sizable segments of a market with equally detrimental consequences for those immediately affected. A new and superior product or advertising campaign, a sharp reduction in prices, some particularly effective selling—any of these may give a competing firm a major advantage, even if only temporarily. The salesperson who suffers heavy losses under such circumstances may respond with emotional and motivational changes that seriously affect future performance. There is no question but that economic conflicts can take a heavy toll among the contestants.

When government actions intrude upon the economic arena, they too may become strategic for failure. So also may union activities. Again, the impact usually hits hardest at the top of the organization, but involved specialists such as company lawyers, tax experts, and labor relations experts may also be affected. The fact that union negotiations break down and a strike results, or that an antitrust action is successfully prosecuted against the company, can have important implications for the future performance of those intimately involved. Failure to measure up to personal expectations at such times can have a severe emotional and motivational impact on some people, even if they have met the standards established by the company.

Dealing with Economic Causes: When economic forces cause performance failure, every effort should be made to bring the person's own standards into line with actual standards. The employee should be persuaded that personal failure was not involved, since the problems were caused by factors beyond his or her control: economic circumstances, a competitor's actions, a government edict, or union decisions. Once the employee is convinced, there should be a rapid improvement in performance. The situation is more complicated if the individual was partially responsible for the way events developed but still is overreacting, with unfortunate consequences for job performance. This makes the job of reestablishing effective performance more difficult. The person must be helped to realize that irrespective of past events, his or her present competence is what counts. Providing a small dose of success can do wonders.

In more severe cases, the anxiety, shame, or depression produced by the sense of personal failure may bring on a true emotional disorder. At such times, the solutions discussed in Chapter 3 are appropriate. Some emotional reactions become so inflexible that a manager cannot realign the individual's personal standards with actual standards. The employee will remain convinced of personal inadequacy no matter what superiors may say or do. The employee's overt behavior may, however, represent an attempt to deny this, making it difficult to determine exactly what provoked the disorder.

It may also be possible to remove the economic forces that have produced failure. A salesperson who is overreacting to the impact of depressed conditions or aggressive competition should ideally be shifted to a territory where there is some possibility of success. At the same time, an attempt should be made to counteract any feeling the person may have that accepting the transfer represents an admission of defeat. Unfortunately, this kind of solution is not generally available for top-level executives and staff specialists. For them, there is seldom any appropriate "new territory" where a sense of success and a revival of effective performance can occur. At this level, there is less chance of solving failure problems short of dismissal or demotion simply because of the shortage of positions to which a lateral transfer might be made.

How Geographic Location Can Cause Employee Failure

Many of the strategic factors involving geographic considerations are obvious. Climatic conditions, for instance, can be so severe as to physically affect performance. Similarly, rough terrain can be a significant factor in industries based on the extraction and development of natural resources. In such cases, where nearly all employees could be expected to suffer some loss of effectiveness, standards are usually adjusted to take the situation into account. For example, a laborer is not generally expected to perform at the same level in the tropics as in a more temperate climate.

When emotional and physical reactions to geographic factors differ among individuals, however, true performance failure may occur. Some people become severely sick whenever they board a ship. Whether the basic cause is physical or emotional, they are incapable of effective work in any job requiring them to spend much time at sea. Similarly, some people develop severe and incapacitating sinus or bronchial conditions in cold, wet climates. Emotional reactions can occur with extended exposure to extreme conditions, such as those in the Arctic, equatorial jungles, or deserts. Environments like these contribute to severe and lasting depressive states in some people, although others are left unscathed. In part, the emotional reactions appear to be precipitated by the isolation that characterizes such regions.

Under conditions of this kind, it may be possible to treat the disorder and so restore effective performance. Through medical research, drugs and other remedies have been developed that permit individuals to continue living in harsh environments. Should treatment prove inadequate, however, it is best to remove the person from the situation as soon as possible. Many people who could not adjust to isolated assignments in extreme climates during wartime have recovered rapidly when returned to the United States. This solution is particularly appropriate when the situational reaction is primarily emotional.

In discussing family ties as a cause of performance failure, we talked about separation as an important contributor. Some people fail because they are assigned to jobs that remove them from emotionally important family and other group associations for long periods of time. Very similar reactions can be caused by separation from a familiar *environment* and exposure to a new situation. In such cases, a thorough discussion with the individual is usually needed to determine whether it is the separation from a family or the strangeness of the new environment that is disturbing. Generally, with sufficient patience it is not difficult to distinguish between the two.

The problems associated with being in new and strange situations appear most frequently when employees are assigned to work in a foreign country. It can be an overwhelming shock to face people whose customs seem unintelligible and with whom communication is difficult because of language barriers. Satisfying the simplest personal wants becomes a complex problem—getting a meal, making arrangements to have laundry done, finding a toilet, and so forth. The strangeness of everything, the potential for getting into embarrassing situations, and the sense of being unwanted provide fertile ground for the development of emotional problems. So too do the value conflicts inevitably aroused by the demands of an alien culture.

Experience with employees in overseas assignments indicates that emotional problems are most likely to develop in unemployed wives who have reached middle age and who have spent most of their lives in some stable U.S. community. The husbands are somewhat less vulnerable, probably because their work remains much the same even though the environment in which it is carried out has changed drastically. Alcoholism is a particularly common response to the stress of a strange country and unfamiliar work situation. Physical disorders of emotional origin also occur frequently. Many of these reactions make normal behavior of the kind required for effective work performance quite impossible for long periods of time. Although psychoses are not very prevalent, neuroses are—especially those with anxiety and depression predominating. In most cases, the symptoms appear for the first time during the foreign service; the individual has usually been emotionally and physically healthy up to that point.

These reactions may also occur within the United States itself when a person is uprooted from a familiar environment. The move from a rural area to a large city is probably the most frequent source of difficulty. Rush-hour crowds, subways, and traffic jams can be almost as disconcerting as a foreign culture. But even the move from a city in which one has grown up to another that presents a new problem of adaptation can cause emotional upset and performance problems in some people.

Dealing with Geographic Factors: In general, the solutions to ineffectiveness caused by novel situations parallel those recommended for family separation in Chapter 6. It is important to get the person out of the new location and back to familiar ground as soon as possible. Ideally, screening should prevent or reduce such occurrences, both in the employee and in other family members.

There is, however, another valuable solution to situationally caused cases, especially those involving foreign assignment. People can be prepared for the new situation so that the shock is eased when they arrive. Ideally, people to be sent on trips or permanent assignments to unfamiliar places should be given as much information as possible about the various situations they may face and ways in which they might deal with those situations. Language training and education about the new culture should be provided before the move is actually made.

Some companies send large numbers of employees to countries very different from the United States. For example, many oil company employees have been sent to the Near East. In these situations, special company-sponsored training programs can provide substantial benefits. Members of the employee's family should also be invited to attend. Training should be conducted by experts who are fully informed regarding both the part of the world involved and the language spoken there, as well as by company employees who have worked in the unfamiliar country. Participants could be given an opportunity to play the roles that they will assume in their new environment. In this way, they can explore and become familiar with their own reactions and emotions before being actually exposed to the situation. This type of training will almost certainly reduce the number of people who have to be recalled from foreign assignments because of performance failure. It should more than pay for itself.

Detrimental Conditions in the Work Setting

Factors like noise, overall illumination, atmospheric conditions, and the condition of equipment can affect performance acutely. However, these factors tend to have a uniform impact on everyone exposed to them. When there is a detrimental workplace environment, standards will generally be adjusted downward to compensate. Generally, the variations in employee reaction that do occur are more a consequence of individual characteristics than of working conditions. Performance failure may occur, however, when an employee suffers from some physical deficiency that increases his or her sensitivity to the effects of the detrimental condition. Or some employees may be more exposed to the condition than others.

In some cases, management may be unaware that the physical environment is contributing to poor performance and so may fail to adjust standards accordingly. It may incorrectly assume that the problem is with the employees themselves, when actually the machines were inappropriately designed or are operating improperly. Similarly, a manager may fail to recognize the effects that noise, temperature, and other conditions have on performance. These effects have been extensively reviewed by Professor Ernest McCormick of Purdue University in his book *Human Factors Engineering.*

Excessive noise can mask speech, making communication difficult and misunderstandings frequent. It can also interfere with tasks requiring concentration. Mental work is affected primarily, but manual activities are not immune. Errors in the quality of work produced are influenced most. But in industrial settings, noise has little impact on quantity, so efforts to make the workplace quieter are unlikely to produce higher output.

Illumination levels are equally important for performance. Because the lighting conditions under which various individuals work can differ even within the same room the potential contribution to ineffectiveness is somewhat greater than for noise. Normally, more light will increase productivity as well as substantially reduce the number of errors and accidents. Improvements in performance can also be expected when glare is removed or reduced to a minimum.

Among the various atmospheric conditions, temperature is the most important. In general, poorer performance may be expected when the temperature reaches around 90°. Performance will get still worse as temperatures rise above that level and as humidity increases. Complex physical tasks are affected most. Cold has similar consequences: at 32°, performance will be noticeably poorer than at room temperature. Below 0°, the impact becomes pronounced. Other atmospheric factors, which appear less frequently, include lack of oxygen at high altitudes, rapid reduction of barometric pressure such as may occur during work under water (creating the "bends"), and noxious gases and vapors that become concentrated because of poor ventilation.

Another important factor is equipment design and maintenance. A machine can demand more strength, muscular speed, coordination and dexterity, perceptual speed, visual competence, or auditory capacities than the operator can possibly provide. Similarly, the design may be incompatible with the size and proportions of a specific individual. Human engineering aims at achieving optimal adaptation of equipment to the operator, but if this is not achieved and if managerial standards are not adjusted, performance is likely to be affected.

Excessive Danger: In studies on the effects of introducing automated equipment, it has been found that workers respond emotionally to the new danger they perceive in their environments. Naturally such feelings can be provoked in a situation where injury is potentially possible or where an accident could have serious consequences. Many examples might be cited—work on high buildings and other construction projects, work with explosives or radioactive materials, mining activities, tests of new and untried equipment, or military service in combat. Some people are apparently almost immune to anxiety in these situations, but others—especially if they have been sensitized to them by prior experiences—can have extreme emotional reactions. Situational and emotional factors can thus combine to impair performance to the point where the employee is totally ineffective in the dangerous situation.

Actual accidents, of course, can also affect performance. A serious injury can require continued absence from work. An occasional accident need not mean that the person is ineffective, but repeated accidents or a severe injury can seriously disrupt performance. Either absenteeism is excessive or the employee becomes physically incapable of meeting quality and quantity standards. When an accident occurs, the employee's misfortune deserves sympathy and understanding— but accidents are also important because of their effect on performance levels.

Injuries are most likely during an employee's first few months on a new job, when he or she has not yet learned how to guard against the dangers in the new environment. Furthermore, higher accident rates are quite frequently found among employees who also lose more time from work for other reasons. In part, this may indicate that the employee is unconsciously resorting to accidents as a means of escaping intolerable emotions aroused in the work situation. This is similar to the reaction that occurs when an employee develops physical symptoms of emotional origin. In other instances, an underlying physical or emotional disorder results in frequent absenteeism, while also providing a major source of distraction and thus contributing to accidental injury. Or it may be that irresponsibility on the part of the employee contributes both to the injuries and to absenteeism.

The Special Case of Accident-Proneness: Why do some employees have more accidents than others? Research shows that the determining factor is not necessarily the amount of danger on the job or the level of the employee's skill. It is true that industrial accidents are particularly likely to occur between the ages of seventeen and twenty-eight and to decline to a minimum in the late fifties and sixties. Although training deficiencies coupled with the fact that younger people are more likely to be new on the job might partially account for these data, it's not the whole story—the higher number of accidents among younger workers is far too striking. Also, skill levels are lowest in the very youngest age groups, but injury rates do not reach a peak until age twenty-one or twenty-two. There appears, therefore, to be something in specific individuals which makes them more susceptible to accidents, at least during an early period of their lives. Studies of the emotional patterns and motives of people who have had an excessive number of accidents tend to support this conclusion. Some employees apparently develop accident-proneness that is attributable to their individual characteristics, although the intrinsic danger of the situation also contributes.

A study by Professors Anthony Davids and James Mahoney of Brown University compared the personality characteristics of two groups: one with a high incidence of industrial injuries over a two-year period, and the other completely injury-free. The accident-prone employees were found to have negative attitudes toward their superiors, their jobs, and work in general. In addition, they were relatively lacking in optimism, trust in others, and positive feelings toward the people around them.

Similar but more comprehensive results were obtained from another study by Lawrence LeShan in which tests were given to fifty-four people with very high accident rates. Again there tended to be a lack of warm emotional relationships with others. Although most of the accident-prone had a wide circle of acquaintances and were considered good conversationalists, they did not really get emotionally close to people. They were frequently concerned about their health and physical condition, yet actual illnesses were rare. Also, many wanted to achieve a higher social status, although usually they had not been successful in doing this. There was an excessive tendency to deny disturbing emotions. As a result, many made bad mistakes in perceiving their environments. People in positions of authority, especially their superiors at work, seemed to arouse their hatred consistently, often for no real reason. Planning for the future was poor and erratic. The accident-prone appear to be living only in the present and to be a rather impulsive group. People with high accident rates are characterized by high levels of adventuresomeness and very little cautiousness. As a result, they take risks impulsively without adequate thought.

These studies, and others, present a consistent picture. The accident-prone appear to be emotionally immature and somewhat socially irresponsible. Yet people meeting this description are not necessarily emotionally ill, and many are not even accident-prone. To this discussion must be added the fact that the tendency to have repeated accidents is rarely a fixed characteristic. High accident rates don't usually last more than a few years, and sometimes not even that long. Accident-proneness is usually caused by transient maladjustments, mostly occurring before the age of thirty.

The most likely explanation seems to be that when people with the appropriate personality patterns are under stress, they experience relatively brief shifts in their motivational hierarchies that result in a series of accidents. Usually the original hierarchies reestablish themselves within a few years or sooner, although occasionally accident-proneness persists through much of the person's life. There is evidence that the motivating forces responsible for accidents often are a wish to impress others through impulsive, risky actions and an intense hatred of people in authority. Presumably this hatred leads to general defiance of rules and regulations, including those on safety. Such motives can result in frequent exposure to dangerous situations and inevitably some accidents.

On occasion, hostility toward superiors may generate strong feelings of guilt, coupled with a conscious or unconscious wish to escape this unpleasant emotional experience through behavior that actually represents a punishment. Here there may be a sufficiently strong *need* for injury so that the accidents are not merely chance happenings in a personally created context of excessive risk, but specifically contrived events. Sometimes a desire to escape other distressing emotions aroused at work may also serve as a direct stimulus to injury.

Counterbalancing these forces is the normal fear elicited by danger and the threat of injury. Self-preservation is a strong motive, and in most cases it remains dominant. When it does not, the forces contributing to accident-proneness break through and may result in repeated and sometimes severe injuries. Unfortunately, the factors responsible for producing this shift in the motivational hierarchy have not yet been identified.

Dealing with Danger: What can the manager do to minimize employee ineffectiveness caused by dangerous work environments? First, there are accident-prevention procedures: poster campaigns, safety discussions and committees, formal competitions for low injury rates among groups, studies of jobs and accident reports to locate trouble spots, safety policies and regulations, special training in accident prevention for new employees, placement of those with physical defects and handicaps in safe work stations, and the design of equipment to maximize safe operation.

Unfortunately, many of these techniques achieve their results by making employees constantly aware of safety problems and the presence of danger. Such awareness has without question been a major factor in reducing industrial accidents, but it may also raise the anxiety levels of people who are particularly sensitive to dangerous situations. Thus, some methods currently used to reduce injuries contribute, at the same time, to performance difficulties in people who become distracted by anxiety.

Design of the workplace and its equipment is a desirable accident-prevention approach that avoids this problem, because it does not rely on the consciousness of danger to achieve its results. Actually, safety devices and other engineering solutions are of value not only in reducing injuries, but in giving many employees a feeling of confidence and security. As a result, anxiety may be significantly reduced among those who must work under potentially dangerous conditions.

With engineering solutions, an important goal is to design in barriers that make it difficult for the employee to get into trouble. Safety devices and protective clothing can prevent a person from getting into a dangerous situation. Controls should be designed and placed to minimize the chances of error. Devices should be installed to provide reliable information on malfunctioning and the presence of danger. If trouble does arise, there should be available methods for eliminating it. Controls and releases should be readily at hand and should be designed to fully utilize the individual capabilities of the employee.

What if an employee has had a significant number of accidents and exhibits the motivational and emotional patterns characteristic of accident-prone people? There are several possible courses. As we've said, such people tend to correct their own problems eventually, but often not until they have suffered considerable disruption of performance, contributed to major equipment losses, left the company precipitously, or received substantial disability payments. Therefore, managerial intervention is called for when accident-proneness is suspected. Perhaps the danger inherent in the work situation can be reduced so that tendencies to show off and take risks have less chance of producing an actual accident. A person who is working in a really dangerous job should be transferred. Such people may try to find risky situations on their own, but management should do nothing to help them in this quest.

The manager faces a major challenge in supervising such employees. We have already noted that accident-proneness can be linked with hatred of people in authority, together with their rules and regulations. It follows that when accident-prone employees are forced into frequent close contact with their superiors, they are most likely to injure themselves. Considering this, the subordinate who has recently had several accidents should be supervised as loosely as possible. Certainly constant checking is not recommended. The manager should try to keep the employee's resentment at a minimum and to eliminate any sources of conflict with authority. Of course, there must be limitations on such kid-glove procedures, but if contact between boss and accident-prone subordinate can be kept to a minimum, both may benefit.

Subjective Danger Situations: Previously we noted that various aspects of the individual and the environment can coalesce to produce emotional symptoms. Among the factors mentioned were the number of situations that mesh with the person's sensitivities to produce disturbing emotions, the frequency and duration of exposure to these situations, the intensity of the emotions aroused, and the capacity to withstand unpleasant experiences. Although the sensitivities and emotions involved exist in the individual, some aspect of the environment generally sets off the symptom. Furthermore, the individual may react as if the situation were truly dangerous, frequently experiencing fear or utilizing symptoms such as those of a physical nature to escape the fear. In contrast to perception of an actual dangerous situation, however, the person's interpretation is based almost entirely on subjective factors. There is little real chance of injury or death.

Following are some situations, objects, and phenomena that can provoke reactions of this kind:

Open streets

Being alone

High buildings

Narrow spaces

Arguments and fights

Animals such as cats or mice

Knives and scissors

Speaking before a group

Seeing a crippled person or an accident

Crowds

Examinations and tests

Toilets

Boats

Noisy places

Airplanes

Darkness

Riding on buses or trains

Receiving orders or criticism

Physical examinations and shots

Social affairs

Talking to the boss

Talking on the telephone

Disorder and confusion

Separation from loved ones

Being in a position of authority

A new and unfamiliar environment

These are typical, but there are others. Each individual has his or her own unique pattern of sensitivities.

The motivational and emotional processes involved in the reactions are complex. Somehow, as a result of previous learning or experience, these subjective danger situations trigger strong impulses and feelings of an unpleasant or unacceptable nature. When the impulse or emotion is one that the individual has learned to consider bad, at least in the context where it has been aroused, it may never reach consciousness. Instead of actually experiencing an emotion such as shame, fear, or guilt, the person may develop a headache or go through a period of vomiting. Sometimes, however, fear does break through, and the person feels scared every time a certain type of situation presents itself. The impulse is aroused, is kept out of consciousness because it is considered bad, and is replaced by the experience of anxiety. Severe physical punishment for harboring such thoughts is unconsciously felt to be deserved, and the expectation of punishment serves as a stimulus to fear. Thus, in a sense it is the unconscious motive which is feared, not the situation, although environmental factors set off the process and are consciously perceived as causes.

Reactions in subjective danger situations are similar to those where real danger is present. There are essentially four possibilities. The individual may experience intense fear, but because of more dominant motives, may remain in the situation and be willing to face it whenever necessary. Many public speakers have continued to address large groups for years while remaining on the verge of panic. In the same way, a salesperson who experiences anxiety every time he or she approaches a customer may continue in this type of work for long periods. Performance may well be seriously affected in such cases, but the person continues to face the situation.

On the other hand, a person may attempt to escape that which is feared, by resorting to defenses and symptoms. The employee may experience physical symptoms that are emotionally based, or may constantly behave in a way that is symptomatic of emotional disorder, or may resort to pathological perceptions and beliefs. All of these are likely to interfere with job effectiveness, either by reducing efficiency or by making it necessary for the manager to remove the employee from the situation.

There is a third alternative in cases where a person has come to recognize the sources of the anxiety. Having learned from past experience that certain situations are emotionally disturbing, the employee may attempt to avoid experiences of this kind. The result can be an outright refusal to work in some environments and under certain conditions. On the other hand, various excuses may be developed in an effort to provide a socially acceptable reason for the avoidance. Some of these can be very ingenious, others quite far-fetched. On occasion, people caught between their fears and the demands of supervision become very emotional. A young woman may break out in tears when told to work in a small and stuffy room alone. A man may become belligerent when informed that he must take a physical examination.

Finally, and this is considerably rarer, the person may enter the situation only to be overcome with terror. In spite of the absence of real danger, he or she may bolt from the room much as a person might attempt to escape from a burning house. Sometimes there will be a few muttered excuses on the way out. At other times words will not come, and the departure remains completely unexplained.

It is important to reemphasize that these reactions to danger situations, whether actual or subjective, are not unusual or entirely in the realm of the abnormal. Many people have experiences of this kind at one time or another. They become relevant from a managerial viewpoint only when performance is seriously affected. On occasion, fears such as these do spread. The conditions under which anxiety is set off increase as the individual thinks of similarities between existing sources of distress and other situations that have in the past been relatively anxiety-free. This, however, is probably the exception. Most people remain sensitive to a group of situations which they have dreaded for years, which they generally try to avoid, and which provoke fear and emotional symptoms when exposure does occur. Yet the number of situations remains essentially the same. Or occasionally people even learn to enjoy circumstances which have previously been a source of distress.

Whether the reaction involves an actual danger situation or is purely subjective, the manager's first step should be to identify the specific cause. What element in the environment provokes the fear reaction? Only with this knowledge can the manager take steps to restore an adequate performance level. Once the strategic situation has been spotted, the manager can make appropriate changes in work requirements or, if this is impossible, transfer the employee to a job less likely to arouse negative emotions.

Handling Problems Inherent in the Work Itself: Often, subjective danger reactions relate to aspects of the work itself. As we will see in Chapter 12, for example, managerial work can arouse such feelings—and, in fact, this response to the demands of a managerial job is a major source of performance problems. Many other aspects of jobs may fail to mesh with a person's intellectual, emotional, motivational, or physical capabilities and characteristics and thus may contribute to performance problems. A job may require knowledge, skills, and information that an incumbent simply does not possess. Or it may lack any potential for the satisfaction of dominant motives.

We have already considered problems associated with personnel placement, and certainly transfer to another position is one possible solution when a person is in an inappropriate job. However, another approach that has achieved considerable popularity in recent years is job redesign, and in particular job enlargement or enrichment. With this approach, problems inherent in the work itself are handled through a redivision of labor.

Job changes of this kind are aimed at satisfying important motives by expanding the scope or size of the job. This strategy is emphasized by Robert Ford of AT&T and Professor Edgar Bargotta of Queens College. They indicate that the following factors are involved when a job is enlarged:

- The work itself is interesting.
- The job is not wasteful of time and effort.
- There is no feeling of a need for more freedom in planning the job.
- There is a reasonable say in how the job is done.
- The job provides opportunities.
- The job provides feedback.
- The job is not too closely supervised.
- It is worthwhile putting effort in the job.

Studies by Ford presented in his book *Motivation Through the Work Itself* demonstrate that the job-enlargement approach can solve motivational problems. Subsequent studies by Professors Richard Hackman and Greg Oldham at Yale University indicate that the approach is particularly effective with people whose dominant motives are for independence and freedom, self-development and achievement, and varied stimulations as contrasted with dull routine.

Yet it is also clear that jobs can be too large and that people may fail because they are overloaded. Professor Stephen Sales considered this problem in some detail and presents convincing evidence that coronary disease may be one consequence of too large a job. Thus, job simplification may be the best solution in certain cases where a problem resides in the work itself.

Whether job enlargement or job simplification is appropriate can only be determined by a close analysis of the employee's job demands, capabilities, and dominant motives. There appears to be an optimum job size for each person, but this optimum varies considerably from one individual to another.

11

Communication Skills: Their Role in Solving Employee Performance Problems

Until now, we have been primarily concerned with decision making—the decision making that managers carry out to deal with the performance problems of their subordinates. First, the manager must decide what factors caused the problem, and we have considered some thirty-five possible causes. Then there is the decision on what should be done to solve the problem once it has been identified. But dealing with people problems of this kind requires more than decision making. Getting to the heart of a problem and carrying out corrective action also require substantial communication skills.

The Nature of Communication Skills

In dealing with ineffective performance, the communication skill that matters most involves speaking and listening between manager and subordinate. It is through this interpersonal communication that much of the information needed to understand a particular performance problem is developed. In addition, a number of corrective actions, such as counseling and applying discipline, require this type of skill. Furthermore, interpersonal communication skills may be needed to get others to support or carry out corrective action. Often this involves discussions with a superior or a personnel representative, either in person or on the telephone.

On occasion, oral communication must be supplemented with written. It may be necessary to document a subordinate's performance problems in a memorandum or letter. Sometimes agreements are worked out with the employee that need to be recorded for future reference. Not infrequently, a recommended course of action to improve a subordinate's performance must be put in writing in order to get the endorsement of a superior or personnel manager.

Thus, interpersonal and written communication skills are an important part of dealing with performance problems. In fact, they can be just as important as the decision-making skills.

Communication skills of this kind derive from the various aspects of the individual considered in Chapters 2 through 5. Clearly intelligence, particularly verbal ability, plays an important role. So, too, does knowledge of how to communicate most effectively, and that is what this chapter attempts to provide.

Good communication tends to be facilitated by positive emotions and disrupted by negative ones, particularly anxiety, depression, and anger. Communication requires some degree of motivation to maintain it. People speak or write well at least in part because they try. They listen well because they try. They observe and interpret the body language of another because they try. In contrast, distraction and lack of interest can undermine communication completely. Finally, communication requires certain physical capabilities—to speak and to write. We tend to assume these as given, but speech defects and muscular handicaps can present problems on occasion.

Effective communication, then, is not a consequence of one aspect of a person, but rather results from a number of aspects. Many of these cannot be influenced by the ideas in this chapter. However, certain guidelines can be provided for the manager who has the motivation and the basic abilities to communicate effectively.

Some Key Findings Concerning Interpersonal Communication

Some key factors in effective interpersonal communication have been brought out in studies by Rudi Klauss of the National Association of Schools of Public Affairs and Administration and Professor Bernard Bass of the State University of New York at Binghamton. One crucial factor is trust. Trust between superior and subordinate is essential to open and undistorted communication. Without it, discussions aimed at determining the causes of poor performance are almost certain to result in the subordinate withholding important information. In many cases, subordinates will distort the truth in order to present themselves in a more favorable way. Perhaps this tendency can never be eliminated entirely, but it can be reduced if the subordinate trusts the superior and feels some security in the relationship. However, building a relationship of this kind inevitably requires considerable time.

Closely related is the factor of credibility. If a manager is viewed as a credible source of information, the communication process is facilitated. In addition, interpersonal communication should be carefully planned and transmitted, open and two-way, frank, relatively informal, and involve careful listening on the manager's part. Each of these factors may be more important in one situation than another, but all can be significant.

Two things stand out from these studies. First, relationships and understandings established over time with the individual and with a whole work group play an important role when it is necessary to discuss a performance problem with an individual. These discussions do not occur in a temporal vacuum. Second, such discussions need to be carefully planned, not only in regard to what is desired as an outcome, but also in regard to how the desired outcome can be achieved. Discussions intended to collect information to test several hypotheses regarding possible sources of a performance problem are very different from those intended to correct a problem in which motivation is already known to play a significant role. When a goal for the discussion is clear, a strategy for achieving that specific goal should be mapped out in considerable detail beforehand. Then one must marshall all communication skills one has to carry out the strategy envisioned.

How to Use Planning in Interpersonal Communication

Planned interpersonal communications between manager and subordinate (or potential subordinate) are used to achieve a number of purposes. Among these are to:

1. Select new employees (or transfers)
2. Orient new employees to company policies and practices
3. Secure knowledge and experience (and thus, to varying degrees, facilitate participative decision making)
4. Appraise employee performance
5. Handle disciplinary problems

6. Counsel employees

7. Train and instruct

8. Explain new company policies and procedures as well as problems that need solving

9. Deal with employee complaints and dissatisfactions

10. Handle and learn from separations (exit interviews)

Clearly, these communications occur for a wide range of reasons, and different purposes call for very different approaches. Accordingly, managers should establish in their own minds, perhaps even write down, what they are attempting to do before they engage in one of these types of communication with a subordinate. After the discussion is over, it is a good idea to go back and compare what actually happened against the initial objectives. Did the discussion achieve what it was supposed to, or did it fail to some degree? It is through honest comparisons of this kind that communication skills are developed.

Professors Otis Baskin of the University of Houston and Craig Aronoff of Kennesaw College, in their book *Interpersonal Communication in Organizations,* distinguish between two major types of communicators: director/controllers and understander/facilitators. Director/controllers prefer to assume command and maintain a psychological distance from subordinates; they feel more comfortable telling others what to do than listening. Understander/facilitators want to analyze the behavior of others and develop mutual trust; they find listening easy, but may be less at home when it comes to giving specific instructions. The point is that people differ in the types of communications that they find easiest, and in the situations they handle best. A director/controller may be excellent in dealing with disciplinary problems, but lack the skills needed to bring out the knowledge and experience subordinates possess. An understander/facilitator may be a superb counselor, yet fail miserably in handling performance appraisals.

Unfortunately, however, managing and dealing with performance problems do not give one the luxury of selecting only communication situations that fit one's temperament. As a result, some managers will have to force themselves to cope effectively with the entire range of such situations. It is important to know when one is on firm ground and when there is a danger of being sucked into quicksand. When the going does not look so good, and it is necessary to conduct a type of communication that does not come easily, that is the time to plan carefully and think through reactions to anticipated events.

One reason managers fail in communication situations that do not fit their personalities is because they get anxious and upset; a type of subjective danger situation arises. As a consequence, they cannot think clearly and make mistakes. A widely recognized example is stage fright when a person cannot perform, or performs poorly, out of fear of the audience. Many people find public speaking very difficult for this reason. What is not so widely recognized is that much the same thing can happen in interpersonal discussions that put a manager to the test and in which considerable significance rides on the outcome.

Again, planning and advance preparation can help in these situations, whether they involve public speaking or interpersonal discussion. Perhaps a degree of spontaneity is lost, but at the same time complete communication breakdown becomes less likely. With most people, the very fact of prior planning instills a degree of confidence, thus reducing anxiety levels. Further, planning and rehearsing can help the manager deal with problems that come up during the discussion.

Thus, it may be possible for a manager to cope effectively, despite being quite uncomfortable, simply because preplanned solutions can be called upon without the need to create new solutions as the discussion unfolds. Many managers find it helpful to bring notes into a discussion for this reason. The notes may not be needed, but it is reassuring to know that they are there.

The most important part of planning involves the objectives of the discussion—what outcome is desired? But there are many more aspects. Where should the discussion take place? If interruptions are not desired or privacy is important, then the necessary provisions should be made in advance. Turf is an important consideration. Having a subordinate come to your office is fine if you want to mobilize all the authority you can. For some types of communication situations, that is what needs to be done. However, if the need is to put subordinates at ease and foster openness, then it is better to go to their turf or move to neutral ground.

It is often desirable to learn as much as you can about the other person before undertaking a discussion. It may be useful to check the file in the personnel office, or talk with other managers for whom the individual has worked. The objective is to prevent unpleasant surprises—surprises that may make excessive demands on a manager's communication skills.

Finally, planning should deal with how the discussion ought to progress. What questions need to be asked? What information should be provided? What is the subordinate likely to do? What responses are desired from him or her? What approach needs to be taken in terms of interviewing style, degree of structure, and the like? What documents need to be introduced when? It is well worthwhile to work out these, and perhaps other matters also, in advance of the actual discussion.

Facilitating Communication

Perhaps the most important thing to keep in mind is that many, although by no means all, subordinates have a tendency to become anxious in dealing with superiors. The results vary with the degree of anxiety and the particular ways in which individuals express their fears. At the extremes, subordinates may be unable to communicate at all; blocking and a desire to escape the situation may predominate. Or there may be simply reticence, or distortion, or even lying. Discussions about performance, whatever their form, can be expected to put people on the defensive. The natural consequence is that communication is blocked or distorted. Part of this is a realistic process of self-protection; part of it goes beyond the realistic to overreaction and panic. The greater the expectation of criticism, the greater the reluctance to communicate openly.

This situation presents managers with a major challenge, especially when they are trying to obtain information regarding the causes of performance problems or to use counseling in an attempt to solve them. Clearly, the need is to reduce anxiety and defensiveness so that more genuine communication can occur.

One approach that we all recognize is to start out with "small talk"—to set people at ease. The idea is to talk, at least briefly, about matters that are not a source of anxiety so that emotions can be brought under control. Small talk often relates to the weather, health matters, family considerations, jokes, and the like. It is well to recognize, however, that small talk for one person may not be for another. Nerves can be struck. Thus, a remark that was originally intended as a buffer against anxiety may instead move the conversation precipitously to an emotion-packed subject area. Sensitive people can see problems and become upset over the most innocuous of comments, so the manager should be prepared for this eventuality.

If the objective is to get a person to speak out and provide important information, a manager should be positive rather than negative. Everything possible should be done to prevent the subordinate from going on the defensive. Whenever the conversation begins to open up, that process should be encouraged: "You were saying . . . ," "That makes sense to me . . . ," "You make an interesting point." Affirmative leads of this kind do a lot to keep communication going.

Nondirective interviewing can also help. The manager summarizes what has been said in a completely unevaluative manner. In the process, the subordinate is encouraged to continue in the same vein. Basically, this approach involves a restatement in which the manager uses much the same words and tries to reflect the other's feelings. Statements such as "I hear you saying something along the following lines . . . ," or "You seem to be saying . . . ," or "You give me the feeling that . . . " fall in this category. They not only encourage further, open discussion but provide a method of verifying communication, so that you can be sure that you have understood correctly. Feedback of this kind can emphasize the content of communication or its emotional meaning. Either way, it represents an effective facilitator.

Closely related are interpretive statements such as "This seems to make you upset" or "That seems to make you happy," which are intended to bring out not only the fact of emotions but the reasons behind them. Other interpretive comments may be introduced, aimed at explaining why people have behaved as they have. The result can be a real breakthrough, with much greater mutual understanding. But be warned that interpretive comments can also elicit resistance and defensiveness, either because a person is not ready for them or because they are wrong. As a result, shifts from purely reflective statements (from which one can back off easily) to interpretations of underlying motivations (which are hard to bury subsequently) should be made with extreme caution. Interpretations have great potential for empathy, but when resisted they can create a major barrier to subsequent communications. Thus, a statement such as "What you are saying suggests you feel a bit uncertain about yourself" has the potential for creating considerable understanding, but whether it does depends on what has taken place previously. Sometimes, the result can be the end of meaningful communication. Trust is lost and communication breakdown occurs.

Then there is the problem of silence. Silence is a two-edged sword. Managers should not avoid silence by jumping in with small talk, because silence often precedes important communications or the expression of strong emotions. On the other hand, long, embarrassed silences can stifle the whole communication process. If there is no reason to believe that a silence is occasioned by a subordinate's intense thought or strong emotions, then it is probably appropriate to break in with a general question to reinitiate the conversation. But if the individual is clearly thinking something through or attempting to deal with strong emotions, it is best to remain silent. Not infrequently, the result may be an outburst of anger or a bout of crying. Emotional expressions of this kind cannot be handled by rational argument and they often serve a therapeutic purpose of their own. They should be permitted to run their course, even though managers may find this very difficult to handle.

In all of this, a crucial consideration is the extent to which valid communication has occurred. A manager may end a discussion by saying, "We need to understand each other better." The subordinate may interpret this as an invitation to intimacy that was never intended. The result can be confusion and conflict in subsequent conversations. The way to avoid such misinterpretations is to obtain feedback on what the other person has heard and give feedback on what you have heard, so that each party consistently reinterprets the other. The consequence is a great deal of redundancy— saying the same thing over again, at intervals and in somewhat different ways. Yet this may be the only way to achieve valid communication in situations where emotions are continually threatening to blot out the content of communications. Outsiders overhearing such conversations might think they're listening to a broken record, but participants attempting to cope with the emotions involved may perceive them quite differently.

Listening

We have just noted that subordinates often do not listen well, so it may be necessary to repeat a point over and over again, while checking continually to determine whether the message has been received. But listening problems are not restricted to subordinates. If discussions are to produce useful information for solving performance problems, managers above all need to listen. They need to stimulate responses from subordinates and give close attention to what those responses mean. Above all, managers must avoid any tendency to talk others to death so that responses never occur in the first place. Some poeple cannot stand conversational pauses, let alone silences of any length, and others are so afraid they might hear something they don't want to hear that they cannot resist dominating a discussion. Either way, the art of listening is eclipsed. Yet listening is an important aspect of communication skills.

Studies indicate that people appear to hear, or at least recall immediately, roughly 50 percent of what they are told. Clearly, listening is frequently not very effective. People may be distracted; they filter what others say through their own frames of reference, expectations, needs, attitudes, and vocabulary knowledge; their emotions can blot out all or part of the messages others send. A problem also arises from the fact that we can comprehend at a much faster rate than others can speak. Most people talk at about 125 to 150 words per minute, while the capacity to listen is roughly five times that. As a result, we tend to fill in the extra time by thinking about other things, daydreaming, and the like. It is very easy to become so immersed in these thoughts that we fail to listen at all over considerable periods of time.

Many communication experts have suggested ways in which listening skills can be improved. For example, Professor Norman Sigband of the University of Southern California makes a very useful distinction between listening for facts and listening for feelings in his book *Communication for Management and Business.* Obviously, both of these are important in dealing with poor performance.

In listening for facts, he recommends the following:

1. Catalog key words.
2. Resist distractions, both external and internal.
3. Review key ideas as the discussion continues.
4. Be open and flexible.
5. Evaluate, but do not tune out ideas.
6. Work hard at listening.

At the same time it may well be necessary to listen for a subordinate's feelings and emotional meanings—what Professor Sigband calls empathic listening. Here's what he recommends:

1. Listen empathically for emotions, hopes, desires, perceptions, points of view, values, and the like.
2. Appreciate the speaker's meanings for the words used.

3. Listen for nonverbal communication.

4. Listen to what is said and what is not—the hidden meanings of words.

5. Recognize your own biases.

6. Select, if possible, the right time and place.

It can be very difficult to put all of these recommendations into practice. So in talking with a person with performance problems, try concentrating your listening on those matters and cues that relate to the hypotheses you have developed about possible causes of the poor performance. Thus, if previous evidence suggests that the person is often emotionally upset at work, either because of family problems or because of something happening in the work group, listening can be concentrated in these areas. Empathic listening can particularly focus on signs of negative emotions that might disrupt work. Listening for facts can concentrate on events in the family or the work group. If at the end of the discussion some or all of these hypothesized factors appear to have little support, it is usually best to formulate another set of hypotheses and have another discussion at a later date. The basic approach is to reduce the demands of listening by concentrating on what you are particularly looking for at the time. This should not preclude keeping an ear out for the unexpected, however. Sometimes unanticipated cues can provide very useful insights that help in formulating new hypotheses for the next discussion.

If the objective of the discussion is not diagnostic, but rather carrying out some corrective action (such as discipline) or getting the person to undertake a corrective action (such as medical treatment), then the primary listening need is to pick up feedback. Empathic listening lets you know how an individual feels about what has been said. Has the discussion produced anger and defiance, or sorrow and depression, or what?

Knowing about these emotional reactions helps you predict the outcome of your efforts. Listening for facts provides data on whether what you have said is understood. If in a corrective-action interview the person does not understand your statements, arguments, and directives, then you are unlikely to achieve your desired outcome. The same may be true if the person responds with resistance and counterarguments. In such interviews, it is necessary to listen for the facts coming back in order to deal with them.

Whatever the purpose of the discussion, it may be necessary to supplement listening with questioning to move on to understanding. Often, a manager hears something that sounds as if it has important implications, but is not sure that is the case. At such times, merely repeating what was said in a questioning manner may serve to bring out further information. Or direct questions may be asked. If the matter appears sensitive, it may be advisable to hold off for a while, waiting to see if the person returns to the subject or reintroducing it yourself at a point when the emotional climate is most conducive.

Finally, it is often a good idea after the discussion to take notes on what you have heard. If most of us actually hear only about half of what others say to us, we surely will remember even less. Note-taking during a discussion can impede spontaneity, but afterward it has much positive value. It can help to improve on the rather dismal performance that memory alone typically turns in, and it helps the manager to rethink and reformulate what has transpired when free of the pressures of the face-to-face discussion itself.

Nonverbal Communication

Nonverbal communication includes facial expressions, postures, gestures, physical appearance and dress, certain aspects of behavior, and perhaps more—any communication not expressed through words. You can learn a great deal from and about subordinates through attention to their nonverbal communication. You can also convey a great deal by the way you communiate nonverbally yourself.

Facial expressions are particularly important because they say a lot about emotions. Primarily this involves the eyes, eyebrows, and mouth. Facial expressions may convey happiness, surprise, fear, anger, sadness, disgust, contempt, interest, bewilderment, determination, and so on. Failure to make eye contact—or the nature and duration of such contact when it is made—can express a great deal; so, too, can the positioning of the corners of the mouth.

In "reading" facial expressions, however, two points should be kept in mind. First, interpretations can be wrong; there is a sizable margin for interpretive error, and accordingly you should seek out confirmatory evidence from other sources before jumping to conclusions from nonverbal evidence. Second, people can mask and distort facial communications, just as they can withhold verbal communications and lie. Some are extremely good at using facial expressions to convey the messages they wish, rather than the feelings they actually have. This is a form of acting. It takes considerable skill, on occasion, to see through intended distortions of this kind.

In contrast, postures are much more difficult to control, and thus more likely to yield valid information. The positioning of arms and legs, the head, and the body as a whole can say a great deal. For example, moving toward or staying close to a person says something quite different than maintaining distance. In general, people approach those to whom they feel positively through more direct eye contact, moving closer, leaning forward or asking questions. Conversely, negative feelings are reflected in moving away, leaning backward, looking away more, or becoming silent. However, in either case, fully correct interpretation of the postures requires additional information.

Gestures most commonly involve using the hands while speaking. Most often, these gestures convey emphasis: they can indicate what is really important to a person. Hand gestures may also communicate care and sympathy, aggression, anxiety and tension, and other emotions. Cultures differ in the extent to which gestures are used and sometimes in their meanings as well. Thus, a person's gestures need to be interpreted in light of the particular cultural context.

Any aspect of an individual's environment that he or she can influence personally may also serve to communicate something about that person. Thus, to the extent that a person can determine the decor of an office, work station, home, or other setting, that decor becomes a reflection of the self. This observation clearly extends to dress and appearance. Yet in this regard it is important to distinguish individualistic communication of the self from conformity to some group norm. Failing to wear a coat and a tie to the office is one thing, if the same attire characterizes all or most members of a given age group. It is quite another thing if the person is the only one to dress this way.

Other aspects of nonverbal behavior can communicate important information as well. Being late or early for an appointment to discuss a performance problem is an example; it can reflect a desire to avoid or get on with the discussion. Similarly whether subordinates do or do not get up and greet you when you enter their offices, can indicate how they feel about you. Also, emotions can frequently be inferred from the physical changes that occur with them, as noted in Chapter 3. Fear and anxiety tend to produce paling of the skin, sweating, rapid breathing, and trembling hands. Anger may cause reddening of the face, protruding veins, and tense muscles. These reactions are automatic, and accordingly they may provide valid information on emotional arousal. It is often difficult, however, to clearly differentiate one emotion from another on this basis alone. When signs of this kind are combined with other nonverbal and verbal clues, interpretation becomes much easier.

Telephone Communication

Clearly, nonverbal communication can provide a great deal of information about a person—feelings, attitudes, reactions to questions, and much more. All of this is completely lost in telephone conversations. Furthermore, static, transmission delays, being cut off, and other problems can disrupt a conversation so that the issue at hand does not get full attention.

Consequently, the telephone should be used only as a last resort in dealing with performance problems. There is simply less communicated over the telephone than in a face-to-face discussion, and as a result, less is learned and opportunities for error increase. This is particularly true if the other person is not expecting the call. A telephone call typically demands immediate attention and interrupts something else. The person called may have someone else in the room, may be in a hurry to leave for an appointment, and so forth. Such factors are not immediately evident to the caller and may never become known. Yet they can have an overwhelming influence on what transpires.

Performance problems are important problems—at times, the most important ones a manager will face. They need to be handled well, and that means through in-person discussions whenever possible.

Written Communication in Dealing with Performance Problems

Written communication is also not a preferred method for dealing with performance problems. Yet there are instances where it is needed, often as a backup to face-to-face discussion. Perhaps the facts about a discussion need to be recorded so that they can be referred to later. In such cases, terms like "memo to file" and "memo for the record" are often used. The discussions recorded may be with a subordinate or with a superior or personnel representative. In the latter cases, the content may be an agreement that has been reached on how to deal with a particular subordinate's problems. Whether a memo goes to someone else, such as the other participant in the discussion, will depend on the circumstances. Frequently, such memos simply go in the file as documentation.

One reason for writing memos of this kind is that today it is increasingly likely that a performance problem will become a legal problem later on. A dispute may go to arbitration, particularly if termination occurs, or may even get a full-scale hearing in court. Against these eventualities, it makes sense to have a written record of what was done, prepared at the time the situation occurred. If there *is* any prospect that a memo for the record might later be used as evidence in court, it is wise to have this thought in mind when writing. The memo should focus directly on the issue at hand: it should say what needs to be said, but no more. Extraneous material can prove embarrassing later on in a context that was never anticipated at the time of writing. Thus, the essential guideline for writing these memos is to be brief and to the point.

A second type of written communication is one aimed at persuading someone else to endorse or help in carrying out a particular approach to the performance problem. Examples would be obtaining an exception to policy or getting a subordinate shifted to another job or work group. Ideally such matters are handled through in-person discussions with those who can make the decisions, but in many companies it is necessary to supplement such discussions with a written statement. Sometimes it is not possible to have a personal discussion with those who will ultimately make the decision, and a written report is all there is available to achieve a desired action.

Writing Persuasive Memos and Reports: Most memos that you write about performance problems will be intended to persuade somebody to do something— perhaps to provide needed information for a performance analysis, but more likely to aid in corrective action once the diagnostic phase is completed. There are ways to pursue this objective well, and also not so well.

The initial need is to arouse interest, perhaps by building on previous discussions if that is possible. The opening paragraph, or perhaps two, should pursue this end. Tell the reader how the proposed action will be of benefit to the organization, the department, and/or the individual reader. Naturally, a brief description of the action itself is needed. But this should be kept short at the beginning—just enough so the reader can get the idea.

The body of the memo should be as long as needed to do the job, but definitely no longer. In written communications of this kind, repetition of a point to get it across is rarely needed as it is in oral communication. A memo can be reread, while oral communications disappear once stated, except insofar as they are retained in memory or recorded. The body of the memo should contain an expanded description of the proposed course of action, as well as arguments pro and con. Presumably the balance of these arguments will favor the action indicated, or you would not be writing the memo in the first place. Yet it is important to present an objective, rational picture that permits the reader to go through essentially the same steps that you did in reaching your decision originally. This makes it easier for the reader to end up at the same place you did. Also, if you are sure the reader will think of certain objections, it is usually better to raise them yourself and deal with them than to pretend they do not exist.

The closing section should assume that the argument has been accepted, the benefits recognized, and the proposed action endorsed. If the action ultimately is not endorsed, then the closing statement will make no difference in any event. Accordingly, the goal at the close is to explain exactly what the reader needs to do. This may represent the reader's share of a concerted action involving others as well, or it may be intended that the reader act alone. In either case, the need is to "close the deal"—to get the person to act as desired, and to be sure that he or she fully understands what the desired action is. Here at the end it is particularly important to write well.

Ingredients of Good Writing: Interestingly, most managers are capable of distinguishing the well-written from the not-so-well-written. They tend to agree on such matters and are quite sensitive to poorly written letters, memos, and reports. What, then, is involved in writing well? The following points do not represent a complete listing, but they cover a good deal of the ground.

Above all else, writing should be clear. The intended message should be thought through before writing starts, words should be chosen carefully, and topic sentences should be used at the beginning of paragraphs. If necessary, an outline should be prepared in advance.

It is common practice to argue against the use of technical terms or jargon in memos and reports. Yet so-called jargon can facilitate understanding and a sense of mutual identity among those who come from the same technical background. Thus, the crucial point is to know your reader, and choose terms accordingly.

Another important objective is coherence. Sentences and paragraphs should create a logical flow of communication. Accordingly, phraseology that can give rise to multiple interpretations should be avoided. Often coherence can be facilitated by listing points in order and by effective use of headings.

Communicaton should also be tactful—one should avoid statements that may unnecessarily arouse negative emotions in the reader. This requires some understanding of and perhaps empathy for that person. It is not just a matter of considering what would offend oneself, but rather of knowing the reader's feelings sufficiently well to avoid problems. It is important not to either insult the reader's intelligence or demean the reader personally. When one is not sure in these matters, it is best to err on the conservative side.

Writing should be personally directed to the person for whom it is intended. It should focus on the needs of the reader, taking into account what you know about him or her: it is important to convey "I took the trouble to write this specifically for you." That can help a lot in getting a memo read and in getting its message across.

Good grammar and proper format are important because they contribute to greater clarity and coherence. But such mechanical soundness is also important because without it there may be a sizable amount of distraction from the intended message. Some readers get so engrossed in mechanical problems of this kind that they miss the intended point; others come to question the writer's credibility.

As noted previously, it pays to be concise. Difficult concepts may need to be restated to get the meaning across, but even so, the fewest possible words should be used. Managers are busy people, but beyond that they generally prefer oral to written communication. The shorter the written communication, the more likely they are to read it, all else being equal. Don't be wordy, or repetitious, or use abstract terms when more concrete words are available.

In general, it is best to write with a positive tone whenever possible. Negative writing often arouses negative reactions. Often, one can positively restate a point that initially comes out in negative terms. To take a simple example—"Mary's performance is very poor" might best be changed to "Mary's performance can be improved" if one is advocating Mary's retention and some course of corrective action.

Readability is a two-edged sword. Much has been made of the need to avoid writing over the head of an audience—as, for example, when a college graduate is writing to recipients who do not even have high school diplomas. In this view, long and seldom-used words should be avoided. Yet it is also possible to write down to people in a demeaning way. Within management, a reasonably high level of reading ability can be assumed. It is not smart to try to one-up people with difficult words, but it is smart to maintain a reading level roughly similar to that of the other managers around you.

Where feasible, it is generally best to use the active voice in your writing. Active-voice sentences move more rapidly and are more empatic. They tend to catch the reader, and to hold interest. Yet there are instances, as in reports of research studies, where convention calls for the passive voice—"The study was made . . . ," "The conclusion was reached . . . ," and the like. In these cases, it is probably best to stay with existing conventions.

Whenever possible, a sentence or paragraph should be restricted to a single idea. Variety in sentence structures and wording is important, but unity of ideas should not be sacrificed in the process. Often, in the rush of getting ideas down on paper, several ideas get scrambled. This is fine in a first draft, but most people need more than one draft. And it is in rewrites that scrambled ideas can be separated and unified communication achieved.

These suggestions are neither all-inclusive nor presented in sufficient detail to serve as specific guidelines for preparing memos and reports. They are at best a beginning. A more comprehensive treatment of the subject is available in Richard Hatch's *Business Communication: Theory and Technique.*

The major point of this chapter is that dealing with people problems requires communication as well as decision-making skills. These communication skills are usually interpersonal, but they may extend to the written word as well. Primarily, they are learned skills that a manager can develop through practice and through observation of feedback. Developing them to a high level requires much hard work—but that work will pay off in more effective diagnosis and correction of employee performance problems.

12

Dealing with Problems of Managerial Subordinates

Much of what we have said about nonmanagerial subordinates can also be applied to managerial subordinates: any of the thirty-five types of factors considered as potential causes of unsatisfactory performance in nonmanagers can also contribute to the failure of a manager. But because of the nature of managerial work, certain of these factors are more likely to operate than others. Moreover, some requirements of managerial work are unique. When managerial subordinates are not doing well, it may be because of the way they are responding to these requirements. This chapter will focus on which causes of poor performance particularly affect managers, and how their reactions to managerial requirements can bring about failure. Such knowledge can help a manager with managerial subordinates to pinpoint and act on problems that may be dragging down their performance.

Factors within the Individual Manager

Intellectual deficiencies are especially likely to create problems for managers. Managerial work clearly requires a broad capacity to make decisions, and decision making is largely an intellectual process. In particular, a lack of essential job knowledge can hamper a manager's performance. Also, as a study of AT&T managers by Douglas Bray, Richard Campbell, and Donald Grant has demonstrated, managers who fail are often deficient in verbal ability. It is not enough just to possess the intelligence to get through four years of college. As one moves into middle and upper management, more is needed, although, of course, intellectual abilities do tend to increase to some extent after college also. In addition to verbal ability, numerical ability may be a key factor for many managers. Other special abilities, such as the mechanical and spatial, are less likely to be crucial.

As discussed in Chapter 3, emotional problems are less common among managers than among nonmanagers, but the problems that do occur are much more likely to cause unsatisfactory performance. In particular, decision making may be disturbed by the intrusion of emotional states and symptoms. Managers with serious emotional problems should be urged to seek professional help. On the other hand, many managers appear to suffer from a chronic low-grade anxiety which is specific to the work situation and which, although destructive to effective managerial performance, is not usually sufficient to justify major psychological or psychiatric treatment. I will elaborate on this point shortly.

Performance difficulties associated with excessively low personal work standards and generalized low work motivation are relatively rare in managers, except among those who have attained their positions through nepotism. People with serious motivational problems do not normally make it into management in the first place. But a manager's work does commonly suffer when a strong motive is frustrated, and the manager may resort to unintegrated means of satisfying the motive. In particular, managing appears to require the will or desire to manage. If certain aspects of the managerial job arouse anxiety and strong avoidance motives, motivation to manage is likely to be lacking and satisfaction in managerial work will be minimal. This problem, which is uniquely managerial in nature, is closely related to the chronic low-grade anxiety just mentioned.

Physical factors that detract from performance are no more common in managerial failure than with other occupations, and some of them are less common. Insufficient muscular or sensory ability or skill, as well as physical characteristics inappropriate to the job, are not usually considerations in management because the job demands in these areas are minor. When job demands are excessive and the manager is overloaded with work, coronary disease and certain physical disorders of emotional origin may become more probable. However, managerial jobs are probably no more likely to become too large than are many other professional or highly skilled jobs. Anyone with scarce skills and capabilities usually finds that his or her job tends to expand and require more time.

Key Group Factors in Managerial Failure

As with other jobs, failures in management rarely have a single cause. Typically, aspects of the individual interact with aspects of the environment to create the problem, and frequently the social or group environment is involved.

Certainly, managers are no less vulnerable to the effects of family crises than anyone else. Fortunately, separation reactions appear to be less frequent at the mangerial level simply because managers tend to be older and have typically faced this hurdle already. However, the nature of many managerial jobs may serve to foster an excessive intrusion of family considerations. Managers often have considerable freedom in scheduling their work. As family members become aware of this, they may make increasing demands on a manager's time, often without being fully aware of what they are doing. The manager who cannot say no often suffers in performance as a result.

In some instances, a problem originates with the group consisting of the manager's subordinates. In other instances, managerial performance problems may arise out of the group consisting of the manager's superior and all those reporting to that superior. Because managers are members of multiple groups at work—they may serve on committees and work on temporary project teams as well—every type of work-group factor is likely to contribute to performance difficulties. Among the factors related to group cohesion, "group-think" is particularly likely to be a problem (see p. 175).

The organization may be equally at fault. The only organizational factor that seems to affect managerial performance less than it affects nonmanagerial performance is excessive span of control. (As discussed earlier, such spans are often extended excessively at the lowest levels to keep managerial overhead costs down.) Failure of organizational action, particularly with regard to management development activities, placement errors, and overpermissiveness, are just as likely to affect the managerial level as lower levels, because such problems tend to permeate an organization as a whole. Inappropriate standards and criteria often plague companies in evaluating their managers. In view of the widespread publicity given to governmental bias charges and costly settlements, it might be assumed that the primary culprit is prejudice against minorities or women, but there are many other inappropriate criteria as well.

At the societal level, legal actions of a kind that might involve jail sentences are least likely to cause failure at the management level, although this has happened more often in recent years. However, strong pressures have been brought to bear on top mangement concerning pollution, consumer protection, and false advertising, including the filing of class action suits. Some managers have experienced performance failures as a result of these pressures. Conflicts between personally held cultural values and job demands are less frequent as one moves up the managerial ladder. Typically, problems of this kind are filtered out at lower levels. In most companies, the person who moves up to high management levels is likely to have made peace with organizational values long before.

Key Factors in the Work Context and the Managerial Job Itself

Economic factors can contribute to performance difficulties at any managerial level, but they are most likely to operate at top levels where vulnerability is greatest. Geographic factors can be just as important for managers as for anyone else. In fact, as managing increasingly takes people to all corners of the world, geographic considerations become a more and more frequent source of performance problems.

Factors such as poor lighting, high temperatures, noise, and other detrimental conditions of the immediate work situation are less likely to affect managers above the first level. Managerial work environments can generally be adjusted to make them as conducive to effective performance as possible. Although excessive danger may be present on occasion, it is not a continuing factor. For this reason, and because most managers are over age thirty, accident-proneness is not a common managerial problem.

However, reactions to *subjective* danger are a major source of managerial failure. When a managerial job comes to represent a subjective danger situation, the result can be serious performance deterioration or perhaps complete failure. Such reactions occur often enough to be considered a primary cause of managerial ineffectiveness.

Among first-line supervisors, subjective danger responses are probably the biggest cause of failure. Above that level, the frequency appears to be somewhat less but is still high. As a major contributor to reduced managerial efficiency, fear reactions provoked by the managerial situation quite often affect the attainment of organizational objectives.

What happens in this situation? Basically, a person responds to the demands of the managerial job by perceiving a personal danger situation. As a result, fear and anxiety are either aroused or anticipated: the chronic low-grade anxiety condition. Avoidance motives are then activated, and the individual attempts to escape from those aspects of the managerial work which are disturbing. Performance is affected accordingly. If many aspects of the work provoke this reaction, and their anxiety potential is strong, the avoidance needs can dominate a person's motivational hierarchy to the point where practically nothing else matters. The result is the opposite of the motivation or will to manage—the crucial ingredient that probably contributes more than anything else to managerial success.

Key to Success: Motivation to Manage

There are several unique motivational and emotional requirements of managerial work. These add up to what has been termed *motivation to manage.* Data confirming the role that these requirements play in managerial work are reported in detail in my books *The Human Constraint* and *Motivation to Manage.*

Let us now look at how these managerial job requirements can lead to the arousal of anxiety and subjective danger states.

Most obvious is the fact that managers must accept and perhaps even enjoy holding a position in which they wield power over other people. They are required as managers to use sanctions, both positive and negative, to control certain aspects of subordinate behavior. People who cannot bring themselves to influence others toward behavior in accordance with their wishes will have difficulty in any kind of supervisory work. Probably more than a mere willingness is needed. Actual enjoyment of power may well be desirable, although this should ideally be coupled with ability to keep the pleasure from becoming too evident to others. In any event, subordinates must be induced to perform in a way that will help to attain organizational objectives.

Closely related is the requirement that the manager must accept, and perhaps enjoy holding, a unique and highly visible position. The managerial job requires a person to stand out from the group and assume independent responsibility for behavior which at times differs markedly from that of others in the same environment. The job forces a manager to behave in ways that subordinates do not, so the manager cannot look to those subordinates for guides to conduct. Managers must be capable of acting entirely on their own initiative. Furthermore, they are inevitably highly visible. Because they have a potentially important role in satisfying the motives of subordinates, they are continually watched and discussed. Thus, the managerial job requires not only a willingness to differ, but also an ability to handle being the center of attention without becoming disturbed. In a sense, managerial work makes demands similar to those made of an actor. Managers are almost constantly on stage. They are required to play a part and to do so without succumbing to stage fright and forgetting their lines. For sufficient motivation to be present, managers probably need to actually obtain pleasure from this kind of activity.

To these job requirements must be added the necessity of getting the work out and keeping things moving. These routine functions vary in different positions, and many are not unique to management. They range from working up budget estimates and turning in employee rating forms to participating in committee activities and talking on the telephone. Administrative demands of this kind are constantly present and if neglected will accumulate until the backlog becomes overwhelming. Thus, managers must be willing and perhaps even eager to devote time to routine matters. Certainly a manager cannot afford to consistently avoid more than a few of the myriad duties that are required as a regular part of the job.

The relationship between a manager and his or her superiors is also important. For one thing, effective supervision requires a capacity to represent the group up the line and to obtain support at higher levels. To accomplish this, a manager must be on relatively good terms with his or her boss. Ideally, the relationship would be quite close. If a manager really likes and admires a superior, it will be easier for them to work together on mutual problems. Naturally, a generalized hatred of people in positions of authority will almost certainly impair a manager's capacity to obtain support and approval up the line. Perhaps even more important, managers who detest their superiors tend to assume that their subordinates feel the same way about *them*. Thus, relationships downward as well as upward will suffer. And the manager will probably fail to make efforts to enlist the assistance of subordinates on the assumption that they will not respond.

Managerial work also involves a strong competitive element, which has important implications for performance. Although competition might not be required if the job existed in an organizational vacuum, it becomes crucial within the framework of a specific company. Individual managers do compete for scarce rewards, including promotions. The person who is unwilling to compete does not even maintain the status quo, but gradually loses out to those who do compete. This means that managers must accept and even seek out competitive situations. They must try to make their group the best and be willing to accept challenges to their authority and position made by other managers. Managers who are unwilling to fight and try to win may see their group disappear from the organization chart or become subordinated to some other activity. Especially at the top levels, a real love of competition would seem to be almost essential.

Finally, management requires assertiveness. A manager is expected to take charge, to make important decisions, to discipline, and to take steps to protect subordinates. Someone who prefers not to assume this role, who becomes upset at the prospect of being assertive, might be expected to have difficulty as a manager.

Since assertiveness is widely considered to be a masculine trait, some believe that this requirement would rule out women as managers. This, of course, is

---

Six Motivational Requirements for Managerial Work

1. Willingness to exercise power over others
2. Willingness to be highly visible
3. Willingness to meet administrative demands of the job
4. Willingness to establish a positive relationship with one's superior
5. Willingness to be competitive
6. Willingness to be assertive

not the case. Women can and do function effectively as managers. As with men, part of their motivation to manage must include the willingness to meet the assertiveness requirement.

The Managerial Job as a Subjective Danger Situation

Some readers may generally agree with the list of managerial requirements given here, yet may feel a certain sense of uneasiness. That is understandable. Unfortunately, many of the job requirements cited are almost inextricably interwoven with behaviors and thoughts that are widely considered undesirable. Therefore, managerial work can stimulate emotional reactions and motives that are socially condemned. Some people will experience anxiety, shame, or guilt in response to one set of requirements, and some people will react similarly to other requirements. Under certain circumstances, any one of the six managerial requirements can be considered bad. As a result, a manager may unconsciously expect severe punishment for fulfilling these requirements. For this person, the work environment can become a subjective danger situation along the lines discussed previously and a constant source of unpleasant emotional experience. How can this happen? Let us consider the negative interpretations that may be placed on the six requirements of managerial work.

The power requirement can, of course, easily be viewed negatively. To get satisfaction from manipulating others to achieve one's own ends is widely considered Machiavellian and undemocratic. Yet it is not unusual to enjoy being in a position of power—to look forward to making others behave according to one's wishes. Most people probably have such feelings at one time or another. In my experience, they are particularly prevalent among managers of outstanding competence. Nevertheless, the manager who experiences a sense of omnipotence and superiority may well feel guilty about those feelings. There is ample evidence that when this happens, he or she may express the feelings and desires involved by relegating them to the level of the unconscious. An unconscious expectation of punishment or physical injury often remains, however. And anxiety may well result.

Visibility: The uniqueness and high visiblity of the managerial job carry with them additional risks. Being the center of attention can stimulate a wish to "show off" that might result in boasting and excessive egotism. Assuming a role that is different may imply a negative evaluation of others, an "all of you are wrong and I'm right" attitude that is not only clearly aggressive but also superior. The fact that a manager is often required to play a part, much as an actor does, can carry with it a certain implication of "phoniness" and superficiality. Further, based on evidence obtained during psychotherapy, constant visibility may tempt a male manager to go beyond showing off to more clearly sexual behavior. Apparently, some male managers do sometimes experience a desire to exhibit themselves while carrying out their job duties. People who are prone to exhibitionistic wishes are particularly likely to have such desires arise in managerial situations. Usually these impulses and thoughts can be expected to remain unconscious, if they have become associated with a previously learned anticipation of punishment. Anxiety, however, often continues to force its way into consciousness. This phenomenon has been studied primarily among males. However, it seems likely that females are no more immune.

Administrative Demands: On the surface, routine administrative duties would appear to be relatively free of negative implications. However, this is not always the case. Certain administrative activities may arouse strong impulses that in turn contribute to subjective danger reactions. For instance, constructing a budget estimate may provoke a temptation to be dishonest. For some, the document is merely a budget estimate; for others, it becomes an invitation to cheat and lie. The budget task can also reactivate a long-standing desire to put something over on the company, to prove that higher management is as stupid and gullible as any lower-level supervisor. To take another example, filling out an employee rating form is no more free of potential danger than constructing a budget estimate. A vindictiveness may be aroused of which the manager was not even aware. Quite unexpectedly the manager may experience an intense desire to make the employee being evaluated suffer "the way I have." Should repression take over, none of these wishes will become conscious, but anxiety may well remain. While working with ineffective managers in an effort to improve their performance, I have seen a number of instances of such reactions. Similar processes apparently can be activated by almost any of the routine administrative requirements of managerial work.

Positive Relationship: The need for a relatively close relationship with one's superior introduces the possibility of a different type of problem. If such positive feelings are openly displayed, they may elicit derogatory comments. That is, the manager who openly expresses admiration and affection for his or her boss runs the risk of being considered somewhat peculiar. So, too, do managers who constantly praise their superiors' ideas, laugh at their jokes, and spend as much time as possible with them. If the manager and superior are of the same sex, some particularly vivid descriptive terms may be applied to such behavior—and all of them carry homo-sexual implications.

The prospect of being branded a homosexual can provide real terror in certain people, which may be felt even when they have no real idea of what they fear. All that reaches consciousness is the anxiety, which appears to have no obvious cause.

Competitiveness: Another possible problem has to do with competition. While competition is not generally considered bad in itself, the competitive drive can lead to behavior that *is* considered harmful. Competing within the rules is one thing; cutthroat competition is quite another. A person may want to win too much, become too aggressive, and come to hate adversaries. This type of manager may be tempted to engage in prac-tices that are considered bad and deserving of punish-ment. For some people, even the thought of resorting to "dirty" tactics and going all out to win is very disturb-ing. They do not consider themselves capable of such behavior and will not permit such thoughts to become conscious. Yet I have seen cases where such a person has become extremely anxious while walking down a steep flight of stairs behind another manager who is viewed as a competitor. Making the impulse uncon-scious does not seem to eliminate it entirely; the fear remains.

Intensely aggressive wishes of this kind can contrib-ute to particularly severe anxiety when a manager sees the boss as the adversary. Evidence derived from psy-chotherapy indicates that the desire to take away a superior's job can be a major source of emotional dis-turbance. Under such conditions, competitive wishes tend to carry with them an assumption that extreme retaliatory measures will be applied. Fighting with another person on one's own level is one thing; fighting with a person who has all the power is quite another. Subjective danger situations that are provoked by impulses of this kind can be terrifying for individuals who are specifically sensitized to them.

Assertiveness: Even the assertiveness inherent in managerial work can become a potential source of danger. For men, the desire to prove and demonstrate their maleness can be carried to what, in the work environment, might well be considered an extreme. Some male managers appear to experience considerable sexual excitement on the job. Since expression of such a feeling would be considered inappropriate, a potential for anxiety and repression is clearly present. Some men tend to react to sexual stimulation as if it were bad, and thus the situation may well be converted into one of subjective danger.

Among women, this particular requirement of managerial work has an additional threat inherent in it. Meeting the assertiveness requirement causes some women to seriously question their identity as women. Research conducted by Virginia Schein of Metropolitan Life Insurance Company demonstrates that managing does tend to be viewed as essentially a masculine occupation. Successful managers are considered to possess characteristics, attitudes, and temperaments most commonly ascribed to men. To the extent that women accept this view, either consciously or unconsciously, the managerial job poses a potential threat, and a uniquely feminine type of identity crisis may emerge.

In all of these cases, wishes and impulses—and how they are interpreted—lead to fear only when the manager associates them with punishment and injury. It is then that they are converted into unconscious motives in an attempt to blot out the sources of distress. As a result, all that is usually experienced is a strange and unaccountable fear of being found out, caught, punished, or rejected by others, a fear that appears to be aroused only when managerial responsibilities must be carried out. Actually, the difficulty can usually be traced back to the learning of cultural values about acting superior, improperly exercising power, showing off, being superficial or exhibitionistic, taking unfair advantage of others, cheating and lying, being vindictive, behaving in an unsportsmanlike way, attacking those who cannot defend themselves, being disrespectful of those in authority, and engaging in inappropriate sexual behavior.

Impulses and desires of the kind just described are in no sense unique to people who react with fear when given managerial responsibilities. Culturally condemned feelings and motives occur in all of us and, in fact, are amazingly widespread among people who do not permit this type of motivation to manifest itself in behavior. Many competent managers consciously experience feelings and reactions aroused by the nature of their work that other managers would not permit to enter consciousness. The difference is that the more effective manager is able to tolerate the wishes and does not interpret them as so inherently bad that they must be suppressed and denied. Thus, the conditions for intense anxiety are not created.

How Managers Fail

If we now look at subjective fear reactions in terms of their performance consequences, several types of managerial ineffectiveness emerge. One possiblity, relatively common according to my experience, is that a person may hold on to a managerial job but experience so much anxiety that concentration on the work becomes impossible. This person becomes so bound up in personal problems and unpleasant emotional experiences that there is little time to deal effectively with managerial duties. Decisions are delayed and forgotten, or are made impulsively and incorrectly at the last minute. Sensitivity to the desires and requirements of subordinates is minimal. The extended logical study required for adequate performance control becomes almost impossible. For long periods, the manager is immersed in anxiety and loses the capacity to react effectively to events in the world outside. "Stupid" mistakes thus become commonplace. This person's managerial style is primarily laissez-faire.

The manager may also, of course, develop various emotional or physical symptoms as a means of protection against disturbing emotions. We have already discussed these symptoms and their performance effects. In this connection, there has been much talk about managerial work as a cause of ulcers and heart attacks. To the extent that these conclusions have any basis in fact, the physical problems result from the kind of processes we have discussed. It is not merely the external pressure of high-level responsibility that produces emotional disorders and physical symptoms of emotional origin. It is also the inability to tolerate personal motives that are aroused without resorting to protective measures that are themselves potentially debilitating.

Some people are very aware of the potential for anxiety inherent in a managerial position. They may not know why they are afraid when faced with the demands of managerial work, but they know that they do feel fear. As a result, they may refuse to accept a promotion to management or to a job with greater managerial responsibility than they already have. Although such refusals are not common in the business world, they do occur. Unfortunately, the monetary rewards offered often tend to outweigh other considerations. Thus, many people who are apparently well aware of the personal difficulties they will experience nevertheless accept promotions because of the money.

These decisions do not always hold up under the test of time. A manager may well overestimate his or her capacity to withstand the stress of job demands. If this is the case, avoidance may occur later, after the duties have already been assumed. While still retaining the title, an individual may bolt from the managerial situation, avoiding one or more requirements of mangerial work. Situations that call for wielding power, standing out from the group, carrying out certain routine duties, competing with others, maintaining close contact with superiors, or being actively assertive can become a source of anxiety. Decisions may be avoided. The person may make practically no effort to maintain an adequate performance level among subordinates. In short, anything that is considered part of the managerial job may elicit an emotional reaction so intense that escape becomes the only objective. Under such conditions, absenteeism may become excessive—and when at work, the manager is consistently laissez-faire in style.

The manager who spends time working alongside subordinates rather than planning the work, observing group performance, and motivating may well be trying to avoid crucial job demands. Merging with the group can be a method of escaping from anxiety-provoking requirements connected with standing out, having considerable visibility, and being different.

Excessive supervision to the point where subordinates feel that they are being constantly watched and instructed in the most minute details, can also be a response to fear and guilt aroused by the managerial situation. Managers with this style view the various motives and feelings that we have discussed as bad, and unconsciously anticipate punishment as a result. This can make them extremely sensitive to criticism and blame—they expect to be condemned and punished for almost everthing they do. In reality, of course, the source of their guilt is within themselves. But since the motives involved have become unconscious, such managers will view almost anything in the environment as a potential source of harm. This anticipation of punishment may be extended to include others: the manager may become convinced that his or her subordinates are also certain to do something wrong. They become, in a sense, an extension of the manager's own being. Being responsible for their work, the manager expects to be blamed for their mistakes. The only way of escaping is to watch and instruct each person in such detail that no mistakes are possible. If subordinates can be supervised closely enough, perhaps the expected errors can be stopped before they occur and thus punishment of self can be avoided. Reactions of this kind are not uncommon in the business world.

Or, a manager may fail to take any real interest in subordinates out of fear of getting emotionally close to them. Such managers don't want subordinates to get to know them too well. They're afraid that their subordinates will have the same low opinion of them as they have of themselves. These managers try, therefore, to escape this expected condemnation by being very formal and appearing so strong and righteous that they could not possibly be suspected of evil deeds and thoughts. For such people, to be kind is to be terribly vulnerable to attack. Thus, any show of considerate behavior carries with it a potential for arousing intense anxiety. In some of these instances also, managers may have even greater expectations of hatred and condemnation by subordinates because of their strong negative feelings toward people in authority. These managers may assume that since they themselves have a defiant and rebellious attitude toward their superiors, they must be hated by their own subordinates just as much.

Of course, negative feelings toward those at higher levels may also make it difficult for a manager to represent subordinates upward in the organization and gain support for his or her actions. This need not be entirely the result of bad relations between the manager and a superior. If the manager's aggressive impulses are repressed so that they become unconscious and only fear is experienced, any contact between the two individuals will arouse unpleasant emotional reactions. This is particularly likely when the manager strongly desires the higher-level position and is tempted to use competitive methods that are generally condemned. The fear and guilt aroused by even the thought of the superior may be so great as to lead to almost complete avoidance. The manager does not exert influence up the line out of fear of facing those at higher levels.

Avoidance reactions of this kind, which preclude obtaining support from a superior, may also occur when very strong positive feelings are present. If a manager harbors an intense affection for a superior, the impulses associated with this positive emotion may arouse shame and guilt. The only way of avoiding these unpleasant experiences may be to remain as far away from the source of the feelings as possible.

Finally, managers can easily fail to exercise influence over subordinates or to establish performance standards because they are afraid of their own reactions in the leadership situation. The problem may be in exercising power, standing out from others, carrying out routine functions, or competing with other managers. Whatever the particular difficulty, managers may fail to exercise their authority and accept the role their position requires because of the anxiety and guilt they anticipate if they should do so. In this sense, they may be said to fear success. They fear their own impulses— impulses that are frequently provoked by positions such as those of a managerial nature that represent success in the business world.

These are some of the subjective danger reactions that managers may experience when faced with the job itself. All tend to reflect a low level of motivation to manage with regard to one or more aspects of the job.

How to Handle a Lack of Motivation to Manage

Most managerial problems can be handled along the lines suggested in previous chapters. However, a lack of motivation to manage, which may reflect a subjective danger reaction to the particular type of work involved, presents a uniquely managerial problem.

Historically, the solution in these cases has been to remove the person from managerial duties. When a manager doesn't work out, someone else takes over. At higher levels, this usually is the preferred solution today. However, in some instances an individual can be demoted to a lower-level management position. Here the consequences of poor performance are less pronounced, and somewhat less motivation to manage is usually required.

But what about the possiblity that a manager might learn to cope effectively with the subjective danger reaction? Can the fears and anxieties aroused be reduced or even eliminated? In other words, can motivation to manage be increased? The answer is a qualified yes. A measure of success has often been achieved, although not everyone can be changed in this way.

The primary approach used is a management development technique known as managerial role-motivation training. This approach gives people a greater understanding of what managerial work is like and also provides insight into the sources of the subjective danger reactions that can occur among managers. Managers thus come to understand relationships between themselves and their work more fully. The approach works best with those who are already active and independent people by nature. Studies indicate that from 60 to 75 percent of those who take such training improve their managerial motivation to some extent; they are much more likely than managers who go untrained to receive favorable performance ratings and move up in management rapidly.

The basic process involved in managerial role-motivation training is much the same as that in psychotherapy and counseling: people come to understand themselves better and thus are able to cope with their unconscious motives more effectively. Thus, certain types of psychotherapeutic help may achieve much the same results as managerial role-motivation training. Either approach is worth trying, because a lack of motivation to manage is one of the performance problems that can be remedied in a relatively high proportion of cases by changing the individual.

Checklist: 35 Causes of Poor Employee Performance

Here's a checklist you can use when you are trying to identify and remedy problems of poor employee performance. After each category is a figure that represents the percentage of cases that might be expected to involve that particular category. These percentages are based on my own experience with employee performance problems in a wide range of occupations—about 25 percent being at the managerial level. Use the percentages as a rough guide only, as your own experience may differ. Also keep in mind that there is often more than one key factor contributing to an employee's failure; that is why the percentages add up to more than 100 percent. In my experience, the median number of key factors was three, and the number sometimes went as high as seven.

GAUGE BASED ON ~~NOT~~ EFFECT ON WORK PERFORMA[NCE]
ONLY STRATEGIC IF EFFECTS WORK PERFORMANCE

must have or cannot perform →

Intelligence and Job Knowledge Problems (25%)

→ Has person done this or similar b/4 ? yes = NS

Would additional training solve problem ?

1. Insufficient verbal ability
2. Insufficient special ability
3. Insufficient job knowledge
4. Defect of judgment or memory

Emot
1. Is response appropriate ?
what takes to provide, how many diff situations evoke ?
1. to provide
2. frequency
3. Intensity (How long reacts)

Emotional Problems (60%) → *INFLEXIBILITY*

Inappropriate Reactions
Disruptive to group

5. Frequent disruptive emotion: anxiety, depression, anger, excitement, shame, guilt, jealousy
6. Neurosis: with anxiety, depression, anger predominating
7. Psychosis: with anxiety, depression, anger predominating *(divorced from reality for long periods of time)*
8. Alcohol and drug problems

see - model Notes 4/12/90

Motivational Problems (62%) - *almost Always accompanied by Emotional problems*

MOTIVE FACTORS
1. New experiences
2. Recognition
a) Professionally
b) Personally
3. Security
a) Financial
b) Psychological
"Sense of well being"

9. Strong motives frustrated at work: pleasure in success, fear of failure, avoidance motives, dominance, desire to be popular, social motivation, need for attention *→ demand superv time*
10. Unintegrated means used to satisfy strong motives
11. Low personal work standards
12. Generalized low work motivation

Physical Problems (10%)

13. Physical illness or handicap, including brain disorders -

14. Physical disorders of emotional origin

15. Inappropriate physical characteristics

16. Insufficient muscular or sensory ability or skill

Family-Related Problems (20%) – *ask if would be different if diff set of family*

17. Family crises: divorce, death, severe illness – *rapid change in performance (maybe initial improve) then decrease in performance*

18. Separation from the family and isolation – *Salesman traveling Supportive family*

19. Predominance of family considerations over job demands

Work-Group Problems (33%)

20. Negative consequences of group cohesion – *p. 175 & 174*

21. Ineffective management – *laissez faire management (do nothing) managers do not tell employees what needs to be done*

22. Inappropriate managerial standards or criteria – *too high to reach.*

Organizational Problems (90%)

23. Insufficient organizational action

24. Placement error – *over or under, emotional*

25. Organizational overpermissiveness

26. Excessive spans of control

27. Inappropriate organizational standards and criteria

Society-Related Problems (12%)

28. Application of legal sanctions

29. Other enforcement of societal values, including the use of inappropriate value-based criteria

30. Conflict between job demands and cultural values: equity, freedom, moral and religious values

Problems Related to the Work Situation (30%)

31. Negative consequences of economic forces

32. Negative consequences of geographic location

33. Detrimental conditions in the work setting

34. Excessive danger

35. Problems inherent in the work itself

INDEX

About the Author

John B. Miner is Research Professor of Management, Industrial Relations and Psychology at Georgia State. He is a former editor of *Academy of Management Journal* and former president of the Academy of Management. He currently conducts seminars in "Policy/Strategy," "Organizational Behavior," and "Personnel Management." He has served as a consultant to various corporations, universities, government agencies, and law firms. Winner of the James A. Hamilton Hospital Administrators' Book Award, he has written forty books and monographs and has prepared ninety-eight articles on management, industrial relations, and psychology.

A Note on the Type

The text of this book was composed, via computer-driven cathode ray tube, in a typeface called Bookman. The original cutting of Bookman was made in the 1850's by Messers. Miller and Richard of Edinburgh. Essentially the face was a weighted version of the popular Miller and Richard old-style roman, and it was probably at first intended to serve for display headings only. Because of its exceptional legibility, however, it quickly won wide acceptance for use as a text type.

This book was composed by University Graphics, Atlantic Highlands, New Jersey.
Printed and bound by Halliday Lithographers, West Hanover, Massachusetts.
Text and cover design by M.R.P. Design.
Production supervised by Richard Ausburn.